The Complete Guide to Learning through Community Service

Related Titles of Interest

101 Ways to Develop Student Self-Esteem and Responsibility
Jack Canfield and Frank Siccone
ISBN: 0-205-16884-1

100 Ways to Enhance Self-Concept in the Classroom, Second Edition
Jack Canfield and Harold Clive Wells
ISBN: 0-205-15415-8 Paper   0-205-15711-4 Cloth

Teamwork Models and Experience in Education and Child Care
Howard G. Garner (Editor)
ISBN: 0-205-13783-0

Transforming Middle Level Education: Perspectives and Possibilities
Judith L. Irvin
ISBN: 0-205-13472-6

Bridges: A Self-Esteem Activity Book for Students in Grades 4–6
J. Victor McGuire and Bobbi Heuss
ISBN: 0-205-16504-4

Creating and Funding Educational Foundations: A Guide for Local School Districts
James J. Muro
ISBN: 0-205-15573-1

Multicultural Teaching: A Handbook of Activities, Information, and Resources, Fourth Edition
Pamela L. Tiedt and Iris M. Tiedt
ISBN: 0-205-15488-3

The Complete Guide to Learning through Community Service

Grades K–9

Lillian S. Stephens
State University of New York
College at Old Westbury

Allyn and Bacon
Boston London Toronto Sydney Tokyo Singapore

Copyright © 1995 by Allyn & Bacon
A Simon & Schuster Company
Needham Heights, MA 02194

Library of Congress Cataloging-in-Publication Data

Stephens, Lillian S.
    The complete guide to learning through community service : grades K–9 / Lillian S. Stephens.
        p.   cm.
    Includes bibliographical references and index.
    ISBN 0-205-15132-9
    1. Student service.   2. Student volunteers in social service.
    3. Education, Elementary—Curricula.   4. Interdisciplinary approach in education.   I. Title.
LC220.5.S74 1995
361.3'7—dc2O   94-23625
                                                                             CIP

Photo Credits:
Cover #1: Fourth graders from P.S. 213 organize for fall cleanup of school trail. #2: Eighth-grade student assists fourth graders' science lesson, I.S. 223. #3: Eighth-grade student, I.S. 223, chats with senior friend at Isabella Geriatric Center. #4: Students from Henderson County South Junior High School monitor pond on school grounds. Photos #1–#3 by Robert Dobbs; #4 by Louis Smith, Jr. Back Cover: Students from Robert Wagner Jr. High School plant bulbs in neighboring park. Photo courtesy Sara-Jane Hardman and National Center for Service Learning in Early Adolescence. Photo by Jane Hoffer.

Inside: Part 1 (p. 7): Henderson County South Junior High School students clean up environmental study area behind school. Photo by Louis Smith, Jr. Part 2 (p. 37): Student from Columbus Academy, I.S. 44, reads to Goddard Riverside Head Start kids. Photo courtesy National Center for Service Learning in Early Adolescence. Photo by Jane Hoffer. Part 3 (p. 135): Student participant in "Magic Me" program, Bala Cynwyd Middle School, constructs crostic puzzle with resident at Bala Nursing and Retirement Center. Photo courtesy "Magic Me" Program. Photo by Nancy Murphy. Part 4 (p. 179): Impromptu mediation session in schoolyard during lunch hour at P.S. 40. Photo by Robert Dobbs.

Printed in the United States of America
10 9 8 7 6 5 4 3 2 1   99 98 97 96 95

Contents

Preface

This book is about joy—the *joy of giving*, the special joy students experience when they have an opportunity to have a positive impact on people's lives.

It is also about rediscovering the *joy of teaching*. Over and over, as I met and spoke with teachers throughout the country, I heard remarks such as "This has been the best year of my twenty years of teaching"; or "I love my job; I wouldn't want to do anything else."

To the above, I would add the *joy of authorship*. My research enabled me to meet an extraordinary population of kids and teachers. "You will be seeing kids at their best," one teacher told me, and I sure did!

I became acquainted with remarkable teachers and administrators in more than twenty states, in rural and urban schools with diverse populations—ethnically and economically. Their dedication, creativity, and energy made every contact inspiring. They generously shared experiences, materials, and expertise. This book is a report of their work, frequently in their own words.

There is not enough space for me to delineate the contributions of each of the educators in the list that follows, but fortunately they speak for themselves throughout the pages. I have tremendous respect for what they have accomplished, and I am indebted to them.

They include: Barbara Akre (MN), Clifford Bishop (NY), Marie Bogle (PA), Beverly Bonkoski (PA), Carl Bonuso (NY), Barbara Boulden (WA), Irma Brown (MD), Nicholas Byrne (NJ), Florence Chapman (PA), Sam Chattin (IN), Michael Chiles (NJ), Claire Delaney (VT), Steve Dibb (MN), Jill Eisner (MD), Linda Epstein (PA), Jean Fazioli, (NY), Tom Gilroy (NY) Fran Greenspan (NY), Mario Guerrero (CA), McClellan Hall (NM), Alan Haskvitz (CA), Sara-Jane Hardman (NY), Bill Henneger (WA), Judy Intraub (NY), Jill Jacoby (MN), Judy Jepson (CO), Carol Kinsley (MA), Janice Lacey (VA), Marc Landas (NY), Pam Lawrence (NY), Ginger Lentz (IN), Brian Loney (CO), Richard Malone (NY), Kris Myers (IN), Ray Myrtle (MD), David Newton (NY), Glenn Pribeck (NY), Carol Schafer (IL), Salvatore Sclafani (NY), John Shaughnessy (MO), Louis Smith, Jr. (KY), Vivian Smith (FL), Judy Starr (NM), Josie Supik (TX), Sonya Thurman (MD), Jim Vaughan (WA), Dian Wurst (NE), Bobbi Wolf (PA), and Angela Vassos (NY).

I am grateful to Victoria Kilanowski and Howard Waldman for information about the New York City Parklands Partnership program described in Chapter 7, and to Katherine Haller of the American Red Cross, who supplied information and material for Chapter 6. The book was strengthened by the thoughtful suggestions of Gwen Fountain of Butler University and Mark Feldhausen, assistant principal at Millart South High School, Omaha, Nebraska, who reviewed the manuscript. In Chapters 6 and 9, I have incorporated some material from a previous book.[1]

Thanks are due to a number of people who directed me to exemplary programs and contacts in the field: Ruby Anderson of the Corporation for National and Community Service; Frank Pomata of the New York State Governor's Office; John Briscoe of Penn Serve in Pennsylvania; Wokie Griffin-Roberts of the Generator School Project; Maggie O'Neil of the Maryland Student Service Alliance; and, in California, Madeleine Wild-Blumenfeld in Sonoma, and staff members of the Constitutional Rights Foundation in Los Angeles: Ingrid Sausjord, Keri Dowggett, and Susan Phillips.

A special note of gratitude goes to the personnel of the National Center for Service Learning in Early Adolescence in New York: Joan Schine, Alice Halsted, Rebecca Lieberman, and Felicia George. I called on them at many points throughout the project.

There are others who must be singled out: Anne Purdy, Central Park East Secondary School; Myrna Schiffman, Mott Hall Intermediate School; and Joanne Urgesse, Shoreham–Wading River Middle School. They shared their materials and expertise freely and repeatedly, and permitted me to accompany and interview their students at their service sites, and to speak with the site supervisors and service recipients. Their help was invaluable.

Finally, there are the members of my family. Four students supported the project and followed it closely: Lauren, Seth, Daniel, and Noah. My sister, Anne Wild, an experienced teacher, made insightful comments. Most of all, I relied heavily on my daughter, Beth, and my son, Mitchell, for their counsel and editorial expertise. They were always available to edit and react to a passage, and to advise at key points. Their encouragement and assistance made this project possible. It is to them that I dedicate this book.

Note

1. Lillian Stephens. *Developing Thinking Skills through Real-Life Activities* (Boston: Allyn and Bacon, 1983).

About the Author

Lillian S. Stephens brings to her interest in service learning an extensive background in education as a classroom teacher, curriculum coordinator, and college professor of education at the State University of New York, where she has taught a variety of courses, supervised student teachers, and was director of secondary education and of overseas education. She has worked with diverse economic and ethnic groups both in the United States and overseas.

Her overseas experience is impressive. It includes teaching students from eleven different island nations at the University of the South Pacific, and working as an exchange professor at the Kangnung University in Korea. She also organized and directed a long-running teacher-training program for State University of New York students in Bristol, England, and a training program for teachers in Jamaica, West Indies. She has lectured in Senegal, Israel, London, and Japan, where she was the keynote speaker at three educational conferences.

Dr. Stephens has long been interested in innovative approaches to education. Her knowledge of curriculum—elementary through high school—has enabled her to suggest practical ideas based on the reality of the classroom. She recognizes the difficulties teachers face in attempting to introduce new programs.

Her books are always based on what is happening in classrooms. Her first book, *The Teacher's Guide to Open Education*, was translated into Japanese and was the main selection of three educational book clubs. This book developed from her doctoral dissertation, for which she observed classrooms in schools in England in areas with diverse populations. For a later book, *Developing Thinking Skills through Real-Life Activities*, activities were again tested in classes, and she was awarded a Department of Energy grant to disseminate the material through inservice courses and workshops to classroom teachers.

In conjunction with research for the current book, *The Complete Guide to Learning through Community Service*, Dr. Stephens again turned to the teachers in the field, reporting on programs in over seventy schools.

Organization

The format of this book is testimony to my belief that service learning must be an integral part of the curriculum, rather than just another educational reform that teachers "don't have time for." It has been designed for teachers who have never engaged in a service project as well as for those who are ready for more extensive programs.

About four hundred different service activities in over seventy schools are included. They range from those that can be performed right in the classroom or school to those that involve multiple placements outside of school. They include projects of varying duration—some that can be completed in a relatively short time and others that require a major time commitment. Each chapter contains descriptions of schools that practice some of the activities described.

Where grade levels are specified, they have been selected to conform with the curriculum guides for those grades. However, it is not always possible to pigeon-hole service activities. Kids from kindergarten to high school, for example, have established relationships with the elderly and the homeless, or become environmentalists. Accordingly, many activities have been labeled "ungraded." I urge all teachers to scan these activities. They can be adapted for many grades.

The book is divided into four parts as follows. Three chapters in Part One respectively introduce and define service learning, present a step-by-step approach to selecting and organizing a service project, and detail the crucial elements in implementing the project.

Part Two categorizes activities by the subject whose curriculum appears most consistent with the activity. This organization was adopted to permit individual classes to incorporate service learning more readily into their curricula. However, the categories are not meant to be limiting. As is true of most good teaching, service learning frequently defies rigid subject classifications. This is particularly true in middle schools, where many service projects originate as part of an interdisciplinary theme. Examples of these appear in Part Three.

The first two chapters in Part Three single out two popular themes for service projects: service with seniors and with the homeless. These can be incorporated in the curriculum of individual subjects or across the curriculum as part of interdisciplinary units. Activities are presented for each approach. The final two chapters in this part present exemplary interdisciplinary and multidisciplinary programs.

In Part Four, individual chapters are devoted to multicultural activities and to students with special needs in order to emphasize the significance of these topics in service learning. They are followed by chapters on conflict resolution, school partnerships, career exploration, and critical thinking, all of which support service learning. They span many curriculum areas. A concluding chapter is devoted to personal reflections.

Although this book is addressed primarily to teachers and administrators concerned with the education of children from kindergarten through middle or junior high school, it is also for parents, community agencies, and educators at all levels who are seeking means of improving education for our kids.

The early grades were selected because many believe that by starting at a young age, a lifelong ethic of service can be developed. It has been demonstrated that all kids, from the time they first enter school, can be made aware of their responsibilities to their communities.

The middle school years have been emphasized because they are particularly favorable for service learning. First, the organization of middle schools, many of which employ an interdisciplinary approach, permits ready incorporation of service projects. There is also a growing recognition of the importance of service learning for youngsters in these years. Increasing numbers of programs are addressed to middle school youngsters, such as the Valued Youth Program in San Antonio, which targeted at-risk middle schoolers instead of high school students because it concluded that by high school many of those kids might already have dropped out of school.

I believe service learning is a powerful tool. There is much evidence of its potential for enhancing learning and benefiting students and the community alike. I trust that this book will encourage you to join with the many educators who are incorporating service learning into their curricula.

Introduction

A FABLE

It's difficult to pinpoint when it started. But everybody agreed the schools had changed. Kids were more eager to attend school; teachers were excited about teaching. Dropout rates were declining; and throughout the country, communities were supporting school budgets.

Many believe it began with the kids' concern for the environment. At some point, the kids decided they could not depend on adults to stop despoiling their planet. So in school after school, the kids organized. They launched campaigns to "Save the earth not just for us but for future generations."[1] They recycled; they reminded their parents to conserve. They beautified their communities—reclaiming littered lots and turning them into vegetable gardens, planting flowers and trees, and painting attractive murals outside of housing projects.

With the help of dedicated teachers, the environment became part of the curriculum of every grade. As kindergartners and first graders explored magnets, they separated aluminum cans for recycling. A unit on rain forests led many kids to institute campaigns to save the forests and to raise funds to buy a few acres to ensure that the forests remained untouched.

Older children "adopted" streams and applied what they had learned in science to test them for phosphate levels. They investigated acid rain and ozone depletion, then graphed and quantified their results to reinforce math skills. Writing improved as they bombarded legislators with letters insisting that pollution be controlled. After a study of the Bill of Rights, a fifth-grade class framed an amendment to the Constitution, an "Environmental Bill of Rights," stating "We believe we are entitled by law to clean air, land and water."[2] This Bill was introduced in the New Jersey State legislature.

Empowered by their participation in environmental campaigns, the kids sought additional ways to serve, and they found many. Today, kids are teaching other kids. Middle school students are acting as Big Brothers and Big Sisters to little kids. At-risk middle school students who know all about failure are undertaking to teach at-risk elementary school kids so they will know nothing about failure. Both groups benefit.

With the power of kids unleashed, service projects are everywhere. Intergenerational relationships are flourishing. Children visit nursing homes and senior citizen centers dispensing cheer and studying history from the seniors' life experiences. Seniors in turn come to the schools to tutor and teach kids. It is clear that there is a special affinity between kids and the elderly.

Recognizing the potency of learning through service, teachers are encouraging the kids—to reach out to the homeless, the hospitalized, and the abused and, in the process, to learn about poverty, health, and society, and also about compassion and civic responsibility. Schools have become active, exciting places; the curriculum makes more sense, and the experiences make the kids feel pretty good about themselves. The teachers, too, are having fun. Discipline problems have eased. Using the community as a lab for their courses enhances their teaching.

Not to be outdone, corporations, banks, and community organizations are signing on, releasing their employees each day to go into the schools to help tutor kids, act as role models, expose kids to careers, and teach them social business skills—how to be interviewed, speak on the telephone, dress, and communicate. The walls separating schools from the community have tumbled, with kids going into the community and community members feeling comfortable going into schools for computer, literacy, or other courses; to enjoy the sports facilities; or to help the teachers. The schools have become true community centers.

And "service learning," a term used to describe learning through community service, is now in every school. All kids participate—the academically gifted and the slow, the athletic and the clumsy, the mainstreamed and "special ed" kids. It is evident that, without any knowledge of Dewey, who had envisioned these kinds of schools almost 100 years ago, the kids have changed the schools.

A fable is customarily defined as "a story that teaches a moral." A secondary definition is "a story about extraordinary persons." The moral of this fable and, in a sense, the point of this book is that kids can experience joy in service—in cooperating, helping, caring, demonstrating civic responsibility—while also learning. The extraordinary persons are the kids themselves, who are proving daily that they are capable of truly remarkable accomplishments.

Unfortunately, fables are fictitious. But if the power of kids is unleashed … you never know!

ROOTS OF SERVICE

Service in U.S. History

Community service has deep roots in the culture of the peoples who populated the United States. It was the ethic of cooperation that enabled the settlers to tame the wilderness and carve out towns. Tales of entire communities cooperating to raise the roof of a neighbor's barn are part of American folklore. And there was more. Food was shared in lean times and the young and elderly cared for. Widows and widowers, the lonely, sick, and disabled were the responsibility of all. Later, as additional immigrants arrived, the earlier ones banded with them to form community aid societies and housed them until they found employment.

Young people were needed. In an agricultural society, children of all ages toiled in the fields. Girls in particular helped with household tasks—cooking, sewing, looking after siblings. The few schools that existed taught children little more than to read the Bible. During planting and harvest time, schools were closed. (The practice of closing schools during the summer months has continued to this day.) In towns engaged in commerce, children received job training by working alongside family members or through apprenticeship to masters.

With the advent of industrial society, families flocked to urban centers. Kids were employed in factories where they worked long hours as cheap labor. To provide trained workers and educated managers, common schools were established. In the Northeast, where children toiled in the textile factories, legislation limiting child labor and later providing for compulsory schooling was passed, often promoted by labor unions, who saw child labor as depressing wage standards.

Because education was a responsibility of the individual states, compulsory schooling was by no means uniform throughout the country. In some states, parents objected because children had to work to help support the family. In the South, kids continued to work on farms. Sons of wealthy plantation owners received private tutoring while education for children of slaves or poor whites was nonexistent or sporadic at best. Not until the beginning of the twentieth century did all states adopt compulsory school attendance laws, and, even then for differing numbers of years.

Gradually, schools have replaced families as the vehicles for providing youngsters with occupational skills. Rich postulates that they were also expected to sort youth for future entrance into society "by a competitive system of grading, promotion, honors and awards. Those who fail will be notified that they were given a fair chance and must now assume societal roles consonant with demonstrated abilities."[3]

Two familiar institutions served as models for schools: the factory and the military. The factory model inspired the division of learning into small, discrete bits. Wood compares the organization of schools to the assembly line: "Every child enters at a set age and is expected to proceed at the same pace. Every child is tested each step of the way. All products are pushed to a norm, and those who come with less 'raw material' are dropped into lower tracks and become substandard."[4]

The chain of command is similar to that of the military: flowing from the superintendent (general) to the principal and administration (officers) and the teachers (noncommissioned officers). As in the military, schools are custodial institutions with an authoritarian structure, strict discipline, and punishment for infractions.

Clearly, the practice of isolating children in schools was a relatively new concept in U.S. history. For the most part, youth were no longer resources to be prized but almost *marginal* to society. Unlike previous generations, youth were given no productive role, no responsibilities to their communities. Instead, they came to be viewed as *recipients* not *givers.* As a consequence, young people experienced a growing sense of alienation.

Service in Other Cultures

Service is also embodied in the Native American culture. "Service to others is a natural extension of Native Americans' traditional sense of communal responsibility," explains McClellan Hall, director of the National Indian Youth Leadership Project. He describes a Cherokee tradition of *Gadugi.* The call for a Gadugi is a call to bring people together to help one another, much as the European settlers came together for barn raisings.[5] "Community service validates our culture," he adds.

Similarly, African-Americans have noted the tradition of service in the African villages. "There are no nursing homes, no adoption agencies in the village," Wokie Griffin-Roberts explains. "The village educates. All are responsible for the others."[6]

This ethic of service and caring for family and group members has also been described as typical of Latino, Asian, and other societies around the world. It is true of Maori people in New Zealand, who endorse the concept of *matrifano*, which means "all children are my children," or "all children are my brothers and sisters," and of Aboriginal peoples whose culture appoints them caretakers of the planet.[7]

Service in Educational Philosophy and Psychology

Throughout the ages, there has been a continuing thread of criticism of schooling, running from Plato and Socrates in Greece, Rousseau in France, Tolstoy in Russia, to Dewey and current theorists. Their common argument has been that schooling needs to include engagement with real life and that students need to be active in their learning. Plato, for example, argued in *The Republic* that knowledge cannot be imparted mechanically by filling the mind as a storage bin. He wrote of a third kind of knowledge—in addition to knowing *that* and knowing *how,* knowing *why.*

It was the ideas of John Dewey and others associated with the progressive education movement in the early and middle twentieth century that were the most influential in the service learning movement. In *The School and Society* and *Experience and Education,* Dewey warned against the isolation of school from society and the passivity of instruction. He stated that it is a fallacy to assume that learning can be separated from experience. "If there be no maturity of experience, the capacity to memorize, to learn by rote, and to anticipate test-response situations can be forcibly developed, but it is wanting in any educational value."

At the heart of Dewey's philosophy was the concept of experience, an *experiential continuum* between the individual and society and between thought and knowledge. According to Dewey, *thought* was inspired by a doubt or problem. Knowledge was the outcome of wrestling with and solving that problem. "To present the knowledge without the problems that it arose to meet is to ask the student to shake hands with a scarecrow."[8] It follows, according to Dewey, that learning cannot be disassociated from contact with real problems.

Dewey also contributed the emphasis on reflection, a key component of service learning. He spoke of reflection as a means of transforming a situation in which there is obscurity, doubt, conflict, or disturbance of some sort, into a situation that is clear, coherent, settled, and harmonious.

George Counts, also associated with the progressive education movement, published a provocative pamphlet in 1932 titled "Dare the Schools Build a New Social Order?" Counts challenged the schools to become the central means of humanizing society and to help correct some of the inequities of an industrial civilization. Earlier he had written that unless the school helped students develop a social outlook, it would deal only with superficialities. "If it [the school] is not rooted in some profound social movement or trend, it can be but an instrument of deception."[9]

The Swiss biologist and psychologist Jean Piaget offered insights into children's thinking, arguing that children develop intellectual structures, or *schemata,* to represent their world. As they are exposed to new experiences, they assimilate these to their existing schemata and then accommodate the schemata to reflect the new elements in the experiences, thus becoming better able to understand the world. Children learn, according to Piaget, by concrete experiences and opportunities to explore their environment. These permit progressive adaptation of the intellect.

Other streams fed into the service learning movement. Jerome Bruner, a U.S. psychologist, emphasized the importance of children being involved in their learning. He claimed that subjects should be taught not to "spectators" but to "participants."[10] The experiential education movement of the last decades, as well as the open education movement of the 1970s, which espoused the notion that students should be "active learners," underscored this approach.

As can be seen from this discussion, the issue of how children should be educated is not solely the province of educators. It has occupied philosophers and psychologists throughout history. Philosophers raise metaphysical issues: "What is the nature of society?" "Who should be educated?" "What should the schools be like in a free society?" Psychologists ask, "How do children learn?" But it is the educators who need to address these questions in the context of practical issues: day-to-day organization, curriculum, and methods of teaching. It is within this context that we examine service learning.

Notes

1. Slogan of Kids against Pollution, Tenakill Elementary School, Closter, New Jersey.
2. Proposed by Kids against Pollution.
3. John Martin Rich, *Innovations in Education,* 3rd ed. (Boston: Allyn and Bacon, 1981), p. 149.
4. George H. Wood, *Schools That Work* (New York: Dutton, 1992), p. 74.
5. Mc Clellan Hall, "Gadugi: A Model of Service-Learning for Native American Communities," *Phi Delta Kappan,* June l991, p. 755.
6. Wokie Griffin-Roberts, director, Generator Service Learning Project. Conference, Minneapolis, Minnesota, April 16, 1993.
7. Gary Howard, executive director, Reach Center, Washington. Speaker at the above conference.
8. Quoted by Roberts S. Brumbaugh and Nathaniel M. Lawrence, *Philosophers on Education* (Boston: Houghton Mifflin, 1963), p. 142.
9. George S. Counts, *Secondary Education and Industrialism.* (New York: Cambridge Press, 1929), p. 68.
10. Jerome Bruner, "The Skill of Relevance and the Relevance of Skills," *Saturday Review,* April 18, 1970, p. 166.

PART I

An Introduction to Service Learning

This part provides an overall view of service learning. Chapter 1 presents its historical background, educational rationale, and a concise definition. The chapter also reviews a number of related aspects, such as the roles of youth and teachers, federal legislation, and research and evaluation.

Chapters 2 and 3 detail step-by-step procedures for organizing and implementing a range of service learning programs in different classes.

CHAPTER 1

Understanding Service Learning

"Youth are a window to the future. Through them we can anticipate the shape of the world to come."

—McClellan Hall, National Indian Youth Leadership Project[1]

Although community service is not a new notion in education, traditionally it has been confined primarily to the high school as an extracurricular activity. When kids engaged in community service activities, such as collecting food or clothing for the poor and homeless or entertaining in senior citizen centers or hospitals during holidays, the activities were add-ons to the curriculum with limited impact on the students.

A number of factors brought community service as an approach to learning into the consciousness of educators. There was the persistent dissatisfaction with schools, the persistent theme of bored, restless, disengaged students going through life as bystanders rather than participants. There was nationwide concern that schools were failing youngsters. They were not providing kids with occupational skills; kids were leaving school with little knowledge of the world of work and work-related behavior. What's more, many were also leaving with questionable academic skills.

Critics focused on the isolation of schools from the real world and extolled the benefits of harvesting youth's energies to serve the community. In the early 1980s, John Goodlad wrote of the need for a partnership between schools and communities.[2] Ernest Boyer went further, recommending "that every high school student complete a service requirement...involving volunteer work in the community or at school."[3]

More recently, the Carnegie Council advocated community service for all middle school students, stating:

Every middle grade school should include youth service—supervised activity helping others in the community or the school—in its core instructional program. Youth service can teach young people values for citizenship, including compassion, regard for human worth and dignity, tolerance and appreciation of human diversity, and a desire for social justice. Youth service also teaches students skills for work such as collaboration, problem solving, and conflict resolution. [4]

There were models for youth service. The ethic of service had been kept alive in the United States by programs such as the Civilian Conservation Corps in the

1930s, by the Peace Corps and the volunteer programs of the War on Poverty during Lyndon Johnson's administration, and by the civil rights struggles of the 1960s. Largely unheralded, many school districts had instituted community service programs by the 1980s and 1990s.

Gradually, more and more schools and districts established service programs. Maryland, in 1992, was the first state to make 75 hours of service a requirement for graduation from high school. Although initially most programs were confined to high schools, there was recognition that service should be initiated as early as kindergarten. If started early in life, it was postulated, service might become a lifelong ethic. Wokie Griffin-Roberts wrote, "It's important to start when students are young—especially if you're working with kids from very economically depressed areas. At age five or six they have an awareness of the importance of doing something for their communities."[5]

Once community service moved into all grades, K–12, the concept changed. It became an integral part of the curriculum, emerging under a new label: *service learning.*

Service Learning Defined

Service learning is a merger of community service and classroom learning that strengthens both and generates a whole greater than the sum of its parts. Service is improved by being anchored in the curriculum and learning is deepened by utilizing the community as a laboratory for the classroom where students can test and apply their curriculum to real-life situations.

Learning is further intensified by reflection. Students are required to contemplate the meaning of their service, to evaluate its context and its impact, thereby reaching a greater understanding of themselves, their studies, and the society. For example, kids who work with the elderly become aware of the special problems of aging, such as declining health, loneliness, the inadequacies of residential facilities, and what these imply about our society. They study and evaluate legislation, such as Medicare and Social Security, not in isolation but as it affects the elderly. In the process, they need to question, analyze, hypothesize, synthesize—that is, to employ critical thinking skills.

A distinction is made between community service per se and service learning. Community service may be an add-on to the curriculum, whereas "Service learning is an innovative concept. It is not simply a field trip to a soup kitchen. Service learning involves students in meeting real human needs as part of the school curriculum, enabling them to learn by doing..."[6]

Youth as Resources, Not Problems

Are young people really capable of assuming the roles service programs would assign them? Different segments of our society are frequently stereotyped—youth, disabled, elderly—although these broad characterizations have little meaning with regard to individuals. Certainly, there have been many stereotypes associated with young people.

Viewed by many as problems—rebellious, undisciplined, frivolous, with uncontrolled sexual energy—and frequently identified in the media with gangs, drugs and violence, youth are often distrusted and even feared. Yet educators such as Joan Schine,[7] who have worked with them in service learning projects, recast them as valued resources for their communities—as concerned, committed, responsible people, eager to help, "grateful for an opportunity to make a difference, and when guided by adults, capable of extraordinary contributions."

Early adolescence is a bewildering period, Schine explains. Youngsters confront difficult choices, experience physical changes, wonder where they fit in. Full of self-doubts, they are a picture of contrasts: at once energetic and lazy, enthusiastic and bored, self-absorbed and altruistic, conscientious and irresponsible, moving away from adults yet desperately needing their support, and frequently most cocky when they are least confident. It is also a period when they need to feel useful, respected, and assigned authentic tasks. Schine adds: "They need to make a difference. If it is not a positive difference, they will make it anyway."

The Report of the Federal National Commission summed up the significance of service to young people:

> *When asked to do something important, something that matters, something that will make a difference in the world, they gain self-satisfaction from having done it well, and respect from others—including adults—from whom they had been isolated. Such an experience transforms who they are—in their own eyes, and in the eyes of others. Community service is not something done for young people; it's something done by young people. By serving, they can become planners and doers and leaders. They become valued, competent resources, rather than clients of schools and police and other social institutions.[8]*

Even younger children, frequently portrayed as self-centered, respond wholeheartedly when challenged to help others, whether they are asked to save pennies to help homeless children or give up a toy to a less fortunate child.

Inclusion

Most important, service learning activities are not the province of any one group the gifted,—the talented, the average, or the exceptional kids. All are involved. All can serve. Furthermore, unlike the classroom, where students are rated individually, service is frequently a collaborative experience. Participants learn to work together and to accept the contributions of each. In many service programs, children in special education classes work alongside mainstreamed kids leading to a new appreciation of each for the other as well as a greater acceptance of disabling conditions. This was borne out by Florence Chapman, a teacher at the Schuylkill Elementary School in Phoenixville, Pennsylvania, who had a quadraplegic young girl in her fourth-grade class. She explained that all the kids made special efforts to ensure that this girl could participate in service.

Learning about Other Segments of Society

By exposing youngsters to segments of society with which they have little contact, such as elderly people in nursing homes, homeless persons in shelters, or retarded individuals in resident facilities, service programs lead kids to appreciate the difficulties these groups encounter, to develop respect for the courage with which they are borne, and to view the individuals free from common stereotypes.

There are many illustrations of this. The author accompanied a group of eighth graders, from the Shoreham-Wading River Middle School on Long Island, on a trip to a school for the retarded. On the bus, the youngsters were exhuberant, boisterous, joking—typical thirteen-year-olds. As they disembarked at the center, however, they became serious, walking quietly to the classrooms to meet the "friends" to whom they had been assigned previously. It was evident that their arrival had been eagerly anticipated. With art supplies they had brought along, the Shoreham youngsters taught their friends to make "bugs" for a Halloween celebration. Later, all joined in spirited basketball and soccer games. On the return journey, the students were quieter, reflective. A young boy summed it up: "I really like them. I learned they are just like us."

A relationship develops between kids and residents of nursing homes. It is surprising to see kids relating comfortably to eighty- and ninety-year-olds. Kids themselves do not anticipate their reaction. Nick, a student at the Redlands Middle School in Grand Junction, Colorado, was visiting nursing home residents as part of his school's service program. Reflecting on his experience with an elderly resident, he remarked, "What I found most interesting was that she was ninety-seven years old and that she was very nice."

Role for Teachers

"We had a group of disaffected, bored fourth graders. We had no choice but to try to reach them. For us, service learning was the crutch that worked."
—Florence Chapman and Beverly Bonkoski, Schuylkill Elementary School, Phoenixville, Pennsylvania

Service learning creates a new role for teachers. They too have been victims of the increasing boredom of life in schools, exhausted from trying to impose a curriculum on uninterested students. They have often expended more energy on just keeping discipline than on teaching lessons. And they too have been isolated from the community.

Service learning offers a change. It is "not just another program to be squeezed into an overpacked curriculum, but a new way of learning or method of instruction," explains James Kielsmeier, president of the National Youth Leadership Council, a pioneer of the movement. By challenging kids to be their best, engaging them in relevant activities, eliminating the constant testing and grading that Ivan Illich, a critic of traditional schooling, described as assigning each child a "level of inferiority," service learning eliminates much of the tension between students and teachers. It engenders trust in kids, a relationship between teacher and student, that leads to the empowerment of both.

Anne Purdy, a service coordinator at Central Park East Secondary School, explains, "I have learned to trust the kids and give them more and more responsibility. When I accompanied my eighth graders on an extended trip, the kids organized it completely. They raised the money for expenses, arranged for the bus, the stay, the program, even the entertainment. They didn't expect or need my help."

Teachers can join this movement. Planning and implementing a service learning program takes an "awful lot of effort." But it permits teachers once again to take control of the curriculum, to be creative, to make a difference in kids' lives, and to recall why they went into teaching in the first place. And there is a growing network of support.

The Federal National and Community Service Act

Nationwide, the service learning movement has been fueled by the Federal National and Community Service Act of 1990, which established a commission to "explore and test innovative ways to renew the ethic of civic responsibility," and provided for grants in four areas: K–12 schools, higher education, youth corps, and national service models.

Grants for K–12 schools were distributed under the title Serve-America "to build service-learning into the curriculum of every school in America." In each of the years 1992 and 1993, the commission awarded $16.3 million to the states, the District of Columbia, Puerto Rico, the Virgin Islands, and Native American tribes. Money from the grants began trickling down from the states to local districts and individual schools. The funds were a catalyst for service learning programs, resulting in a proliferation of programs, many with innovative approaches.

In 1993, the National and Community Service Act created a Corporation for National and Community Service, which brought together various volunteer organizations including the commission, ACTION, and the White House Office of National Service to offer Americans: "From the youngest citizens engaged in service-learning activities through schools to the oldest citizens...the experience of participating in what the President calls 'seasons of service' throughout their lives."[9] The Corporation established a K–12 National Service-Learning Clearing-house "to provide assistance in involving students in community service programs." Fifteen organizations throughout the country, termed Partners in Technical Assistance, were identified by the clearing house for this purpose. (See Appendix B for a list of these organizations and more information about the clearinghouse.)

Appropriations continue through the Corporation. In fiscal year 1994, for example, the Corporation provided $30 million through its Learn and Service America program. Funds were earmarked for teacher training, placement of service learning coordinators in schools, and grants to local partnerships.

Service Learning as Education Reform

Education reform does not have a good track record in this country. For the most part, reforms have been programmatic, relying on alterations within the classroom—new curriculum, grouping of students, scheduling, or extraneous changes such as vouchers or school choice. But the basic organization of schools, such as the departmentalization of subjects, rigid time periods, and single-age grouping has remained the same. The lecture method of teaching and adherence to a text for each subject are still the norm. Modifications that would question the existing organization, challenge authority relationships, empower youth by entrusting them with real responsibility for their learning—or for that matter, provide real empowerment of teachers have been infrequent.

A major obstacle to such reform has been the testing frenzy. The production of educational tests is a billion-dollar-industry in the United States. Not only do schools use tests, but so do corporations, the military services, government agencies, and psychologists. The ubiquitous testing of kids in schools has created a myth: that the items on a test are the crucial details that every child should learn, regardless of whether that child lives in a rural or urban community, regardless of that child's cultural background, regardless of personal aspirations.

Tests have been described as the "tail wagging the dog." Instead of measuring the work of the school, they determine that work because of concern that children will not be taught the specific material tested. This creates an imperative to cover the texts and leaves little time for even the most conscientious teachers to try still another activity in their busy days. Just as serious, tests tend to distort teaching—supporting the notion that skills are better learned in isolation than in context, hence the emphasis in test preparation materials on short paragraphs followed by brief answers.

However, the chorus for education reform keeps growing louder. There are reasons for optimism. Test makers are experimenting with diverse forms of tests. Alternative schools are experimenting with curriculum. In New York City, a host of community schools have been established recently, many with different patterns of organization and many including service learning. "Service learning may be the vehicle to facilitate school reform," Jan Reeder believes. "Specifically, it can assist us in changing the structure of the school day, which I think is a very critical key to any reform efforts."[10] On the horizon and already implemented in many schools are other reforms: the drive for restructuring schools, site-based management, teacher empowerment, cooperative learning, and shared decision making. These are all friendly to service learning. Indeed, service learning may be the catalyst that helps transform education.

Research and Evaluation

There have been consistent reports of the benefits service learning provides to students. Educational practices, however, are notoriously difficult to evaluate. Conrad and Hedin[11] affirm this: "Advocates of almost any practice...can find research evidence in its favor. Detractors and empirical purists can likewise find reasons for discounting the results of any study." Customary assessment instruments, such as pen-and-pencil tests, are not applicable to most programs as complex as service learning. Encompassing as it does an array of projects with diverse populations in varying sites, service learning defies the usual means of evaluation. To complicate the problem further, a complete assessment of a project would have to include both parties—those who serve and those who are served. Yet in many instances, it is not possible to assess the effects of programs on community groups. How, for example, does one determine the effects on the homeless of kids doling out food in soup kitchens?

Research has, therefore, focused primarily on the impact on students. Conrad and Hedin have made a useful distinction between two types of research: qualitative and quantitative. The former employs performance-based methods of studying attitudinal changes in participants. It is based to a large extent on observations, interviews, supervisors' comments, and anecdotal reports in students' journals.

Qualitative Data

There is a growing body of evidence of the positive effects of service on kids. Turning Points,[12] for example, looked at the student participants in the Early Adolescent Helper Program,[13] and reported:

...Helpers said they learned to listen to others, to trust and be trusted by others, to be patient and reliable, and to accept responsibility. They enjoyed getting to know adults at their school outside the usual teacher—student relationships, and especially liked being treated as co-staff, feeling valued for their efforts and opinions, and feeling important to others.

Adults reported...that the Helpers acted without exception in a professional manner, attended regularly and assumed their work roles with complete seriousness. The adults also noted positive attitude and behavior changes.

Other studies have reported that service activities may "significantly reduce levels of alienation...may result in reduced discipline problems."[14] The National Association of Partners in Education summarizes the qualitative gains as follows:

enhanced self-esteem as students affect positive change and as they succeed in an arena not gauged by academic or athletic ability; greater sensitivity to cultural diversity; improved collaborative and problem-solving skills; increased interest in their studies as they begin to see practical applications; and a greater sense of civic responsibility and an ethic of service which they may carry throughout their lives.[15]

Quantitative Data

Attempts to study the effects of service on academic learning have varied. The most consistent evidence of gains is associated with tutoring programs. "Research and evaluation...consistently tends to show positive results for both server and served in terms of academic improvement and personal growth."[16]

Impressive quantitative benefits have been reported by a number of schools described later in this book. The Valued Youth Program in San Antonio identifies potential dropouts in middle schools and trains them as tutors for kids at nearby elementary schools. An evaluation of two years of the program documented significant gains. Of 101 tutors in the experimental group, only one dropped out, contrasted to 11 of the 93 in a comparison group. Furthermore when matched with the latter group, tutors and "tutees" had significantly higher reading grades and higher grade averages in mathematics and English. Tutors also had fewer disciplinary referrals, had improved attendance, and scored significantly higher on self-concept and Quality of School Life scales.

Other schools also have reported notable achievements. At the Suzanne Middle School in Walnut, California, over a period of seven years of the Make A Difference service program, students' state test scores went from the 22nd percentile to the 94th percentile, the largest increase in the state.

Students at the William H. English Middle School in Scottsburg, Indiana, are from a county that had the lowest rank in educational attainment in the state. After many years of a unique science service program, they placed in the 97th percentile in science knowledge, and in the 95th percentile in ability to apply scientific knowledge; and every student tested selected science as her or his favorite subject.

Further studies are currently being conducted to establish a research base. The National Society for Internships and Experiential Education; the Search Institute, affiliated with the National Youth Leadership Council; and the federal Corporation for National and Community Service have all started comprehensive research projects to establish theoretical bases and provide program evaluation models. Hard data from these studies should be available in the near future.[17]

Notes

1. McClellan Hall, "In Our Own Language: Youth as Servant Leaders," *Journal of Emotional and Behavioral Problems.* Winter 1993, p. 29.
2. John I. Goodlad, *A Place Called School* (New York: McGraw-Hill, 1983).
3. Ernest L. Boyer, High School: *A Report on Secondary Education in America* (New York: Harper & Row, 1983), p. 209.
4. *Turning Points: Preparing American Youth for the 21st Century,* Report prepared by the Carnegie Council on Adolescent Development's Task Force on Education of Young Adolescents. The Carnegie Council is a program of Carnegie Corporation of New York, January 1990.
5. Wokie Griffin-Roberts, Profile, *Generator, Journal of Service Learning and Youth Leadership,* (Roseville, MN: Fall 1992), p. 25.
6. *What You Can Do for Your Country,* Report of the Commission on National and Community Service, Washington, DC, January 1993.
7. Joan Schine is director of the National Center for Service Learning in Early Adolescence, 25 West 43rd Street, New York, NY.
8. *What You Can Do, for Your Country,* p. 7.
9. Newsletter, *Corporation for National and Community Service,* Washington, DC, Fall 1993.
10. Jan Reeder, principal, Gig Harbor High School, Washington State, *Service Line, 2* (1), Summer 1991, p. 2.
11. Dan Conrad and Diane Hedin, "School-Based Community Service: What We Know from Research and Theory," *Phi Delta Kappan,* June 1991, p. 746.
12. "Turning Points, p. 24.
13. The Helper Program is a project of the National Center for Service Learning in Early Adolescence.
14. Raymond L. Calabrese and Harry Schumer, "The Effects of Service Activities on Adolescent Alienation," *Adolescence, 21,* 1986, p. 685.
15. Newsletter, National Association of Partners in Education, Inc., 209 Madison Street, Alexandria,VA 22314.
16. "What You Can Do for Your Country," p. 29.
17. "Research Agenda for Combining Service and Learning in the 1990s," National Society for Internships and Experiential Education, 3509 Haworth Drive, Suite 207, Raleigh, NC 27609.

CHAPTER 2

Organizing a Service Project

"It's like opening a new book, but you learn so much more. It gives you a chance to do something instead of just reading about it."
—Eric, eighth-grade student, Mott Hall Intermediate School, New York City

On Monday afternoons there is an exodus of the 100 eighth graders at the Mott Hall Intermediate School (I.S. 223) in Harlem. These kids are going to "work," some by bus or subway. They will assist the elderly and the handicapped; tutor younger children; work in offices, museums, libraries, theaters, health facilities, and more.

The program at I.S. 223 was conceived by Myrna Schiffman, a Home and Career and Health and Education teacher, who started it as a voluntary after-school-activity for her eighth-grade students. Although these kids were designated "gifted and talented," many had low self-esteem, lacked self-confidence, and had no knowledge of the world of work. Their parents tended to keep them close to home. Some kids had never been far from their immediate community.

"I wanted to design a program that would bolster their self-concept and expose them not only to work situations, but also to the different developmental stages of life, part of our health curriculum," Schiffman explains. Students were given a choice of service in pre-K classrooms, elementary schools, or a geriatric center. "The response was astonishing," Schiffman recalls. Ninety of her 100 students volunteered to participate, and 75 remained for the entire term.

After another successful year, the school principal, Miriam Acosta-Sing, decided that "all students should have an opportunity to participate in service learning." Schiffman was asked to design and teach a course in Community Service that would replace other eighth-grade electives. The course meets for one period Tuesday to Friday, and a double period on Monday when students have an early lunch period and then work in their placements for the rest of the afternoon.

These once shy kids, Schiffman reports, are demonstrating leadership qualities, planning and teaching lessons, organizing activities for seniors, and participating in staff meetings in their agencies. They behave responsibly, performing assigned tasks and conscientiously contacting supervisors if they are going to be absent. They are learning life skills while improving academically.

The kids are enthusiastic. "I feel like a teacher," confides Suleika, who tutors math and science at an elementary school. "I now participate more in my own classes." Neirovich, who helps out at a Head Start center adds, "Working with little kids has made me more patient. I feel more like a parent. I am nicer to my little sisters now. I would like to be a kids' doctor."

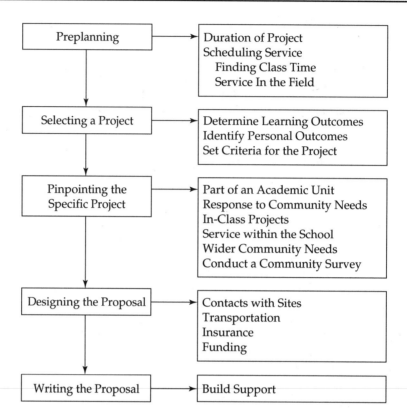

FIGURE 2.1 The Project Development Cycle

Planning for Service Learning

Teachers who wish to initiate a service–learning project need to engage in extensive planning. Decisions will have to be made first as to the duration of the project and time available to schedule service. Before the project is selected, objectives, criteria, and academic and community needs will need to be considered. Finally, other aspects of the plan—sites, transportation, insurance, and funding—will need to be investigated before the actual proposal is written. Each of these topics is described in Figure 2.1, which illustrates a step-by-step approach for developing a service-learning project.

Duration of the Project

Involvement with a project may last anywhere from a few days, to four to ten weeks or even an entire school term or year. Teachers who have had no previous experience with service learning should consider starting with short-term projects, such as raising funds for a specific cause, making cards for children in hospitals or for senior citizens, reading to younger children, planting bulbs or trees on school grounds or a neighborhood street, writing in support of legislation, or mobilizing for an area cleanup.

Projects of longer duration may include weekly visits to or from senior citizens, tutoring younger children, befriending immigrants and refugees, or helping shut-ins, the homeless, and the hungry.

Scheduling Service

Finding Class Time

Everyone knows there's not enough time in the school day as it is, without adding yet another activity. The trick is to link service to the curriculum and then schedule it during class sessions in the period assigned to a related subject or subjects, or as part of a regular community service class, as in the Mott Hall program described in Chapter 1.

A number of schools use the Advisory or homeroom period for designing service learning projects. For example, the Redlands Middle School in Grand Junction, Colorado, plans its service learning curriculum during advisory periods. Likewise, the Lee School in Fort Myers, Florida, originally lodged planning for service in the homeroom period.

At the Nipher Middle School in Kirkwood, Missouri, the period known as "Contact" is set aside each day to "address the physical, emotional, social and intellectual needs of the middle school child." Group dynamics, self-esteem, peer relations, and conflict resolution are some of the topics explored. The Contact period can also be used to involve students "in investigating societal problems and issues and to provide activity-oriented learning." The Nipher Civic Learning Project: Action Through Community Service, described in Chapter 12, was developed in a Contact period.[1]

Kids can serve their community on a host of issues without leaving their classroom. Some examples are presented later in this chapter.

Service in the Field

Many service projects require students to work in the community. It is obviously easier to arrange for this in elementary schools, but a number of practices in middle schools have facilitated the introduction of service learning experiences off the school grounds. Many middle schools have adopted an interdisciplinary curriculum, which includes team teaching and block and flexible scheduling. Service in the field usually requires a minimum of two periods. By scheduling the periods of two or more team teachers back to back, time can be carved out for a field experience.

Even when teachers are not engaged in a comprehensive interdisciplinary program, two or more may decide to team for a service project. Here, too, by arranging to have their classes meet back to back, they can find time for service outside of school. For example, English and social studies teachers may work on a common theme, such as homelessness. The English teacher assigns related reading and writing and undertakes to read the kids' journals, while in social studies the students study the societal issues involved. Field experiences may be scheduled as often as once a week or as infrequently as a few times during the course of the project.

By eliminating some electives and study periods, some schools find time for half a day of service once each week. This approach has enabled groups of seventh, eighth and ninth graders from the Central Park East secondary school to serve in the community on mornings supervised by a community service coordinator. Teachers use these periods at school for planning. The Mott Hall School, as noted, arranges for service on Mondays by scheduling a double period of a Community Service course on Monday afternoons.

In still another pattern, only a few students leave class at a time. The Henderson South Junior High School in Kentucky participates in a project to test the water quality of the Ohio River. Small groups of students leave class for one and a half hours twice a month to collect water samples. These students are expected to make up the work they miss.

Arrangements can also be made for service outside of school hours—before or after school, on weekends, or even during vacation periods. In these instances, service may be mandatory—a homework assignment—or voluntary— an independent study or extracurricular activity.

Voluntary service projects may be associated with student councils or service clubs. Others are organized by faculty and involve large numbers of students. Examples of these are the SHARE program at the Coppachuck Middle School described in Chapter 13 and the BEST program at the Wantagh Middle School described in Chapter 18.

Selecting a Project

Determine the Learning Objectives

"Service learning should begin with clearly articulated learning goals."[2] How will a particular project strengthen the curriculum? Which specific skills or attitudes will the students gain? Will it provide a career experience?

Identify Personal Outcomes

Will the project foster a more cooperative learning atmosphere? Will it contribute to students developing a service ethic? Or, as Alice Halsted phrases it, "What's the point, the overarching idea of the project? What will the youngsters get from it that's going to change them? Will it provide a real service experience?"[3]

Set Criteria for the Project

An effective program should achieve the following:

- Strengthen the curriculum by providing opportunities for students to apply skills from their courses.
- Enhance critical thinking by permitting students to share in the selection, planning, and organization of the program consistent with their maturity and to reflect.
- Develop habits of dependability, responsibility, and cooperation.
- Satisfy a real need, be perceived as relevant and worthwhile by the students and the recipients.

- Be appropriate and of interest to participants of varying abilities.
- Have a concrete and visible outcome within a realistic time frame.
- Strengthen students' sense of worth by enabling them to contribute to others.
- Foster understanding of and respect for the recipients.

Pinpointing the Specific Project

Part of an Academic Unit

Most often, projects are generated from the curriculum of a specific subject that would be strengthened by a service component. This was the scheme used by the Somerset Elementary School in Montgomery City, Maryland, when it introduced a service component to each primary grade's social studies curriculum, starting with kindergarten and succeeding each year to another primary grade.[4]

A Response to Community Needs

Frequently, projects are in response to identified community needs. In this context, the *community* is defined as the class or school community, the neighborhood, and any other entity from the town to the nation.

In selecting a project, kids ask: What should be improved? What actions can they take that will make a difference? They may wish to start with in-class or school projects.

In-Class Projects

These include activities such as writing to government officials in support of legislation on a community issue, inviting senior citizens or local government officials to their classes, and collecting food and clothes for the needy and homeless.

Service within the School

The school or district itself may be the setting for service activities. Students of all ages can organize school energy conservation drives, institute recycling campaigns within the school, identify and propose plans to eliminate wasteful practices, suggest improved lunch or bus procedures, tutor younger children, present science demonstrations, and help supervise the playground.

Middle schools frequently "adopt" an elementary school in the district. Students serve during special periods, free periods, or in after-school programs. They also engage in peer tutoring in their own schools. In a unique project, three eighth graders in the Mott Hall School in New York were trained by the Upper Manhattan Task Force on AIDS to present AIDS prevention programs to their peers by performing skits for classes at their school.

Kilsi, one of the students, explains, "We tell them how you get AIDS and how to prevent it by cleaning needles and using contraceptives. We can help more than parents. Parents can't talk to kids as we can. They tell them to abstain, but we know some kids won't do that. We can save lives."

Wider Community Needs

Projects frequently develop in response to neighborhood conditions, such as an influx of immigrants or homeless children. When Russian immigrants moved into the neighborhood of the Wyncote Elementary School in Pennsylvania, Roberta Jacoby recognized an opportunity for her fourth-grade students to engage in service learning. First, she paired each student with an immigrant pen pal, permitting both to practice writing skills. After a while, the pen pals met and a host of activities followed. Mapping the areas from which the immigrants had come harmonized her pupils' study of geography; collecting oral histories and hosting ethnic feasts helped each learn about the other's culture. The students wanted to do more. With Jacoby's help, they researched the examination immigrants must pass to become citizens and coached the Russians.

When kids become attuned to respond to special needs, it inspires in them a commitment to civic responsibility. Hearing of natural disasters such as a neighborhood fire, a hurricane, tornado, earthquake, or flood, children may be interested in learning the causes, costs, and effects of the disaster. Just as important, they also learn to care and to help.

Reports of a hurricane in Florida, for example, led many youngsters to want to "do something." Students from the Northport School District in Long Island were among those that responded. The district raised money for a truckload of supplies for the Homestead Elementary School in Florida. "Our students have acquired an ethic of service," principal Clifford Bishop of the Fifth Avenue Elementary School in Northport explains. "Over the years, they have adopted a park, worked with senior citizen centers, raised funds for children with AIDS or cancer, fed birds in winter, and more. All students, including mainstreamed and special education kids, work side by side on these projects. Parents participate, too. They are coordinating a plan to join with the kids on relandscaping our school property. And these programs are improving academic learning."

Conduct a Community Survey

Where there is no obvious project, suggest a survey of the neighboring community. As an added benefit, such a survey also makes kids more aware of the communities in which they live.

With younger children, the teacher may take the class for a neighborhood walk so that they can note any eyesores or hazards. Are there sidewalks or potholes that need repair? Any broken street lights? If so, notify the responsible local agencies.

Is there a vacant lot that is littered? One that could be used as a garden or ball field? In many schools in the South Bronx, kids are cooperating with others in the neighborhood to clean up abandoned lots and then plant community gardens or create play areas. Vegetables grown in the garden are distributed free of charge to people in the community.

Older students often conduct a community survey in groups—each assigned to a different area and armed with a list of questions such as:

- What facilities exist in the community?
- Which are needed?
- Are there playgrounds, areas for kids to play ball safely?

- Other recreation facilities?
- Parks?
- Libraries?
- Hospitals?
- Schools?
- Businesses?
- Is public transportation available?
- Which ethnic groups live in the community? What languages are spoken?
- Are there homeless people?
- Senior citizens centers?
- Adequate provision for the disabled?

This last question might be raised with someone who travels in a wheelchair. Perhaps some other kids could try riding in a wheelchair to become familiar with barriers.

Is there an existing effort that the class might join—campaigns by scout troups, 4-H Clubs, Red Cross, Salvation Army, United Way, UNICEF, or fraternal organizations such as Kiwanis, Lions, and Elks? Are there community agencies that need assistance, such as volunteer centers or youth clubs?

By sharing each group's findings, a number of projects may be indicated. Before choosing one, the students may want to do further research.

A community leader, the mayor, a city councilor, a social worker, or parent may be invited to class to discuss community needs. Students can also scan the newspapers for ideas. Reports of pollution of a nearby waterway, for example, may lead a science class to analyze water samples and inspire cleanup activities.

Finally—Select the Project

Let the kids share in the selection. They may first meet in small groups to present their research and formulate recommendations. Remind students of the criteria for an effective program, described earlier. Then, *brainstorm!*

It is advantageous to start with a small project, particularly if there has been no prior service experience. This will allow you to experiment with different activities and strategies.

An added suggestion: as you read the reports of projects later in this book, you will note that many schools have adopted acronyms to describe their programs, such as:

BEST Business and Education Serving Together

ARK Animals Rehabilitating Kids

THRIVE Teaching Healthy Relationships, Individual Values, and Ethnic sensitivity

Others use titles, such as, Helping Hands—Caring Hearts, Grand Vision, or Pennies for Love. You may wish to encourage the kids to institute a contest to select a name for their project.

Designing the Proposal

The plaque on the teacher's desk read, "Let a kid do it." It was a reminder that many of the organizational tasks in service learning can be entrusted to the students, whose early participation may be the key to a project's success. By their involvement, students experience a sense of ownership and empowerment, while learning essential skills—organization, planning, communication, responsibility, and decision making.

Contacts with Sites

Having identified the project, teachers will need to contact the agency, school, or group involved to make arrangements. Suitable sites are without doubt the most important component of the project. The National Center for Service Learning in Early Adolescence, speaking of middle school children, cautions, "These young adolescents are inexperienced and vulnerable. They need the assurance of staff members who are aware of them, can offer constructive criticism and positive reinforcement, and are genuinely pleased to have them at the agency." [5]

As students, parents, or friends become aware of your interest in service, you may receive recommendations for placements. However, it is essential that you personally visit each proposed site—even if the placement is a classroom. Scrutinize the population of the site before you assign students. You will need to brief students on what to expect when they arrive at the center.

It is only by speaking with the people in charge that you can evaluate their ability to accept the students, to offer them the guidance and encouragement that are essential for their growth. Volunteers should not be viewed as mere "gofers" but they should be included as much as possible in the work of the agency. Because the assignment is part of the students' school curriculum, their tasks should provide learning experiences.

Occasionally, particularly if the site has had no previous experience with service, you may encounter skepticism and even unpleasant stereotypes of young people. By presenting a carefully prepared plan that ensures that students will be trained, monitored, and evaluated, you can help overcome these attitudes.

Review your plan with the site administrator and the person who will be assigned to supervise the students. Convey the objectives, the number and ages of the volunteers, and the times they will be available. Make clear what can be expected of the youngsters, their strengths as well as their limitations. Be certain that the administrator is familiar with Department of Labor guidelines which emphasize that no student take the place of a regular employee and that students may not be employed during the course of their program. Site supervisors should be carefully briefed on their responsibilities (see Chapter 3).

Transportation

Some programs limit themselves to sites that are within walking distance—to a nearby school, park, or agency. This is true more often than not for elementary school projects. If transportation to a site is necessary, there are a variety of possible solutions:

- Some districts have vans available.
- Agencies may have vans or buses at their disposal and may agree to transport students to their sites or members to the school.
- Transportation in school buses may be available by including service under the rubric of field trips.
- For children old enough to use public transportation, arrangements usually can be made for free or reduced-rate tokens.
- Many schools provide bus transportation after school for sports or club activities. Students whose service is with kids in after-school programs or in nearby sites may be able to use these buses.

Insurance

In most cases, insurance provided for field trips or other off-site experiences will cover students, particularly if the activity is clearly identified with the academic program. In some cases, a rider to the policy may be necessary. Check with your principal or district business office.

Funding

A modest project may require only limited funds for incidentals. A more involved program will require the commitment of the administration for release time and/or appointment of a full- or part-time program director or service coordinator.

Here are some fund-raising strategies:

- Send a soliciting letter explaining the objectives of your project and funding required to parents, school administrators, student council, and community leaders. Each may have suggestions for raising funds.
- Suggest that the students become publicity hounds—write news releases for the local papers; contact reporters to suggest photo opportunities, or send the newspapers photos of kids at work. The more publicity you get, the better shot you have at receiving contributions.
- Small amounts for incidental expenses such as motivators and limited materials can be raised by the tried and true ways: raffles, walk-a-thons, babysitting, car washes, white elephant sales, lemonade, bake sales. Some kids collect and redeem recyclable cans and bottles. For larger amounts, investigate other sources in the community. Send your Project Design to local fraternal organizations—Lions, Elks, Kiwanis, and to banks, neighborhood corporations, or parent companies of branches in your neighborhood. Ask for donations of products you can sell, seed money, or funds for specific expenses such as transportation.
- More sizable amounts come from government agencies, large corporations, or foundations. Some cities or states provide funds for neighborhood development or other specific community activities. Your mayor's or governor's office may have information on this or may be able to direct you to the appropriate party.
- The federal National and Community Service Acts provide funds for service-learning through the Corporation for National and Community Service, usually distributed by the State Offices of Education. To

determine the criteria for receiving such funds, contact your State Education Agency or the corporation directly.[6]

- Your school district, too, may have money for special projects or someone who can help you write grant proposals. Learning to write for grants is a useful professional skill. Once you have the hang of it, it's not as awesome as it appears.
- Local school libraries have copies of grant registers and directories that list sources of grants from government agencies and from corporate and private foundations. If you believe you are eligible, write for the groups' annual reports which indicate money allocated in the previous year. This information can serve as a guide as to whether your program meets their guidelines.
- An important caveat must be added here. Teachers may participate in fund raising, but for any complex operation, they will not have the time to take full responsibility for funding. Running an effective service learning program requires a large commitment in time and energy. Tasks need to be shared.

Writing the Proposal

Now, put it all together. Prepare a proposal detailing your plans. Include the following:

- Objectives
- Service to be offered
- Number and description of students including their skills and strengths
- Times students will be available and where they will be placed
- Who will be in charge at the site
- Description of site population

Add to this list:

- A projected budget
- Transportation plan (if any is required)
- Provisions for training and evaluation of the students and of the program (described in the next chapter)
- Don't forget to include some motivators in the budget—an occasional pizza party, trip, picnic, jamboree, or T-shirts for added *esprit de corps.*

Although you have consulted while you planned your project, you will seek final approval and any other input at this point. You should emerge with a finished proposal.

Build Support

Distribute copies of your proposal widely—to parents, school administrators, interested teachers, student council members, community leaders, and the school newspaper. Remember, if the students will be leaving the school building during the day, you will need parental permission. Much will depend on the complexity of your proposal. In elementary schools, if the project is limited to one or two classes and to short-term activities, such as planting bulbs in a nearby park, you may not need to do much more than this.

Particularly in middle or junior high schools, however, where multiple sites and larger populations may be involved, seek a broader support base. Send a letter home explaining your intent and describing the potential benefits of service learning. Contact the PTA to request that a student be invited to make a presentation at a meeting. You may wish personally to make a report to parents to overcome some of their typical concerns: "Will service interfere with schoolwork?" "Shouldn't the kids be in school all day?" "Is it unpaid work?" To address these issues, inform the parents of other successful projects, distribute articles on service learning, and explain the relationship of service to learning.

Parents frequently have been partners in service projects: assisting in identifying projects, planning, transportation, fund drives, and media coverage. Weekend activities, such as environmental cleanups or building a playground, are often joint student–parent projects.

Involving other teachers is a must. How about a steering committee? While one person is usually designated as in charge, one or more backups ensure continuity and an influx of new ideas. Network, too, with colleagues at schools who have established programs.

Notes

1. Material on the Nipher Middle School, Kirkwood School District R-7, Missouri, was provided by teacher John A. Shaughnessy. Nipher's service learning program is described in Chapter 12.
2. "Standards for School-Based Service Learning," Alliance for Service-Learning in Education Reform. May 18, 1993.
3. Alice Halsted, assistant director, National Center for Service Learning in Early Adolescence, 25 West 43 Street, New York, NY.
4. For a complete description of the Somerset program, see Chapter 5.
5. *Connections: Service Learning in the Middle Grades* (New York: National Center for Service Learning in Early Adolescence, 1991), p. 44.
6. Corporation for National and Community Service, 1100 Vermont Avenue, N.W., Washington, DC 20525. Telephone: 202-606-5000.

CHAPTER 3

Implementing
A Service Project

"You can be somebody. Somebody who can change someone's life."
—Seventh grade student, helper, National Center for Service Learning in Early Adolescence

Kids do not just step into their roles as service providers. They will need to learn many new skills as they undertake responsible and unfamiliar tasks. As a minimum, most projects may require instruction in procedures such as interviewing, writing to organizations and government officials, telephoning, and even public speaking. Meticulous training is essential.

Training for Service

For some programs, a more extensive orientation is needed. This will include an introduction to the world of work, description of the placement sites and populations, details of the students' assignments, and meetings with the recipients and the site supervisor. Figure 3.1 summarizes the steps involved in implementing a service project.

The World of Work

At the outset, youngsters will have to know how they are expected to behave, how to dress, how to greet their supervisors and recipients, how to work as part of a team, and who will be in charge at the site. If they will be traveling to the site on their own, they will need to appreciate the importance of punctuality and of notifying the agency and the school in the event of an absence.

Description of Placement

Also essential is information about the organization or agency in which they will be placed—how it is funded and its history, mission, and organizational structure. What are its functions? What population does it serve?

Description of Population

Students working in intergenerational settings will require additional details about their populations. If they will be working with younger children, the training should include general developmental characteristics of the age group as well as of the specific group of kids to whom they will be assigned. They will need

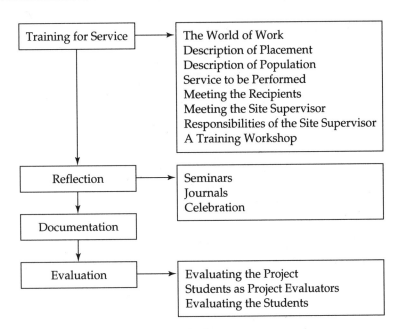

FIGURE 3.1   The Project Implementation Cycle

to know how to handle discipline problems and acceptable ways of relating to the kids.

Similarly, those who work with the elderly will need to understand what they will encounter. For many it will be the first time they will confront issues such as aging, terminal illnesses, and death. Without preparation, a visit to a nursing home can be a confusing experience. It may be helpful to show students a videotape of the site. Teachers and agency personnel can help the youngsters accept aging and death as normal stages of life. Eighth grader Noel, speaking of his work in a nursing home, related: "My grandmother lives with me. I know she is going to die, but I can accept this more now. It is not so depressing."

To further understanding of some of the physical problems of older people, such as impaired eyesight and hearing or arthritic conditions, children have at times been encouraged to simulate these. When such activities are used, however, it is essential that students learn to discriminate among individuals in the elderly population. Not all have physical impairments, and, for those who do, physical impairment does not imply mental impairment.

Contact with other populations also requires specialized training. Those working with the physically or mentally challenged need information on the nature of the problems and on the strengths and limitations these impose.

Service to Be Performed

What will be expected? If students will be reading to kids, they should be instructed on how to read books to children to maintain their interest. Seventh graders in Bleeker Junior High School in Queens, New York, administer an interest inventory to the third graders they tutor. This enables them to bring books from their local library that will be of interest.

Other questions are pertinent. Will the students be expected to help kids with homework? Required to plan lessons? If so, what form should these take? Will the cooperating teacher wish to see these in advance? Also important is an overview of the curriculum for the grades they will be assigned to tutor. How are these skills related to their own curriculum?

In some programs, students either individually or in small groups are paired with a recipient, frequently by chance. That tends to ensure more continuity in the relationship and the possibility of joint planning for future meetings.

Just how confusing a placement can be is illustrated by the report of a student who was asked to answer an agency's telephone while staff members were at a meeting. When the phone rang, she was flabbergasted. Was she supposed to mention the name of the agency? Should she interrupt the meeting for the person called? Others are overwhelmed even when asked to use a photocopier. Simple tasks may be new to the student.

Meeting the Recipients

When students first visit their placement, utilizing the first session as a get-acquainted, walk-through may help both groups overcome their trepidations. Kids will want to observe the staff as well as the population at the site. Large buildings may seem awesome to inexperienced students. By the same token, some adults may not have had recent contact with young children or adolescents and may be wary of their intrusion.

Meeting the Site Supervisor

It is essential that kids know who their supervisor is at the site, whom they can comfortably approach in the event of a question or problem. The supervisor may be able to visit the classroom in advance or else may be available when the kids first visit the site.

In some situations, the teacher or community service director will accompany students to the placement. Particularly where there are multiple placements, however, this may not always be possible. A regular schedule of visits to the site by the school personnel is a necessity, and the supervisor must be able to contact the responsible person at the school quickly in the event of a problem.

Responsibilities of the Site Supervisor

These should include the following:

- Maintain a record of students' attendance; sign-in and sign-out sheets are advisable.
- Assign appropriate and meaningful tasks.
- Act as mentor for the students; monitor their experiences.
- Share information about the agency's services and clients.
- Explain daily activities.
- Contact the school in the event of a problem.
- Prepare ongoing and final evaluations.

A Training Workshop

An extensive service program with multiple placements requires an even more comprehensive training plan. The training workshop conducted by the Mott Hall School, I.S. 223 in New York, deserves mention. It consists of five once-a-week sessions, prior to the students fieldwork, and is part of the Community Service course.

Before the workshop begins, a letter in English and Spanish explaining the program is sent to parents, and also to community agencies that have agreed to participate. All sessions except the first one, are led by volunteers from corporations and agencies. They include the following topics:

1. Orientation/Introduction to Community Service
2. Communication Skills/Interpersonal Relationships
3. Exploring Fields of Service. Students select three workshops of thirty-five minutes each that present an overview of what it would be like working with each of the following populations:
   A. Assisting the Elderly
   B. Working with Preschoolers
   C. Working with the Disabled
   D. Peer Education/AIDS
   E. Tutoring Elementary School Children
   F. Introduction to Administrative/Business Skills
   At the completion of these workshops, students select several choices. Most receive their first choice.
4. Leadership Skills/Introduction to the World of Work
5. Learning Skills relative to students' selection

Reflection

There is an often-repeated anecdote about the student who returns home from a busy day at school and is asked by a parent, "What did you do at school today?" The student replies, "Nothing!" Even though the teachers may have packed numerous activities into the day.

There are many possible interpretations of this story. One is that some youngsters are simply unable or unwilling to communicate about their school day. Unfortunately, there is another: that much of what occurs at school leaves students relatively unaffected. They often function as onlookers, disengaged and present only in body. It is this latter problem that the concept of reflection addresses.

Reflection is the yeast that transforms service experiences into learning. It is the path to development of critical thinking skills. Over half a century ago, John Dewey argued that experience without reflection can be shallow and "miseducative." Education results when we reflect on our experiences. More recently, Jean Piaget, who investigated children's cognitive development, noted that children must be engaged actively in examining their intellectual experiences. There is a difference between a superficial facade of knowledge and knowledge that has actually been incorporated into the child's intellect and that is available to be applied to other situations. For the latter to happen, students must deliberately think about their experiences, analyze them, try to make sense of them, appreciate their meaning and significance, and in this way learn from them and be able to apply what they have learned to other situations. These are the components of reflection—and, incidentally, of critical thinking, as well.

Reflection is not easy to teach in this era of seven-second sound bites. We rarely reflect. Images tend to bounce off us. We forget a movie or a book soon after we see or read it. Students remember information just long enough to repeat it on the unit test.

The key role of reflection in service learning cannot be overemphasized. Without reflection, students may resort to a simple reporting of experiences. We are much better at reporting than reflection. Reporting describes the details and sequence of where the student went and what occurred, such as the following entry in a student's journal: "Today I went to the Head Start Center. I found out my teacher was absent. I couldn't get a group of kids to play with Lego."

Reflection, on the other hand engages students in examining experiences, and in repeatedly asking, "Why?" What were the implications and effects of my work? Reflective activities "have real consequences: the reflection is purposeful, the outcomes make a difference to someone."[1]

New insights can also be gained from examining a critical incident, one that might have been handled differently, and then asking: "What happened?" "What led to it?" "Was it handled well?" "Would another approach have been better?" "Could (or should) it have been avoided?"

A number of activities encourage reflection about service, individually or in a group. They include journals, evaluation sheets, guided observations, seminars, conferences with teachers or personnel at the site, role playing, simulations, letters to the editor, formal reports, and other expressive forms—art, poetry, drama, video, or photos.

Of the activities cited here, the two most frequently employed are seminars and journals.

Seminars

Provision should be made for a regular seminar at which students can discuss and analyze their experiences. In a climate of acceptance, students are more apt to share their feelings, frequently relating initial expectations as they entered the program, problems that arose, experiences that made them feel inadequate or conversely, those that made them feel competent.

The seminar serves as a means of ongoing training. "How do you get a young child to sit still to listen to a story? Or a four-year-old to leave the sandbox?" Kids may not have the skills to handle the problems that arise. They may react in an authoritarian manner—for example, by shouting at the children. Myrna Schiffman of the Mott Hall School uses the seminars to focus on some of these problems. She has devised a useful approach. Groups of students present short skits that depict a dilemma they encountered in their service and how it was resolved. The other students react, offering alternative solutions. "These kids will be better parents as a result of these experiences," Schiffman predicts.

Students often express frustration during seminars, as did the eighth-grade girl who said, "All I do in the day care center is tie shoelaces." Peter Covino of the Federation of Protestant Welfare Agencies, who was present when the student uttered this complaint, countered, "Have you noticed any change since you started?"

"Well," she replied, "my line is always longer than the teacher's."

"Anything else?"

"There's a kid in class," she responded, "who according to the teacher never talks. But he talks to me."

Sometimes students question the larger society. "Why can't we do something about the homeless. I used to think they were all 'mental,' but some of them are just like us."

Many communicate a sense of growing confidence. "I feel I know something about the world now." "It feels good when someone looks up to you. If these kids think you are a great person, you must have done something real nice for them to like you." A new rapport is formed among the seminar participants. They take pride in each other's accomplishments. The seminar also permits students to share materials and plan for their next visits to their sites.

Journals

Journals are individually maintained notebooks in which students reflect on and try to make sense of their service experiences. They may include attendance sheets, service schedules, seminar notes and lesson plans, but the heart of the journal is the student's personal reactions entered after each visit. Some teachers believe students should be permitted to keep their journals confidential. The disadvantage of this approach is that reading the entries permits teachers to assess students' progress and, by commenting, to help students to understand the experience better. One compromise is to permit a student to fold over a page that is personal. The teacher will respect such a request for confidentiality.

To encourage reflective thinking, pose a preservice question, for students serving with seniors, for example: "Write about your previous experiences with older people," or "List five adjectives to describe the aged." Once the students are engaged in service, consider these questions:

- What have you learned—any new insights into the problems of the aged, into their status in society?
- What do you admire most about the people at the center?
- Have you learned anything about yourself? About others?
- What was the best thing that happened to you this week? How did it make you feel?
- Has anything happened that made you feel uncomfortable or unhappy?
- What do you believe is your major contribution?
- Have any people been affected by your service?
- Have you been given more responsibility since you started?
- Which aspects of the service experience have been most meaningful?
- Would you do anything differently?
- What is the hardest part of participating?
- Would you like to return to this site?
- Have you learned about any careers? New skills?

Pupils are usually instructed to answer one or more of these questions after each site visit, but to try to answer all of them by the end of the project.

An interesting side effect of journal writing is that it teaches kids not only to think reflectively but also to write reflectively. Many English teachers team with other subject colleagues for service projects for this very reason and cite the improved communication skills of the participants.

In addition to the journals, it is recommended that each student keep a folder summarizing specific activities performed. In tutoring programs, for example, the folder would include lesson plans, books read with kids, and games played. This may also include a case study about a particular child, as well as ideas for future activities.

Celebration

On a different note, at the completion of a project, *celebrate!* Have a picnic, luncheon, pizza party, dance, whatever. Have fun and recognize the contributions of the kids. The Mott Hall School had a moving end-of-the-year gathering for about twenty-five representatives of the community sites and the students who had participated. The school Home and Career class prepared lunch. Principal Acosta-Sing welcomed the group by stating: "These kids have acquired life-long skills. They have learned what it means to be productive workers, to speak to a supervisor, ask questions, get to a job on time, be responsible."

The participating youngsters presented their site supervisors with plaques carrying inscriptions such as this:

"I look forward to Mondays because I know I will be surrounded by loving, caring people whom I can never repay for all they've taught me and whom I can never forget."

—Alba

At the luncheon, groups of youngsters addressed their placement representatives and described the impact of their service experiences. The following were some of their stories:

"Community service has shown me I'm important, not just another kid. I want to be part of the solution, to help like the people at the center."

"I was very nervous when I first went to my service. I wasn't sure I wanted to go. But I learned so many things I will always remember. I see people trying to help their community. Someday I hope I can be the same way."

In turn, the site representatives praised the students for their contributions. They urged the school to continue sending them students.

Documentation

Many teachers also keep a journal. It is more a diary of the project: its organization, people contacted, students involved, hours contributed, and recipients or organizations served. Include also details of site visits, evaluation of the sites, comments on activities, and copies of correspondence—in other words, all matters pertaining to the program as it progresses.

This documentation is available for reports to administrators, boards of education, parents, and other concerned parties. It will also provide the basic data available for an evaluation of the project at its completion or in the future, and it can be helpful if you are planning to apply for grants.

Evaluation

Evaluating the Project

Build in evaluations of your service projects. Start by reviewing the original objectives of the program and the anticipated outcomes. To what extent has the project met them? Were the objectives realistic? Should changes be made in the program?

Collect qualitative data based on reports from the community sites, your own observations, students' seminar participation, and journal entries. Over the weeks, students' journals should exhibit higher levels of reflective thinking as students analyze their service experiences, appraise the placement site, assess their participation, and evaluate the effects on those served.

Look also for evidences of students' improved academic and social skills, civic responsibility, and job-related skills. Additional data can be gathered through questionnaires, interviews, and objective tests. The extent of the evaluation will vary depending on the time and resources available and on the use to which the data will be put.

For a more intensive study, consider setting up a control group of students, matched with program participants, who will not be part of the project. Students from local universities may be interested in participating in an evaluation study.

Students as Project Evaluators

A unique approach to evaluation, which relies on students to conduct the evaluations, was reported by Alice Halsted of the National Center for Service Learning in Early Adolescence. At the end of each academic year, selected students are appointed as evaluators to determine which aspects of the program have been successful and which can be improved. Aided by a trained facilitator, kids help frame the evaluation design and compose different questionnaires for each population to be interviewed. For younger kids, for example, they may ask, "Do you like it when your Helper comes?" "What do you do with your Helper?"

They work in pairs, collecting data through interviews with site personnel, student participants, parents, teachers, and administrators, as well as through questionnaires. Finally, the evaluators tabulate their data and make recommendations.

In a typical year, about eighteen students in the Center's Helper Program evaluate three schools and present them with useful recommendations. Halsted,[2] who is enthusiastic about the program, cautions, "You must trust kids enough to let them do an evaluation and then take their ideas seriously."

Evaluating the Students

To grade or not to grade the service experience? If service is directly related to an academic subject, the grade will usually include the service experience. If, however, the service is not anchored in a particular course, the procedure may vary from assigning no grade, to pass/fail, to a letter grade. Some students opt for a grade.

At Central Park East Secondary School, students' performances are evaluated in midyear and at the end of the semester. (See the sample evaluation form in

Appendix C) In addition, each student completes an end-of-year project, such as an in-depth paper on the site describing its function, source of funds, clients, personnel, and the like. This project, together with the site and service coordinators' evaluations, determines the final grade, which in this school is either U ("Unsatisfactory",) S (" Satisfactory",) S+, or D ("Distinguished").

Other factors considered in determining the grade are students' attendance, motivation, enthusiasm, performance, and responsibility, as well as projects, written reports, participation in seminars, journal entries, and reports from the sites.

Notes

1. *Reflection: The Key to Service Learning* (New York: National Center for Service Learning in Early Adolescence, 1991), p. 5.
2. Copies of the manual "Student Evaluators: A Guide to Implementations" may be purchased from the National Center for Service Learning in Early Adolescence, 25 West 43 Street, New York, NY 10036-8099.

PART II

Introducing Service Learning in the Curriculum

Service learning, encompassing as it does a wide range of topics, cannot be confined easily to one subject. Students who interview and write oral histories of veterans for their language arts class may also be learning about World War II (social studies); kids who created murals around a long-buried African-American gravesite in Manhattan were in an art class but also discovered history. An extensive environmental program, Kids against Pollution, originated in a social studies class. Furthermore, service projects require students to keep journals of their experiences (language arts).

Nevertheless, to encourage individual teachers to integrate service in their curriculum, it may be necessary to link activities with specific subjects. For this reason, in the chapters that follow, activities have been grouped by subjects whose curriculum is most closely related to that activity. These classifications are not inflexible . The subject listings may in fact lead to interdisciplinary teaching, as teachers combine related activities from different subjects to create an interdisciplinary unit.

Examples of themes that are clearly interdisciplinary or multidisciplinary are described in Chapters 13 and 14.

CHAPTER 4

Language Arts

"I learned you need to give special attention to some kids because they are not all the same."
—Eighth-grade student, Redlands Middle School, Grand Junction, Colorado

The language arts may be the areas most strengthened by service learning. The potential for practicing, improving, and applying language skills is unlimited. Students engage in extensive research, conduct surveys, and keep journals; they write letters, reports, and articles; they address meetings and prepare resolutions. It would be difficult to conceive of a service project that does not include one or more of these skills.

Books related to service topics such as homelessness are read in preparation for service with that population. An excellent example of this was the assignment of Dickens' *Christmas Carol* as a prelude to a unique project on homelessness at the Waseka Middle School in Minnesota. (See Chapter 13 for details.)

TUTORING

One of the most popular and, by all accounts, most successful service activities is tutoring, which involves kids of all ages. Customarily, middle school students work in day care centers or with elementary school kids. However, many elementary school students themselves tutor younger kids. Upper grade classes are paired with lower ones. Students may be assigned to kids who need extra help or randomly to interested participants. During lunch, recess, or special periods, they read to the younger kids, play games with them that reinforce language skills, or inspire them to write. Sometimes each student in a class is paired with a younger child as a "special reading friend."

"Tutoring programs produce significant benefits for the child tutored and the child tutoring," according to research cited in a recent report.[1] Teachers are finding that kids learn best what they must teach to others. And some of the tutors are making progress even with difficult youngsters.

Examples of programs and activities follow.

Ungraded Activities

Tutors from All Academic Levels

A nationwide program, the Coca-Cola Valued Youth Program, focuses on preventing school dropouts among the middle school population by recruiting students who are themselves at-risk to tutor elementary school children. These

39

students frequently have a special affinity for the younger kids, and the tutors and tutees both benefit.

A Nationwide Program to Prevent School Dropouts

Coca-Cola Valued Youth Program
Intercultural Development Research Association (IDRA), San Antonio, Texas

"All students are valuable; none is expendable."

—From Coca-Cola Valued Youth Program Statement

If you were selecting students to tutor elementary school kids with learning problems, would you pick middle school Hispanic students with limited English proficiency, poor academic and attendance records, a record of disciplinary referrals, and at risk of dropping out? This is what educators from the Intercultural Development Research Association in San Antonio, Texas did—with remarkable success.

The premise of the program was that valuing at-risk youths and giving them responsibility for tutoring younger children would strengthen their self-concept and would motivate them to stay in school and improve their grades, language proficiency, and school behavior.

An evaluation of the program confirmed this premise. Not only did it dramatically increase retention and improve academic grades, but there were a host of other benefits. Tutors' work habits improved, as did their attitudes toward school and teachers. Treated with respect, "they began to view themselves differently—as valued and important. They began to believe that they have control over their lives and their futures .... When placed in a responsible tutoring role and supported in their efforts," the report concluded, "tutors gain important social and academic benefits. Simply stated, "He who teaches, learns."

The effect on the kids who had been tutored was equally impressive. "Tutees' posttest scores increased in every subject; and absenteeism and discipline referrals were significantly lower." The kids often developed "powerful bonds with their tutors"[2] (see Chapter 1 for a summary of the evaluation).

Impressed by the results, the Coca-Cola Foundation, which had funded the original project, adapted the program and awarded over $1 million for its expansion nationwide and for the development of guides, brochures, and other training materials. The program was first established in two San Antonio school districts. Today it has spread to over seventy middle and elementary schools throughout the states.

"Helpers" Promote Reading

"You can be somebody. Someone who changes someone's life."

—Seventh-grade student, Reading Helper

Another nationwide program, the Helper Reading Program, is one of the service projects of the National Center for Service Learning in Early Adolescence.[3]

Also involving middle and junior high school students in tutoring, the program trains young adolescents to go into day care centers and elementary schools on a weekly basis. "Helpers" are selected from the entire student body, ranging from advanced readers to those with reading difficulties. They tutor and read to younger children and encourage them to view books and reading as a "source of pleasure." In addition, they discuss the ideas in the books to foster critical thinking.

Prior to the onset of the program, the adolescents receive comprehensive training, including simulation exercises and role playing, as well as an extensive orientation: to the world of work and to the program; to the developmental characteristics and motor skills of the kids; and to specific tutoring skills such as how to hold and read a book, select books, prepare lessons, inspire writing, and help kids with homework. Students are expected to prepare lesson plans and reflect on their experiences.

"Helpers" in Action

At Bleeker Junior High School in Flushing, New York, one of the schools affiliated with the Helper Program, seventh graders are assigned to third graders at two nearby elementary schools. Kids are pulled out of classes to meet their "Helpers." Prior to the onset of the program, tutors asked their young charges to complete an interest inventory, which enabled them to bring related books from the public library to the sessions.

Sitting in on one of the seventh graders' weekly seminars at Bleeker, one is impressed with the level of their planning. They evaluate the books to be used with the kids, share experiences, and plan to encourage the kids to write their own books. Ideas flow: "Could the books be in different shapes?" "Maybe they could write about their favorite character." Enthusiastically, they embrace a suggestion to have the kids rewrite fairy tales from the perspective of a different character—the story of Cinderella, for example, from the viewpoint of the stepsisters.

Tutoring as a Service Option

Schools that have developed extensive service programs usually include tutoring young kids as one of the service options. A group of eighth graders from I.S. 223 in New York City, selected this activity. They worked right in the kids' classrooms at Public School 98, reinforcing reading and readiness skills. Each tutor was assigned to a particular child or small group. Close ties developed between the age groups. There was marked improvement in the young kids' academic work. Parents were so enthusiastic that they hired some of the tutors to continue working with the kids during the summer.

The guidance counselor at the elementary school noted: "These students have been great for our kids. The children look forward to their visits. More and more teachers are requesting that students be assigned to them."

Tutoring ESL Kids

Frequently shy and insecure because of their limited language proficiency, kids in English as a Second Language classes respond particularly well to their student "teachers." With students, they are comfortable practicing English—reading and conversing—and the tutors often assume more extensive roles: helping the kids with homework, introducing them to the school environment, and facilitating their adjustment to a strange country. The tutors may be peers or older children who may or may not have been immigrants themselves. Middle school foreign language teachers may pair their students with immigrant speakers of the same language. Each group has an opportunity to perfect its verbal skills.

Bilingual Students Teaching ESL Kids

When Damaris Rivas, an eighth-grade Dominican student, was asked to tutor a third grader from the Dominican Republic, she was "confused" at first. "I didn't know if I would like it." The third grader had been in the United States for three years and was assigned for the first time to a monolingual class. Damaris explains:

"She had problems listening. She was shy. It was hard for her to put words together. She reminded me of me when I was a little girl. I was really able to help her. It made me feel great, more like a teacher. Now I am more sure of myself."

With Damaris' help, the little girl made remarkable progress. "Children can identify with their bilingual tutors," the third-grade teacher explained.

Tips for Tutors of ESL Students

- Help tutees write essays about their native country—customs, geography, government. These frequently can be used in social studies classes.
- Interview each other: "What would you like me to know about your country?
- Construct picture dictionaries. Have tutees bring in pictures from magazines or newspapers of common objects and create personal dictionaries.
- Help immigrant children construct a rudimentary map of their neighborhood.
- Work together to translate jazz chants and songs from English to Spanish and vice versa. Issue a bilingual music book.
- Role-play real-life skills—asking directions, checking bus and train schedules, shopping, using phone books.

Other Ungraded Activities

Share Books

Publicize a "We Share Books Day." Schedule a collection day for books for kids in hospitals and shelters, or for shut-ins. Students may contribute books they have outgrown that are still in good condition, or the class can raise funds to buy new books. Arrange the books by appropriate age and topic.

Create Bookmarks

Students can decorate strips of cardboard to be used as bookmarks. They add a slogan such as "Read every day," or a humorous one: "Don't read and drive." Donate the bookmarks to the school and public libraries. An advertisement for a particular book may be placed on the back.

Conduct Interviews

Interviews expose students to people with whom they usually would have little contact. They also require research to determine what questions to ask, and experience in taking and transcribing notes. Kids may prepare a list of people they wish to interview, then write or telephone them for appointments. Interviews can be conducted either at school or at the office of the person involved.

First, students draft a list of questions and role-play the interviews. After the interviews have been completed, they transcribe them in a book for the community or select one for a "person of the month" article. A local newspaper may be interested in a regular column on this subject.

Write Letters

Write to:

- Kids in hospitals and classmates who are home ill
- Authors of books the class has enjoyed
- Shut-in senior citizens

Students can also write letters in conjunction with social studies, as described in Chapter 5.

Compare Jump Rope Rhymes

How to account for the similarities of jump rope jingles around the world, crossing oceans, continents, languages and cultures, and spanning centuries? It's a mystery!

One fascinating study originated in Teutopolis, Illinois. Carol Schafer, a computer coordinator for the Teutopolis School District, needed a research project for her graduate class at the University of Illinois. "I was in the schoolyard watching a group of girls jumping rope and reciting a jingle," Schafer recalls. "It suddenly occurred to me that the jingle was familiar, one that I had known as a child."

She wondered how far back these jingles go. The third and fourth-graders at the elementary school were enlisted to gather jingles from their sisters, mothers, and grandmothers. Schafer sent out a general call for jingles on an electronic education network. She expected to hear from a few schools. Instead, she received almost two hundred responses from countries throughout the world: New Zealand, Australia, Ireland, England, Belgium, Jamaica, Canada, the Netherlands, and most of the fifty states. Peace Corps volunteers in Botswana submitted some. Contributions came from great-grandmothers as well as middle-aged men.

Even more surprising was the similarity among them. Versions of "A Little Dutch Girl" came from New Zealand, Australia, Ireland, Canada, Botswana, and the United States.

Here are some examples:

Illinois Version

I'm a little Dutch girl dressed in blue,
Here are the things I like to do:
Salute to the captain, bow to the queen
Turn your back to the submarine.

Irish Version

I'm a little girl guide all dressed in blue.
These are the actions I must do.
Salute to my master,
And bow to my queen,
And run to the corner to buy an ice cream.

Jingles based on "Johnny over the Ocean" were another example:

England, Ireland, and Illinois, Version

Johnny over the ocean, Johnny over the sea.
Johnny broke a bottle and blamed it on me.
I told Ma,
Ma told Pa,
Johnny got a whippin'
Ha, ha, ha!

Iowa Version

Down by the river, down by the sea,
Johnny broke a bottle and blamed it all on me.
I told Ma,
Ma told Pa,
And Johnny got a spankin'
So hah, hah, hah.

Some were variations on similar themes. Sixty-five were variants of "Down in the Valley Where the Green Grass Grows." Rhymes starting with "Teddy Bear, Teddy Bear, turn around" came from such diverse countries as Ireland, Canada, Belgium, Australia, New Zealand, Botswana, and the United States.

The project was integrated into the Teutopolis curriculum. In addition to language arts, the kids studied geography, mapping the countries that had sent jingles. They accumulated the jingles in a book and sent jump ropes and a copy of the book to those who had contributed ten or more jingles. They purchased the rope, measured it into jump rope sizes, and attached the handles. Schafer hopes to raise money for a dedicated line on the computer network to expand this project into other areas.

All students can participate in collecting jingles. Older kids can analyze them and note the slight differences among similar ones. Differences may reflect the culture or history of the country. In Alison Lurie's novel *Foreign Affairs,* for example, a professor who studies jump rope rhymes ruminates on the origin of "Ring Around a Rosy" and relates it to medieval history.[4]

Activities for Grades K–2

Find Initial Letters in Community Spots

Kindergartners or first-graders become acquainted with their community and reinforce beginning reading skills in the process. To reinforce initial consonant sounds, suggest they observe places in the community that start with a particular letter, for example, *T*—trees, town hall, traffic light.

Speak Out against Gender Stereotyping

Even young kids can become sensitive to stereotyping. When Susan Becker's first-grade class at the Rand School in Montclair, New Jersey, received an offer from a paperback book club for summer reading, the kids were surprised that there were two packages offered, one for girls and one for boys.

Becker suggested that the kids write to the club questioning why the books were designated by gender. A reply from the company stated:

I'm sorry to learn that you are disappointed with the designation of 'Books for Girls' and 'Books for Boys.' Your comments have been passed on to our editorial and marketing departments and will be taken into consideration as future plans are discussed...Thanks for sharing your thoughts. We appreciate your input and apologize for any discomfort caused you.

A complimentary book was sent to each member of the class.

Read for a Cause

First graders at the Dr. Bernard Harrif Elementary School in Baltimore, Maryland, wanted to raise money to help the homeless. One of their fund-raising activities was to read to parents and other adults for a set amount per page.

Activities for Grades 3–5

Make Big Books

Youngsters can construct 11″ × 15″ illustrated books based on their versions of popular children's books, such as *Goodnight Moon*, by Margaret Wise Brown. These can then be shared with younger children.

Research the History of Your School or Town

When you are driving down a street or lane, don't you get curious about how its name was selected? Students at the Northside School answered this question and many others for residents of their town, just as researchers at the Schuylkill Elementary School discovered long-buried information about their historical landmarks.

Historical research on a school, town, or neighborhood encourages the participation of many community residents. The project can be limited to an interesting street in the neighborhood or a landmark such as a statue or an old cemetery.

It may be a short-term activity or can become a key part of the language arts curriculum for weeks or months. It is a particularly effective means of reinforcing language skills.

History of a School

Northside School, East Williston, New York

"Being a researcher is like being a detective. Digging up information, going around to find the history of our school; that's what we've been doing for the past months. You can't imagine how we've worked for our school's anniversary, but we enjoyed it."
— Philip Fort, Matthew Singleton, and Adam Cohen, fourth-grade members of the research team

To commemorate the seventy-fifth anniversary of their school, twenty fourth graders researched and produced a twenty-nine-page book about the "world, the community and the school," as each looked when the school was first established

The students worked in committees. Researchers on the World Committee wrote to corporations that were in existence in 1917 requesting information about their products now and then so they could make comparisons.

At the library, another group studied a 1917 issue of the *New York Times* on microfilm. Advertisements were of particular interest. It didn't seem possible that a man's suit once had cost only $9.00. Other students visited the Town Hall, where they were able to examine old photographs of the town. They were surprised to learn that the Town Hall had records of every town meeting dating back to the 1700s.

The finished book also contains a history of World War I, and items such as sports, entertainment, transportation, fashions, technology, life in the community in the 1920s, origins of street names, comparative prices of 1917 and the present, excerpt from a teacher's planbook in 1917, history of the school to the present, reminiscences of former students, and interviews with elderly residents.

Of great fun was a copy of the twelve rules for teachers issued in 1915, which stated:

1. You will not marry during the term of your contract.
2. You are not to keep company with men.
3. You will be home between the hours of 8:00 P.M. and 6:00 A.M. unless attending a social function.
4. You may not loiter downtown in ice cream stores.
5. You may not travel beyond the city limits unless you have the permission of the chairman of the board.
6. You may not ride in a carriage or automobile with any man unless he is your father or brother.
7. You may not smoke cigarettes.
8. You may not dress in bright colors.
9. You may under no circumstances dye your hair.
10. You must wear at least two petticoats.
11. Your dresses must not be any shorter than two inches above the ankle.
12. To keep the schoolroom neat and clean, you must sweep the floor at least once a week with hot, soapy water, clean the blackboards at least once a day, and start the fire at 7:00 A.M. so the room is warm by 8:00 A.M.

The book was widely distributed and appreciated by the community.

History of a Town

> An excellent example of a book on the history of a town is provided by this report from the Schuylkill Elementary School, where the students researched local landmarks. As noted here, this project was a collaborative effort with senior citizens, which resulted in a book that raised funds for the school and established a unique bond between the school and the community.

A Phoenixville Journey

Schuylkill Elementary School, Phoenixville, Pennsylvania

"We've never witnessed such determination on the part of our students to achieve a goal."
—Beverly Bonkoski and Florence Chapman, fourth-grade teachers

The teachers were referring to a book on local history titled *A Phoenixville Journey: Past...Present...Future,* produced by their two fourth-grade classes with help from their "adopted grandparents" from the local Kiwanis seniors' club. (The unique relationship that exists between the two classes and the Kiwanis seniors is described in Chapter 11.)

The project developed from a topic in their fourth-grade social studies curriculum that called for a study of the state of Pennsylvania. Instead, the teachers narrowed this to a study of their town. Utilizing the seniors' knowledge of the town, they were able to develop a list of twenty local landmarks significant to Phoenixville's history. From these the students selected fifteen, including sites such as the Toonerville Trolley, the Bull Tavern, the Colonial Theater, and George Washington's headquarters at Valley Forge.

Numerous interesting facts emerged from their research. For example, they learned that the trolley had never had any passengers, that the tavern had originally been built in 1734 and was the site of archery and wrestling matches between the white settlers and Native Americans, that the theater is the oldest operating motion picture east of the Mississippi. And the army never actually fought a battle at Valley Forge—it was just a training ground.

The investigation started with two bus trips to the landmarks, which the youngsters photographed under the supervision of a Kiwanis senior. A series of interviews followed, with the director of the local historical society and with community residents who were familiar with the landmarks. The youngsters invited the residents to their classes, where they taped responses to a list of questions they had prepared previously. In addition, letters were sent to the community soliciting "humorous, poignant or special memories" about the landmarks.

The research was compiled into an impressive book, which was sold at the school Spring Fair to generate funds for the school. In addition, a coloring book was prepared for the first graders detailing facts about the landmarks.

Parents and teachers were enthusiastic. "What resulted was beyond our own expectations," Bonkoski and Chapman reported. "We were able to allow our students not only to design their own educational experience, but to record and preserve it in book form." The collaboration truly encompassed all aspects of the academic component. And, the teachers concluded, "the students had established a bond with the community that may stimulate our children to continue to preserve the tender reminders of our past and to help build a better future."

Learn the History of a Cemetery

Children at the Sea Cliff Elementary School on Long Island wondered about the ancient cemetery near the entrance to their school. They invited the "oldest man in town," a ninety-year-old man known as the local historian, to the school to tell them who was buried there.

His reminiscences fascinated the kids. They learned that the majority of the graves were of Civil War veterans, some of whom he had known.

Host a Story Hour for Younger Children

Intermediate grade youngsters can take turns hosting a regular reading hour for younger children during recess, lunch or after school. Suggest the kids dramatize some of the books.

Publish, Publish, Publish...

Organize a publishing company. Have the class select a name and publish books of interest to the community. The books may be distributed at no charge or sold at nominal rates to raise funds for worthwhile causes. Here are some suggestions.

A Community Directory. Students can investigate a particular block or a whole shopping area. They map the street and then interview the owners or officers of the companies, banks, libraries, and stores. Students work in teams to garner interesting bits of information. "How long has the institution been at that site?" "What changes have there been in the community?" And of the bakery: "How many pies are sold each day?" "Which is the most popular?" Or of the ice cream parlor: "Which is the favorite flavor?" "Have tastes changed over the years?" Of a pet store: " Do you have any unusual pets?"

A Book of Names. What are the most common first names in school? How does this compare with the names of parents? Grandparents?

What are the origins of different names? Which names are typical of particular ethnic groups?

Suggest that the book include anecdotes about why a particular name was chosen.

A Book of Hobbies. Students first develop a questionnaire to be sent to teachers, other school employees, parents, and community residents inquiring about hobbies or collections. The questionnaire should ask for details: "How long have they had these hobbies?" "What is the size of the collection?" "Where are the items available?" "For which age would you recommend this hobby?"

Students then describe the hobbies in a book. They may also consider having the class sponsor a fair at which the collections are displayed.

In Defense of the Wolf. After reading about wolves, a group of fourth graders concluded that wolves had been given a "bad rap" in literature ever since the story of Little Red Riding Hood. They learned that many wolves were in fact friendly animals, similar in various ways to dogs. Each student set out to write a story in which wolves were depicted as saving kids' lives. One student rewrote the story of Little Red Riding Hood and depicted the wolf as saving the grandmother.

Activities for Middle and Junior High

Continue to Write

A Children's Book for New Mothers. At the Coppachuck Middle School in Gig Harbor, Washington, sixth graders using desktop publishing write and bind a children's book for each new mother at the Tacoma Hospital as part of a literacy packet that emphasizes the importance of reading with kids and suggests titles of age-appropriate children's books.

A Guide to Recreational Activities. What are the nearby recreation facilities—skating rinks, bowling alleys, movie theaters, public library events? List hours, phone numbers, and any other pertinent information. Include also art galleries, landmarks, and coming attractions: holiday parades, street fairs, and flea markets.

Students at the Redlands Middle School in Grand Junction, Colorado, issued a community brochure in Spanish and English titled "Adventure for Kids 5 to 15," listing all the nearby recreational facilities with a map pinpointing where each was located.

Ghost Stories. On Halloween, encourage kids to write ghost stories to be inserted into a plastic pumpkin and presented to kids in a hospital or shelter.

Correlate Research and Writing

Books can be written on themes related to curriculum topics. As part of the health curriculum, students at the Turner Middle School in Philadelphia students regularly write brochures about different diseases—their causes, symptoms, and possible treatments. These are distributed to the community.

Eighth-grade students in Alan Haskvitz's social studies class in the Suzanne Middle School in Walnut, California, participate in a wide range of service activities that entail research and considerable writing. These have included the following unique projects:

- Researched and published an article in the *American Fire Journal* on improved procedures for fire drills
- Wrote to governors of all states to express concerns about the environment
- Wrote letters to embassies of all foreign governments as part of their research for a project on graffiti

(The complete Suzanne Middle School program is described in Chapters 5 and 13.)

Correlate Language Arts with Environmental Topics

Newsletter. Students from the Robert Wagner Junior High School in New York City publish an environmental newsletter in which they report on their activities, offer facts about the environment, and include poetry and other creative pieces inspired by their work.

Poetry. Kids from P.S. 213 in Queens built a trail through a neighboring park. It has been the focus of many integrated activities, including a book of poetry expressing the reactions of the students as they walked silently along the trail. Here is an excerpt:

> *As a leaf dances gently down*
> *Aiming toward the ground*
> *There it lies still*
> *No movement and no sound*
> *There it lies on the ground*
> *Hoping not to be stepped on.*
> —Margaret Chan, Grade 5

(See Chapter 7 for a complete description of the project).

Award-Winning Environmental Books

A trilingual (English, French, and Spanish) book of poetry, *One Voice for Wetlands,* was published by a sixth-grade language arts class at the Georgia Middle School in St. Albans, Vermont. It received a "Class Act" Amway/*Newsweek* award. (The complete project is described in Chapter 7.)

The following books by students received a President's Environmental Award.

- *Green Kids' Book of Issues: A Book for Kids by Kids,* written by a sixth-grade class at the Lafayette Regional School in Franconia, New Hampshire. Topics included oil spills, destruction of the rain forest, and solar power.
- *Prevent Pollution from A to Z—26 Ways: Please Color Me,* an alphabet book, was the product of Project CREATE at the Solomon Schechter Day School in Commack, New York. It was sold nationally and is now in its third printing. Profits from its sales were donated to the National Wildlife Federation.
- *50 Simple Things These Kids Did to Save the Earth* was created by Earth Defenders, an environmental group of two fourth-grade classes at the Blue Ridge Elementary School in Evans, Georgia.

Letters as a Multicultural Bridge

An imaginative approach at the Lee Middle School in Fort Myers, Florida, combines all the students in the school into PODs of nine, each of which contains students in a single grade level mixed by race and gender. The groups remain the same throughout the school year and form the basis for many multicultural activities.

Friday afternoon is devoted to letter writing. Each student is required to write to each member of her or his POD once each month. (Chapter 14 contains a complete description of the Lee program.)

Prepare Tapes

Arrange for students to read books onto audiotapes for the visually impaired and for kids in hospitals. If a cassette player is not available, suggest they raise funds to donate one.

Analyze Readers for Bias

Borrow basal readers from elementary schools and from other schools in your district. Are there evidences of bias related to age, gender, or ethnicity in reading texts? Also try to secure texts published many years ago, even if they are no longer being used, to give you a basis for comparison.

Working in groups, have students arrange the texts by date of publication, then analyze each for indications of bias. For example, in readers for young children, how are older people or grandparents depicted? Are they most often frail or in wheelchairs? How about gender? Do the little girls watch while the boys do important work? How are they dressed? What are the roles of the mother as compared with the father? What responsibilities are assigned to members of different ethnic groups?

What about illustrations? Are members of ethnic groups stereotyped? In which occupations are men generally depicted? Are women shown primarily as homemakers? Compare texts by publication dates? It is interesting to observe how books have changed over the years.

You may wish to scan science and math books too. In the past, only boys were portrayed in science and math books. Do the illustrations in science and math books still depict more boys than girls? Is there still evidence, albeit more subtle, of bias?

After collecting the data, if there are indications of bias in currently used readers, report them to the appropriate publishers.

Book-Talk Program

An outstanding program in the East Williston school district on Long Island seeks to combat prejudice through reading and discussing selected books. Students are introduced to the program through guest speakers and in their English classes. Students choose a book from an annotated book list and are encouraged to discuss it with their parents. Led by a faculty or staff member, they then engage in guided talks in mixed age groups of ten children, to discuss, the content of the book and its wider ramifications.

Originally a program for the middle school, it has now spread to all classes in the district. (See "Prejudice Reduction through Literature" in Chapter 14 for more details about this program.)

Broadcasting on the Radio

It is not unusual for students to broadcast to the school on the intercom to announce birthdays; report the weather, current events, and school activities; or honor a "good citizen." Some schools secure spots on local radio channels for special school announcements.

What is unusual is the program of the Jackson School, which broadcasts regularly on public radio with two programs: "Kids Edition" and "From the Shorter Point of View."

Kids on National Public Radio

Jackson School, Selma, California

"It's the greatest game in town! It adds glitter and spice to the class. Education has to be exciting to compete with television programs like MTV."
—Mario Guerrero, sixth-grade teacher, director, Kids Production, Inc.

Guerrero's goals are admittedly ambitious: to start the first Kids' National Public Radio Program. Somehow, one believes this winner of the 1993 Hispanic Teacher of the Year award might just do it. His sixth-grade students, the majority of whom are Hispanic, have organized a radio company, Kids Production, Inc., which broadcasts to the town on Valley Public Radio, KVPR. They now produce two programs regularly.

One is the Kids' Edition, six to eight minutes in length, broadcast four to six times a year, which focuses on issues that affect youngsters, such as the growth of gangs, the environment, an antismoking bit featuring "Joe Camel," and safety topics, such as reminding kids to wear seat belts.

More recently, another program was added: "From the Shorter Point of View." About fourteen to twenty minutes in length, it allows for coverage of issues in more depth. Guerrero likens it to "All Things Considered" on National Public Radio. Features have included "how gang problems affect families" and interviews with celebrities who are perceived as having "done positive things for kids."

Before a show, the class brainstorms ideas for scripts and engages in research. Each student then writes five stories, which become the basis for the programs. The kids compose the scripts, edit, and rewrite. At the studio they receive instruction in voice delivery, techniques of interviewing, and technical support from station KVPR. Three former students work with the class as "executive producers."

The school uses portfolio assessment. Completed scripts become part of the students' portfolios. Guerrero sees the students' work as part of the "renaissance of radio, which these kids will help to create."

Notes

1. "What You Can Do for Your Country (Washington, DC: Commission on National and Community Service, January 1993), p. 29.
2. Josie Danini Supik, "Partners for Valued Youth: The Final Report," *IDRA Newsletter*, January 1991.
3. The National Center for Service Learning in Early Adolescence is located at 25 West 43rd Street, New York, NY.
4. Alison Lurie, *Foreign Affairs* (New York: Avon Books, 1984), p. 8.

CHAPTER 5

Social Studies

"These students need to understand that they can take control of their own destiny. They are not helpless victims of society…They can become doers, that is, contributing members of the community…the contributions they make can improve the quality of life for everyone."
— Salvatore Sclafani, principal, Public School 59, The Bronx, New York

Sclafani was speaking of students in a school in a depressed section of the South Bronx with an almost total minority population. It was the above beliefs that led him to establish an extensive service learning program at his school (described in Chapter 14). Other educators, noting the widespread disillusionment with politics and government among youth, are echoing Sclafani's views by calling for programs that prepare young people for participation in society as active citizens.

The heartening fact is that many kids are already effecting change: reaching out to the homeless, the elderly, immigrants, and the disadvantaged. They are petitioning their legislators for laws to improve their communities, studying the Constitution and the Bill of Rights not because they may need to answer questions about them on tests, but because they are serious about their prerogatives. They are united by a belief that kids have a right to grow up in a safe, healthful, caring world.

Kids' social actions are not limited to the rubric of social studies. They are part of the service activities of every discipline. For example, multicultural activities, as well as projects with the elderly and the homeless, though frequently tied to the social studies curriculum, may also originate in other classes. (Separate chapters are devoted to these topics later in this book.)

It is true, however, that at every grade level the social studies curriculum is particularly appropriate for service activities; virtually every aspect of social studies can be enriched by a service project. At the Somerset Elementary School, this philosophy led to an award-winning service learning program in the primary grades.

Somerset Kids Participating (SKIP)

Somerset Elementary School, Chevy Chase, Maryland

"Kids need opportunities to see themselves as 'givers.'"
— Ann Proctor, parent, SKIP Coordinator

It was this belief that moved Ann Proctor and kindergarten teachers at Somerset to found SKIP back in 1990. "We wanted to infuse service into the curriculum starting at an early age," Proctor explained. Although, the social studies curriculum provided a ready focus, it was important that other subjects also be reinforced.

It was decided to inaugurate SKIP in kindergarten. At that grade level, the curriculum calls for a study of families. This topic led to a project with a senior citizen center. The kids visited a nearby center once a month: playing bingo (reading numbers and letters), engaging in arts and crafts, and practicing joint rhythmic exercises. In the process, they reinforced mathematics, language arts, and physical education.

The service program quickly gathered momentum. It was agreed that SKIP would move up through the grades, one year at a time, with each grade organizing a service learning project. In first grade, "Instead of studying tepees and igloos to learn about shelters," Proctor related, "they observed a shelter for homeless families" and collected clothing, books, school supplies, art supplies, and toys, as well as bedding and diapers for the nursery children. The activities provided math lessons. Records of collections were kept and illustrated on huge graphs. A cookie and lemonade sale to raise funds netted $200, carefully tabulated by the kids. "It was an empowering experience for the youngsters," Proctor noted. "First graders wheeled their wagons through the school collecting contributions for 'their' shelter."

Taking off from the topic of community, second graders adopted environmental awareness as their service learning theme. They developed a three-part program: collecting aluminum cans and white paper in the school for recycling, composting leaves and other organic material from the school lawn, and reducing waste by auditing the amount of waste generated in the school and at home. Again, students used these activities to further their math skills: estimating, weighing, measuring, and graphing. During the year, the kids went to a recycling facility, worked with parents to construct a composter at the school, and helped organize a school "litter-free day."

By the third grade, the students moved their activities into the community, consistent with the theme of community beyond the school grounds. A partnership was forged with the town's elected officials who permitted the kids to use the town's parks and streams as a "lab" for their activities. The kids undertook to monitor a stream that flows through Somerset County: testing the water, charting characteristics, and checking storm drains for fertilizer runoff while seeking ways to reduce water pollution.

The Somerset program is unique in many ways, among them the fact that it was pioneered in kindergarten. Also noteworthy, is the level of collaboration between parents and school. Ann Proctor was the only parent in Maryland invited to serve on the Governor's Advisory Board for Service Learning. SKIP was cited by the state of Maryland as a model for service learning and received state grants.

Principal Ray Myrtle summed up: "It is important for children to engage in community service. It gives them a positive image of themselves. Research shows that service for others at an early age strengthens kids morally and makes them more resilient."

Ungraded Activities

Who Is Responsible?

In planning any action, it is necessary for students to know which branch of government should be contacted: town, city, state, or federal. Some issues are the concern of many levels of government, but the lowest level should first be contacted. For example, for an environmental concern, there are agencies at each level, but the local environmental agency may be the easiest to reach. (The telephone directory classifies government offices by branch.)

Here are examples of the responsibilities of each branch.

CHAPTER 5 Social Studies   **55**

- *Town or city:* How pure is the water? Are there problems with a local park, sanitation, street lights, fire or police protection, zoning, over-charging by a local store? These are usually the concern of the town.
- *State:* The state is responsible for matters related to safety and health, state highway maintenance, education, school schedules, curriculum, financing, unemployment, labor, consumer affairs, the environment, and miscellaneous items. For example, kids in Utah were able to obtain state legislation establishing a state insignia and state motto.
- *Nation:* Responsibilities relate to defense, federal budget, the environment, labor, mass transportation, Social Security, and Medicare.

Identify Community Agencies

Which public or private agencies exist in your community? What are their functions? How can they be used to help residents? The class can work in groups to contact these for information.

Community Involvement Program

In the Manhasset Middle School on Long Island, this program has two levels. The first is the content level, developing a core body of knowledge, an awareness of how the subjects relate to each other and to the ability to participate in public affairs.

On the second level, by eighth grade, students are expected to apply what they have learned: identify ways to become effective citizens; address civic issues; and become involved in a community, county, state or national issue.

Some of the actions the students have taken include:

- Participating with four neighboring school districts in Martin Luther King, Jr., Student Conference Day, "A Challenge to Find Unity in our Diversity"
- Raising money for Habitat for Humanity
- Organizing a dance to raise money for muscular dystrophy research
- Collecting clothes for Native Americans in Montana
- Decorating a nursing home for Valentine's Day
- Launching monthly drives for toiletry items for the homeless through the Interfaith Nutrition Network
- Adopting a family and engaging in toy drives during holidays

Take a Stand

The Manhasset School also encourages students to speak out regularly in a program called "Speak for Yourself." Students can take a stand on issues by writing letters, organizing petitions, and formulating legislation.

Write Letters

Students express their views through letters—to the president, congressional representatives, other government officials, newly elected officeholders, newspapers, and radio stations—on pending legislation and problems such as pollution, the environment, gun control, substance abuse, and landfill dumping. They write to embassies of countries they are studying in social studies for specific information.

Even young kids can be encouraged to react to news stories. The Union Camp Paper Corporation, whose plant is on the bank of the Blackwater River in Virginia, announced that it would voluntarily replace chlorine, a toxic water pollutant, with ozone, a nonpollutant, to bleach its paper. Furthermore, the corporation stated that it is perfecting a process that will enable it to use 30 percent recycled paper in its product. A teacher of seven-year-olds in Montclair, New Jersey, told her class about this and encouraged them to write to Union Camp. Danny, a second grader, wrote, "What you did, made me very, very happy."

Institute Petition Drives

Petitions can be extremely effective in illustrating the extent of support for a project. When a town decided to close its library two days a week instead of one, students went into action. First, they monitored attendance at the library to prove that it was being utilized fully. Then they organized a petition drive. The next town budget revoked the change.

There Oughta Be a Law

Students in a fifth-grade class in Closter, New Jersey, organized as "Kids against Pollution" and introduced a bill in the New Jersey legislature that would guarantee "clean air and water" as a constitutional right. (See Chapter 7 for further details.)

Ask students to find out how a bill becomes a law in the municipal or state legislature. If there are pending bills related to any of the following, kids can support them. If not, here are some actions kids can take.

Ban Cigarette Vending Machines. In July 1993, the Massachusetts Supreme Court upheld Provincetown's ban on cigarette machines because they enable minors to buy cigarettes. Students can investigate whether their town has a similar law. If not, consider urging that one be enacted.

Smoke-Free Schools. Has your school been designated a smoke-free facility? In New York City, all schools are so designated. A number of other municipalities have similar legislation, but the majority do not. If your school is not smoke-free, the kids may wish to lobby for the required legislation. Note the problems that have been associated with secondary smoke, as described in Chapter 8.

Bike Helmets. If there is no law requiring that bicyclists wear helmets, urge that one be enacted.

Child Restraints. Investigate whether there is a law requiring that infants ride in car seats and whether seat belts are provided for other children. Each year many kids are hurt in accidents because of the absence of such restraints. Research the information and then organize to lobby for appropriate legislation.

Handgun Ban. In 1993, Colorado passed a law making it illegal for anyone under age eighteen to own or carry a handgun. The only exceptions are for licensed hunting, target practice, or shooting competitions. Conviction carries penalties ranging from detention in a juvenile center to three years in prison.

With the proliferation of guns in schools, it may be timely to lobby your state legislature for a similar bill. Write letters to lawmakers and newspapers, organize petition drives and visit your local representatives if possible.

Conduct Polls

Polling is an excellent activity to integrate language arts, math, and social studies. Kids poll the class, school, or community on some of the issues previously identified or others. Also poll during political campaigns. Compare the results of the class polls to those of the media and to the actual results of elections. To what can differences in the various polls be attributed?

The following poll reveals attitudes toward electing more women to Congress.[1]

A woman and a man (the incumbent) are running for a U.S. Senate seat. Both have good ideas on issues that matter to you. Bearing the following two facts in mind, for whom would you vote?

1. The male candidate has more experience in the Senate.
2. Females are underrepresented in the Senate.

Tally the entire class, then male and female students separately. Administer the poll to other classes. Is there a difference among students of different ages?

Community polls have dealt with a variety of issues: Should a street be made one way? How late should the neighborhood swimming pool stay open? Should there be more street lights in a particular neighborhood or park? Communicate the results to the concerned government agencies.

Note, too, the effect of the construction of questions on the results. A poll on the need for a traffic light at a particular intersection might be posed in different ways: "Do you think we need a traffic light at Spring and Broome Streets?" Or "Considering that there have been frequent accidents at Spring and Broome Streets, do you think we need a traffic light there?" The results will undoubtedly vary. Although this is an extreme example of skewing a poll for a desired result, it illustrates how politicians may phrase questions to ensure a certain response.[2]

Students should find out what percentage of the population needs to be polled to make a poll valid?

Serve Your School Community

Social studies classes frequently take the lead in service activities within the school. Chapter 2 includes some suggestions for such activities.

Consider the following additional ideas as extensions of the social studies curriculum's emphasis on good citizenship.

Welcome Newcomers to the School

A class can take the lead in setting up committees from each grade who would be responsible for greeting newcomers. If the child is from a foreign country, arrange for the incoming class to post a notice prominently in the room welcoming the new student in her or his native language.

Introduce the student to children who live close by. Identify neighborhood areas and facilities that would be of interest. Recruit someone to be a special friend—to walk the child through the school, explain some of the rules, and take responsibility for guiding the child until the newcomer is acclimated.

Volunteer During Parent–Teacher Conferences

Babysit for Younger Kids. Noting that some parents could not attend conferences because they had younger children at home, students volunteered to babysit during conferences. They set up a room at school with art materials and toys where parents can drop off their kids. Attendance at conferences increased dramatically.

Translate. To aid parents who are not fluent in English, students in middle school language classes translate for parents of elementary school kids during conferences.

Children: Past and Present

This topic is the title of an interdisciplinary theme in a number of schools. It can be approached from many different perspectives. For example, as part of a unit on U. S. history, investigate the child labor laws in this country. Has child labor completely disappeared?
It would also be interesting to investigate the life expectancies of children at different ages and of varying ethnic groups. Have these changed? Consider also comparing attitudes toward children over the years. How have these varied? What about children in other countries?
Your unit should culminate with an activity designed to help children—perhaps in hospitals, in shelters, or living in poverty.

Children for Children

Another activity on behalf of children frequently arises from a study of world communities. Students become aware of the shortage of school supplies in many Third World countries. They contact embassies or U. N. representatives for information. They collect school supplies—paper, pencils, pens, compasses, crayons, and the like and send these regularly. Kids in the other countries may be studying English. Texts and easy children's books are also helpful.

Organize Walk-a-Thons

Kids walk to raise pledges to alleviate hunger, to house the homeless, for Special Olympics, AIDS, "Christmas in April" for the needy and for victims of natural disasters.

Activities for Grades K–2

Interview Community Workers

Invite some of the following people into the classroom in conjunction with a study of the community:

- *People who make the community work:*
  - —*At school:* Principal, teachers, secretaries, custodians
  - —*In the community:* Police, firefighters, mail carriers, crossing guards, or people with interesting jobs or hobbies
- *People behind the scenes:* Sanitation workers, meter readers, gardeners
- Anyone else the kids would like to meet

By interviewing them, kids gain an appreciation of their contributions to the community.

Be Aware of Gender Stereotyping on Television

Young children can scan television cartoons to see whether boys and girls are equally represented. Are boys generally depicted as stronger, braver, or more active?

Examine Violence on Television

Are TV cartoons violent and frightening? Encourage kids to write letters or send drawings to television stations telling them which cartoons and other programs are "too violent."

Activities for Grades 3–5

Study the Ethnic Composition of Your Community

Does your community include recent immigrants? Reinforce geography skills by indicating on a map of the world the countries from which residents have emigrated.

If possible, have students interview some recent arrivals then create a book made up of their stories. Why did they leave their native countries? Did they leave family members behind?

More Gender Stereotyping

A fifth-grade class in Milwaukee was asked to list adjectives describing boys and girls respectively. Boys were labeled "strong," "adventurous," "athletic," "mean," and "brave." Girls were described as "weak," "scared," "pretty," "patient," and "tearful."[3]

Try this exercise in your class. Then demonstrate how false these stereotypes are. It would be interesting to administer this to younger children in the school. Give them a list of adjectives and ask them which they identify with each gender.

Store a Time Capsule

Invite community members to contribute an item that represents today's culture. Store and seal these in the school to be opened at a future date—ten or twenty-five years from now.

Activities for Middle and Junior High

Active Citizenship Today (ACT)

ACT is a four-year service learning project for middle and high school students that is jointly planned and implemented by the Constitutional Rights Foundation (CRF) and the Close Up Foundation.[4] The project's goal, according to Susan Phillips of CRF, is "to develop effective citizen participation in democracy by improving social studies education through integrating community service and the study of public policy into the social studies curriculum."

Though based primarily in the social studies, ACT also links service with all subjects, aiming to "open the school to the community and challenge students to learn by becoming active citizens." Districts around the country are piloting the program.

Students follow a carefully designed framework that includes assessment of community problems, analysis of policies and how they are made, and options available to effect change. In the final step, students are expected to identify and carry out a specific service project followed by a period of evaluation and reflection.

Lesson plans have been prepared on a number of topics, such as drugs, crime, violence, and homelessness. In the Northside district in Texas, for example, students completed a project on crime. They studied teenage violence; interviewed legislators, politicians, and other community residents to assess the reasons for the increase in crime; noted the conflict of values among different groups; examined constitutional issues such as gun control; and identified pending bills that they wanted to support. They prepared and presented educational programs on the topic for younger kids at their school.

Another topic was "children." Students examined this theme historically, around the world, and in the United States—how society has viewed children in different periods compared to the present day. Then they contemplated related topics, such as the effects of violence and crime on children.

Two middle schools in the Jefferson District in Colorado, the Mandalay and Carmody Middle Schools, have completed projects on the homeless following the ACT guidelines. Seventh-grade kids organized collection drives for clothing, books, and food; raised funds; prepared meals; and visited the shelters. As indirect actions, they wrote letters to state legislators inquiring why the problems of the homeless were not being addressed more actively, prepared an educational "infomercial" and skits for elementary classes, and presented data to government officials and the public. Armed with detailed information, graphs, and charts, they sought to counter public misperceptions on the homeless, raised money, and suggested public actions.

The ACT director for the district, Brian Loney, declares that although ACT was designed for both middle and high schools, he sees more of a demand for programs in the middle schools. He attributes this to two factors: kids at the middle school level seem more sympathetic to people with problems, and the interdisciplinary approach of middle schools permits more ready incorporation of projects.

Looking at a Local Industry

A seventh-grade class in Southampton, Long Island, became interested in the lives of the local fishermen known as baymen. The baymen came to class and presented information and demonstrations of their work. The students noted that the unique lifestyles of the baymen were "threatened by overdevelopment, pollution and excessive regulation." In a booklet that they prepared, they concluded that "we may have witnessed the last of a dying breed of local heritage bearers."

Debate Conflicting Views

People frequently have sincere conflicts or disagreements, some resulting from different interpretations of the Constitution or other documents used as a basis for lawmaking..

Students can research and organize debates. How would students vote on the following?

- A law is passed holding parents financially responsible for the costly actions of their children.
- The town wishes to build a shelter for the homeless in a particular neighborhood. Some residents object. This is sometimes known as the NIMBY syndrome ("Not In My Back Yard").
- The school board recommends an increase in the school tax to build more classrooms. People in the community, particularly those with no children in the school, complain that taxes are already too high.
- Local theaters decide to eliminate the senior citizen discount for admission.

First Amendment Rights: Another Topic for Debate

A number of interesting issues have been raised with regard to *freedom of speech.* One is the right of hate groups to march in communities and express their views freely. Another is related to renting city facilities to groups who may express biased viewpoints. These have been deemed to be protected by the freedom of expression provisions of the First Amendment.

Issues related to the First Amendment also have surfaced with regard to student newspapers, particularly in colleges. Some campus papers have printed editorials offensive to various groups. Courts have usually upheld the newspapers' actions under First Amendment rights.

Students at one college took matters into their own hands by stealing thousand of copies of a college newspaper that they deemed insulting. They claimed their actions were a legitimate form of expression, not censorship. Many First Amendment scholars would disagree.

Students find out about such instances of attempted censorship and how they relate to the First Amendment. They organize a debate on the subject and might solicit opinions from the community.

Study Immigrants Who Arrived in Ellis Island

Students can obtain statistics on the number of immigrants who have arrived through Ellis Island. They can send an open letter to the community inquiring about any grandparent or relative who arrived in this country through Ellis Island. Would it be possible to interview a person to find out about the experience?

Aid for Immigrants

When immigrants move into a community, students can go to work to help the immigrants in a variety of ways: translating government papers, writing letters in English, completing applications, and helping to prepare them for the citizenship examination. Students frequently act as interpreters. They tutor immigrants in survival skills: how to shop, ride buses or trains, and use a map of the neighborhood. In turn, the immigrants can help students learn a foreign language, introduce them to foods of their native country, and describe the countries from which they came.

Students also interview immigrants for oral histories to learn about their cultures and countries. An opening question might be: "What are five (or ten) things I should know about the country in which you were born?"

This information is shared and becomes a useful part of the social studies curriculum.

Entire School Districts Befriend Immigrants

When Cambodian refugees moved into a school district in Massachusetts, the schools went into action. Every person in the school was involved—kids, teachers, secretary, custodians, administrators. Each Cambodian child was paired with a student. Study of the country of Cambodia became part of the curriculum. Children studied the language, culture, and history. They learned of the hardships the immigrants had suffered and helped prepare them for citizenship.

Encourage Voter Registration

Students have gone door to door to help residents complete registration forms and to urge them to vote. Where necessary, foreign language classes or bilingual students translate the information on the ballots for non-English speakers.

Serve in a Government Office

Students from the Central Park East Secondary School in New York serve in the Ombudsman's Office of the president of the City Council. They speak with constituents about complaints against city agencies and are assigned specific investigations.

Analyze History Texts

An eighth-grade class studying the history of the United States from nineteenth century to the present focused on history texts, past and present. Students secured copies of texts that had been published many years ago and compared them to their modern texts.

Working in groups, the students arranged the books chronologically and analyzed each for examples of bias and stereotypes, particularly as related to gender and ethnicity. Were women and members of minority groups represented? Did the books rely primarily on white male achievements? How about the illustrations?

Although students found many improvements over the years, they also found areas of concern. In each case, they wrote letters to the publishers.

The Suzanne Middle School in Walnut, California, discovered a disturbing fact while engaged in a similar exercise. They examined history textbooks to see who were described as "heroes." Sixty percent of these "heroes" were acclaimed for having killed somebody. Students concluded that the prevalence of violence is not only the fault of the media, but also of school texts, which give tacit approval to violence by glamorizing such acts.

Rewrite History Texts

Sensitive to the claim that U. S. history is written largely from the standpoint of the white male population, some students are projecting events in U. S. history from the perspective of women or minority groups.

What would history texts say about Columbus, Davy Crockett, or Kit Carson, for example, if they were written by Native American historians?

Persistent Television Stereotypes

A survey of television shows concluded that TV still abounds with obsolete and offensive stereotypes. The mentally ill are portrayed as evil. African-Americans, Hispanics, the poor and the foreign-born are cast as victims. Minorities are seen more often in crime news than as business people.

Students should be encouraged to view television critically. Have different committees check prime time, daytime, Saturday morning children's shows, and the news for evidences of stereotypes. They can tabulate the results and write to the networks if they find reason for concern.

Build a School Museum

Students have organized historical museums in their schools devoted to topics such as the American Revolution or the Civil War, the civil rights movement of the 1960s, war in general, or other units of study.

Members of the community who have participated in the more recent events are invited to speak at the museum and share artifacts. Videos of some of the events are available and could be scheduled for showing to the community.

Become Human Rights Advocates

Students have advocates through Amnesty International[5], which supports people throughout the world whose human rights have been violated. Their activities include the following:

- Education, organizing, and training in how to document and publicize human rights violations
- Monitoring and researching countries around the world to sound an early warning when human rights are in jeopardy
- Urgent Action/Freedom Writers Network, which organizes campaigns and letter writing to help free "prisoners of conscience" anywhere in the world, who are victims of torture and being held illegally.

In the face of an immediate threat to a prisoner, Amnesty institutes an emergency letter-writing campaign to the government involved, as well as to our own representatives and the United Nations. Students can participate in this campaign. Ask to be placed on Amnesty's mailing list.

At the Fieldston Ethical Culture School in the Bronx, the entire school gathered in the lunchroom to write to major world leaders in response to an emergency call from Amnesty International.

Correlating Social Studies with the Entire Curriculum

Frequently, in the process of furthering the social studies curriculum, students find that they are meeting curriculum goals of many other subjects. This is true of the activities of eighth-grade students in the Suzanne Middle School in Walnut, California. They have tackled a host of community problems and have received recognition for the breadth and quality of their service activities.

Make a Difference

Suzanne Middle School, Walnut, California

"Knowledge is only valid when it is usable."

—Alan Haskvitz, eighth-grade social studies teacher

There is a clear-cut way to assess the service learning program of the Suzanne Middle School, grades 6–8, located at the eastern edge of Los Angeles County. Back in 1985, when Haskvitz started the program, the school's state test scores were in the 22nd percentile. After four years, they reached the 94th percentile (the largest state gain in history). The "Make a Difference" program has received national recognition, including the Program of Excellence award of the National Council for the Social Studies. What's more, students at this multicultural school have justified the title of their program. They *have* made a difference!

Haskvitz integrates social studies with all subjects. The list of students' accomplishments spans every discipline. They achieved the following:

Science (Environment)

- Planted and maintained a drought-tolerant garden to convince the county to save water by using xeriscape landscaping. Wrote legislation and lobbied, which succeeded in a bill that has saved the state millions of dollars and countless gallons of water. (See Chapter 7.)
- Testified before the United Nations (winning the right to do so over classes throughout the country) on the environment.
- Sponsored efforts to save endangered animals.
- Purchased acres of rain forest.
- Conducted a water awareness campaign that saved the city 23 million gallons of water a year.
- Translated city environmental information into four languages.
- Introduced legislation to ban mass balloon releases.

- Participated in community-wide cleanup days.

History

- Acted as the official historian archivists for the City of Walnut collecting both written and oral history for the community library.
- Computerized this information.
- For History Day, each student researched a character, event, or invention that changed history. They created short poems or stories with descriptions of the period of their character or object. These had to be explicit because they were then put on audiotapes for blind children. For example, "What did Paul Revere look like?" "What did he wear?" "Describe his horse."
- Designed a U. S. history game.
- Corresponded with General Noriega about the war in Panama. Theirs was the only school that received a reply from Noriega.

Language Arts

One of Haskvitz's students was selected as the national champion over 12,000 other entrants for his letter to encourage his congressional representative to support education.

Other language arts activities by Suzanne students are described in Chapter 4.

Additional Student Action Projects

- Rewrote the Los Angeles County voter instructions, which they considered too difficult. The instructions were subsequently altered in accordance with their recommendations.
- Wrote and helped distribute a tape in Spanish on the meaning of the Bill of Rights to schools all over the United States.
- Translated city documents into various languages to benefit the influx of immigrants.
- Registered voters and held voter information nights.
- By selling plants, they raised money to buy a seeing-eye dog for a blind person. In this annual project, the recipient comes to the classroom and the youngsters observe how the blind person and the dog learn to work together. (This project spawned a study of different dogs in history.)
- Learned to "sign," which enabled them to aid hearing-impaired people during voter registration.
- Wrote and computerized a children's travel guide for Interstate 40, which runs from California to North Carolina. The guide includes the history of cities on the route, geographical features, bridges, trains, landscape, wild flowers, temperature extremes, and activities for kids in each city.
- Conduct annual seatbelt checks with the Los Angeles County Sheriff.
- Learned to fingerprint youth and now fingerprint all new district pupils on a community health day.
- Received the national traffic and safety award for their work with the County Sheriff.

A commitment to action defines the entire service curriculum at Suzanne. "The students want to change society," says Haskvitz. In every assignment, students do not merely participate, but conduct research and determine if there should be changes.

Haskvitz's eighth-grade students complete six to eight research projects every year. Students who wish to improve a grade or receive extra credit can do so by engaging in an additional project outside of school, such as sitting in on a city or community board meeting or writing to national leaders. Each year, Haskvitz also assigns one extensive interdisciplinary project to the entire class, which runs about three weeks. This past year's project was "tagging" or "graffiti busting" around the world. (A description of this project is in Chapter 13.)

Notes

1. Suggested by *CRF BRIA*, Summer 1993, Constitutional Rights Foundation, Los Angeles.
2. Polling is also suggested in Chapter 9.
3. Reported in *Teaching Tolerance*, Fall 1993, p. 26, published by Southern Poverty Law Center, 400 Washington Avenue, Montgomery, AL 36104. The Center provides Teaching Tolerance materials including Civil Rights Kits and videotapes free of charge to schools on written request from the school principal on school letterhead.
4. Constitutional Rights Foundation, 601 South Kingsley Drive, Los Angeles, CA 90005; Close Up Foundation, 44 Canal Center Plaza, Alexandria, VA 22314. The project is funded by the DeWitt Wallace Reader's Digest Fund.
5. Amnesty International USA is at 322 Eighth Avenue, New York 10001.

CHAPTER 6

Science

"It started with showers. My daughter informed me that she thought she should start taking showers instead of baths to save water."

—Parent of a seven-year-old

Changes in science education were proposed in October 1993 by a commission appointed by the American Association for the Advancement of Science (AAAS). Criticizing the existing curriculum for expecting kids to memorize useless information, such as the 109 known chemical elements in the periodic table, it recommended instead practical applications of science, drawing conclusions from experimental data, and integrating science with math and technology. These recommendations describe the approach to the teaching of science used in service learning projects.

The majority of science service activities focus on the environment, an area where kids have been singularly effective in applying their classroom learning as recommended by the AAAS. These activities are discussed in the next chapter but many of the topics in this chapter also can be in a unit on the environment. They include:

- Sources of energy: fossil fuels, alternative sources
- Energy conservation
- Respect for living things

A brief review of sources of energy is presented primarily as a background to a discussion of energy conservation. The activities described here are intended to be completed in the classroom to create an awareness of fossil fuels as a finite resource, and a recognition of the increasing attention being given to alternative sources other than nuclear power.

FOSSIL FUELS: A LIMITED RESOURCE

Ungraded Activities

Coal, natural gas, and petroleum are all fossil fuels. Their use poses several problems. First, the reserve of these fuels is exhaustible. Second, their use makes the United States dependent on foreign countries for fuel, and this has led to war and tension around the world. Finally, burning fossil fuels has undesirable environmental impacts in that it releases carbon dioxide and chemicals, which pollute the atmosphere.

The fossil fuels were formed over a period of millions of years. Originally, the surface of the earth was moist, and plants and animals lived in mud or shallow water. As they died, their remains settled, accumulating in succeeding layers. More mud, rocks, sand and water settled over the remains. Over the eons, the pressure of these materials created heat and, together with the action of bacteria, formed the fossil fuels.

Locate Reserves of Fossil Fuels

On a map of the world, students are asked to indicate where there are deposits of petroleum, natural gas, and coal.

They integrate this project with social studies finding out more about the countries with the largest reserves. How do these reserves influence relations among nations? Relate your findings to the need for conservation.

Sources of Energy Can Be Depleted

To illustrate this concept, do the following: Distribute materials to students to light a small bulb by completing an electric circuit using a dry cell battery. When they have completed the circuit, suggest that they add additional bulbs. Gradually, each bulb will become dimmer and dimmer and will eventually be extinguished because the energy stored in the dry cell was depleted. Older children may demonstrate this activity in classes for younger kids to reinforce the need for conservation.

ALTERNATIVE SOURCES

Scientists keep searching for alternatives to fossil fuel as sources of energy. Most of the present alternatives are still not feasible for wide-scale use, but their use is increasing. Eventually, a number of small, varied, alternative projects, catering to local communities and utilizing local resources, may provide a partial solution to our overdependence on fossil fuels. Perhaps, as new technologies are perfected, many of these alternatives to fossil fuels will in fact become more practical.

The most common alternatives include:

- Nuclear power
- Renewable energy sources: sun, wind, and water
- Biomass

Nuclear Power

This is the most common alternative to fossil fuels. Concerns have arisen, however, about the safety of nuclear plants, their effect on fish and plant life in the surrounding waters, and the potential dangers of an accident. Serious questions have also been posed concerning the disposal of nuclear wastes. Students can research how these wastes are disposed; how long they remain radioactive, and the regulations for monitoring nuclear plants. Are there any plants in your area?

Students should answer these questions to become familiar with the advantages and disadvantages of nuclear power.

Solar Energy

Direct use of the sun for energy is an attractive concept. Solar energy is plentiful, free, and nonpolluting. Since it is produced from sunlight, it is a renewable source of energy. In the course of a year, more than 500 times as much solar energy reaches the surface of the United States as is consumed in all other forms. To fully utilize solar energy, however, we must be able to collect, store, and concentrate the heat of the sun. Currently, the process employs photovoltaic cells, which convert sunlight to electric current by charging batteries that store electricity. Advances are being made in the production of solar panels that will make them more cost- and energy-efficient.

Is Solar Energy Used in Your Community? The most common use of solar energy is to heat homes and water. Are there any solar heated homes close by? If so, students could interview someone who lives in a solar-heated house to discover its advantages and disadvantages.

Can the Sun's Rays be Harmful? In the summer, many young people enjoy spending long periods of time in the sun acquiring a flattering tan. Students should be aware of some of the dangers of overexposure to the sun. They can research these and then inform their peers and families about their findings.

Wind Power

This proven source of energy has been employed extensively to sail ships, pump water, turn mills, grind flour from grain, and activate generators to produce electricity. In the Netherlands, windmills were used to regain lands from the sea.

In California, windmills are generating enough electricity to supply power to San Francisco. They are installed in sites where winds whip through at high speed. The power created by the wind is used to spin the blades of turbines, which then turn generators to produce electricity.

Small communities have also experimented with windmills. At one point, two windmills made it possible for Navaho children in a remote reservation to attend their own school. The children had been commuting to schools outside the community. In order to build a school on the reservation, they needed electric power. It would have cost $100,000 to bring in electricity. Instead, they built windmills at a cost of about $20,000 (labor was donated by the Navaho). The windmills charged batteries that provided electricity.

Other communities have experimented with power-generating windmills. However, serious obstacles exist to the development of power from the wind as a feasible alternative source. Large land areas would be required to install windmills; and the strength and frequency of winds vary. Here, too, small projects may be the answer. Some families have been able to install wind generators near their homes to produce electricity.

Learn about Wind Farms. These are areas where people build windmills to harness the energy of the wind. Students need to investigate where they exist and evaluate the advantages and disadvantages of wind farms as alternative sources of energy.

Water Power

Long ago, water was a key source of power. Unlike the power of the wind or the sun, water power can be stored and released as needed.

Expanding the use of water power is deceptively appealing. Water is cheap, safe, nonpolluting, and naturally recycled. But there is a down side, too. There are limited additional sites for large hydroelectric plants. Most important are the concerns of environmentalists, who oppose flooding sites to create new dams because of the potential danger to wildlife and the encroachment on natural areas.

Where are Hydroelectric Plants Located? Identify states where large hydroelectric plants are located. Ask students to determine how effective they have been as sources of energy. Debate the pros and cons of building additional plants.

Biomass

Biomass refers to growing crops for use as fuel. Plants are a natural storehouse of energy. During photosynthesis, they capture energy from the sun. Some of this is utilized by the plants for their own growth, some by animals and people who eat the plants as food; but much of the solar energy remains in the plants. It can be released when the plants are burned, creating a potential alternative source of energy.

Crops such as alfalfa, switch grass, fast-growing trees, desert shrubs, corn, and beets, have been employed. Arguments against cultivating biomass for fuel note the danger of growing plants with chemical fertilizers that would later pollute the atmosphere, the tremendous amount of water that would be required, and the moral issue of growing crops for energy rather than food.

ENERGY CONSERVATION

People in the United States consume about seven times as much energy as people in other nations. Millions of barrels of oil are wasted each day through inefficient use of energy in homes, buildings, industry, and transportation.

Young people are among the largest consumers of energy for personal use. They leave lights, television sets, and even air conditioners on when they leave a room. They drive or request transportation when they might just as easily walk or ride a bicycle. They may use appliances, such as hair dryers, to excess. Yet youngsters are becoming energy-conscious and can influence adults to conserve.

The possibilities of power shortages remain. A cold wave in the northeastern United States in January 1994 led to the closing of all offices in Washington, D.C., and neighboring cities for varying periods to avert blackouts.

Ungraded Activities

Imagine Life without Energy

Have students recall a power blackout when there was no gas or electricity, and a shortage of gasoline as well. Suggest their families participate in these activities. Start with the morning. They have to wash with cold water, eat cold foods, and not turn on any lights. As the day progresses, note all the everyday activities that would need to be eliminated if there were no fuel.

Invite others in the school to complete this activity as a way of building energy awareness.

Be an Energy Private Eye

Kids can investigate the following practices that waste energy.

Heat is wasted on cold days because of drafty areas in the home. To check for such areas, they make a "draft detector." Tape a strip of plastic food wrap, about 5" × 10", to a stick or pencil. Place it near windows or doors. If the plastic blows, there is a draft. Can it be sealed?

Try to slip a coin under the door. If it goes through easily, the door needs weather stripping.

Are lights left on in empty rooms? How about the radio or television? Do family members keep opening the refrigerator door unnecessarily? Or keep it open while they decide what they like? What other example of wasteful practices can the kids identify?

Shower or Bath?

Which uses more water, a shower or a bath? Design an experiment to find out.

Conduct a Contest for a Slogan

One class used "Kill-A-Watt," another "Don't Be Fuelish, Save Energy." Make buttons out of felt with the winning slogan. Popularize it.

Issue an Energy Fact Sheet

Send this fact sheet home with students:

- *Turn off:* lights, radio, television, air conditioner, faucets, when not in use. Avoid heating or cooling unused rooms.
- *Turn down:* thermostats.
- *Use less:* make fewer car trips, take shorter showers instead of bathing, use only necessary bulb wattage, don't let water run when you are brushing your teeth, wash clothes with cold water.
- *Save energy:* stuff cracks, close doors and windows when air conditioner is on, close refrigerator door quickly, do fewer washes of dishes and clothes, dry clothes outdoors if possible, keep doors of unused rooms closed to avoid heating or cooling them, use fluorescent instead of incandescent lights, use mass transportation.

Facts to Consider

If the thermostat in every house in the United States were lowered by an average of 6 degrees for 24 hours, there would be a savings of more than 570,000 barrels of oil each day.

Assuming that a person bathes in water that is half hot and half cold, substituting one five-minute shower for one bath each day would save 2,000 gallons of hot water in a year.

Two lightweight sweaters provide more warmth than one heavy one.

Monthly Conservation Day

Identify one day each month as a schoolwide energy conservation day. Encourage students to seek means to conserve energy both at home and at school. Note suggestions in the energy fact sheet above.

Complete an Energy Report Card

Ask students to rate themselves on the report card shown in Figure 6.1.

Name _____

Week _____

	Needs No Improvement	Needs a Little Improvement	Needs Lots of Improvement
Ways I saved energy this week:			
Turned off lights when not needed			
Turned off radio and TV when not in use			
Checked doors and windows for drafts			
Requested fewer car trips			
Closed refrigerator quickly			
Closed water tap while brushing my teeth			
Used fewer electric appliances			
Wore warmer clothes on cold days so thermostat could be lowered			
Showered instead of bathing			

FIGURE 6.1   My Energy Report Card

Activities for Middle and Junior High

Save Energy When Cooking

Which boils quicker, water in a covered or an uncovered pot? To test this, students boil different quantities of water, from one quart to six quarts, and record the difference in seconds.

Lower Thermostats

The following chart indicates the percentage of savings on the price of heating fuel if thermostats were lowered from 70 degrees Fahrenheit to the temperatures shown for the period indicated.

If a heating bill for a year was $1,000, students can compute the savings if the thermostat was lowered from 70 to each of the degrees noted below.

Temperature	Four Hours	Eight Hours
65	2.5%	5%
60	5%	9.5%
55	7.5%	14.5%
50	9.5%	19.5%

Learn about Kilowatts

A kilowatt is the equivalent of 1,000 watts. Electricity use is measured in kilowatt-hours (KWH).

The number stamped on an electric light bulb—100, 75, 60, and so—on reveals the number of watts of electricity the bulb will use in one hour. For example, a 100 watt bulb will use 100 watts of electricity in one hour, 1 kilowatt in ten hours.

Cost of a Kilowatt-Hour (kwh)

The local utility company can supply information about the cost of a kilowatt-hour and other factors that are included in an electric bill. This information will enable students to compute the cost of the electricity used over a given period by learning to read the electric meter.

Read Electric Meters

Meters are maintained by utility companies to indicate the kwh of electricity used and the cubic feet of gas. The resident is then charged accordingly.

To learn how to read an electric meter, see figure 6.2. Read the dials from the smallest number to the largest. When the indicator falls between two numbers, record the smallest number. Note that some of the dials read clockwise and some counterclockwise.

The number in Figure 6.1 reads 12,594. To determine how many kilowatt-hours of electricity have been used over a period of time, you would have to know the previous meter reading and subtract this from the current one. For example, if

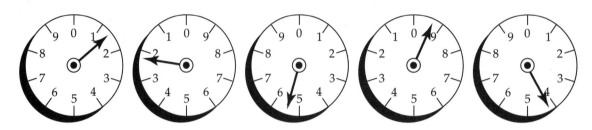

FIGURE 6.2 Electric Meters

the previous reading had been 11,232, then 1,362 kwh of electricity would have been used in the period.

Gas meters are read in a similar fashion.

Monitor Electric and Gas Use

Students read the meters to determine how much electricity and gas were used over a given period of time. If one period shows a large increase in use, try to determine the reasons and seek methods of conservation.

Students can help their families learn to read the meters, too.

How Much Does a Family Pay for Electricity?

Check the number of kilowatt-hours used monthly, and calculate the savings that would accrue if a family used 10 percent or 20 percent less electricity. Could students devise such a plan in cooperation with others in their families?

What Is the Cost of Electricity to the School?

Students research this figure. Can they help reduce the cost? Organize a group to brainstorm a plan, submit it to other students and enlist their help to put it into effect.

Electricity Uses Fuel

Here's an interesting math problem:

Electricity is generated by burning fuel; about 75 percent of our gas, coal and oil is used to manufacture electricity.

It requires about one gallon of oil to produce 12.7 kilowatts of electricity. How many gallons of oil were needed to produce the electricity used in the school last month?

Encourage Car Pooling

Kids submit the following questionnaire to adults who drive to work:

- How many people ride in the car with you?
- How many miles do you drive to work (round trip)?
- How many miles can you drive on each gallon of gasoline?

- What is the average price you pay for a gallon of gasoline?
- What is the cost of tolls, if any?

Tabulate this information and compute the following:

Assuming that each person's car used about the same amount of gasoline, how much gasoline could be saved if each car included one or more additional passengers? How much money?

Do Commuters Car Pool?

Working in teams of four, older students can stand on a corner during commuting hours to record the extent of car pooling. Have one person record all the cars with one passenger, another those with two, the third all cars with three, and the fourth person all cars with more.

Compute the savings in gasoline if each car contained three or more passengers. Estimate that the cars will drive about sixty miles round trip, covering about 20 miles per gallon of gas.

Investigate Electric Cars

As a way of conserving gasoline, scientists have been experimenting with automobiles that run on rechargeable batteries instead of gasoline. Corporations have already built some of these cars.

Students can gather information about electric cars. Where do they exist? What are the problems that currently prevent them from being used widely? What government regulations are projected mandating their use in the future? Can you locate someone in the community who might have this information?

Broadcast Energy-Saving Tips

Use the school intercom for students to broadcast energy tips. They read the names of "super energy savers," students who have instituted savings based on the energy report card (previously described in this chapter).

RESPECT FOR LIVING THINGS

Science education fosters a respect for all living things and stresses the interdependence of each species on earth. Kids have been organizing in defense of endangered species, adopting and caring for animals, helping in animal shelters, and even rehabilitating orphaned and injured wildlife.

Ungraded Activities

Endangered Species

The Federal Endangered Species Act is intended to protect endangered plants and animals. But unfortunately, it has been difficult to enforce. It has come into conflict with people whose jobs are threatened by attempts to safeguard a particular species. In the Pacific Northwest, for example, loggers have been posed against those who would protect the habitat of the spotted owl. In the same areas's Columbia River, it is hydroelectric plants and industrial development versus threatened species of salmon. In the Southwest, desert tortoises conflict with ranchers. This is conflict exists in many areas of the country.

Some would amend the Endangered Species Act to include a provision that the economic impact of any decision be considered before making an environmental rule. Environmentalists fear this would weaken the act. Once a species has become extinct, it is too late. Unfortunately, it comes down to jobs and development versus the environment, a difficult choice at any time, but particularly so in depressed economic times.

The World's "Ten Most Wanted" Species

A number of species have been identified worldwide as at risk of extinction. These change from time to time. A number of organizations maintain lists of endangered species.[1] For example, the World Wildlife Federation issues a list of the "Ten Most Wanted," those species most in danger.

Unfortunately, most species make the list because of human greed. The species are poached because their parts may be valuable, or, as in the case of the beautiful Moluccan cockatoo, a native of Indonesia, they have commercial value as pets. (Cockatoos may sell in the United States for up to $3,000.)

Publicize the Endangered Species

Design "Ten Most Wanted" posters to be placed in the school, neighborhood stores, and libraries to build awareness of the problem.

Protect Endangered Species

Students can contact organizations dedicated to protecting endangered species worldwide. What is being done to protect them? What actions can students take to make their views known? Check the status of the Federal Endangered Species Act. Write to congressional representatives for information, and encourage them to support legislation to protect endangered species.

Activities for Grades K–2

Select an Animal in the Zoo

Kindergartners at the William Penn Elementary School in Indianapolis "adopted" an animal at the zoo. Before they went to the zoo, stations were set up in the kindergarten classroom where students learned about each animal and kids imitated some of their characteristics—hopping like kangaroos; drinking like elephants by trying to use a straw to fill a glass with water; wearing manes like lions, striped tails like zebras, and so forth.

Sixth graders came to the class and read stories to the kids about animals. The kids then visited the zoo and decided on an elephant. They raised funds for its care, interviewed zoo attendants about its habits, visited regularly, and received a photograph of it.

Activities for Grades 3–5

Protect a Whale

A fourth-grade class in Springfield, Massachusetts, was interested in providing a safe environment for a whale in Boston harbor. As a result, they became more concerned about harbor pollution and wrote to their senators to communicate their feelings about keeping harbors clean.

Assist an Animal Shelter

Classes can select a nearby shelter. Youngsters identify a pet, usually a dog or cat, they learn to handle it, brush its fur, help to clean the cages, check its ears for infections, and walk the dogs. Kids have also collected old blankets, towels, and sheets for shelters. In Evanston, Illinois, when an elementary class decided to assist a shelter, a visiting nurse trained the kids to care for the animals.

This activity is important for kids who want a pet but cannot have one of their own.

Activities for Middle and Junior High

A Traveling Zoo

Science teacher Louis Smith, Jr., in the Henderson County South Junior High School in Kentucky, recalls that when he was a child his favorite sleeping companion was a stuffed snake. It is therefore not surprising that he brought snakes into his science class. "Animals make good teaching devices," he believes.

Today, Smith's classroom in Henderson, Kentucky, is host to a variety of animals brought in by students, parents, and teachers. Before the winter, kids add animals from the wild that would not survive if left outdoors. "The population changes," Smith explains, "based on what becomes available and what dies." It has included snakes, an iguana, a tarantula, an Argentine horned frog, hermit crabs, toads, turtles, a rabbit, lizards, and common pets such as hamsters. A favorite was a baby opossum whose mother had disappeared. The students trained it to eat cat food.

Students learn to handle, nurture, and protect the animals, as well as their characteristics and which can live compatibly together. "They also learn responsibility, respect for other life forms and about careers related to animals," Smith adds.

Accompanied by a knowledgeable cadre of students, Smith visits elementary schools teaching kids to respect animals, sharing information about animal growth, and demonstrating how to handle them. "It helps young children and teachers overcome their fears of animals," he explains.

Students also conduct a program to study animals that cannot be brought into their classroom. These have included a whale and a dolphin.

A Wildlife Rehabilitation Center

It is not unusual for science teacher Sam Chattin to be interrupted in middle of teaching by a knock on the door from someone bringing in a wounded animal. With the aid of his seventh- and eighth-grade students, Chattin runs the largest wildlife animal rehabilitation center in three states: Indiana, Ohio, and Kentucky. The project has received international recognition and been has rated one of the ten best science programs in the United States.

Animals Rehabilitating Kids (ARK) (a.k.a. Kids Rehabilitating Animals)

William H. English Middle School, Scottsburg, Indiana

"Most of what we do is hard, unpleasant, smelly—not all that much fun—cleaning cages, mopping, feeding, washing, changing bandages, but what keeps us all going is that it is IMPOR-TANT, and kids are not allowed to do important things anymore."

—Sam Chattin, science teacher, director, ARK

Before he came to Scottsburg, Chattin had taught high school science. At the middle school, he discovered that the lecture style he had used at the upper levels didn't work. Kids were bored, uninterested.

At a science convention, Chattin met an elementary school teacher with a classroom pet, a boa constrictor.

"I couldn't believe the excitement he created with that snake," Chattin recalls. He convinced his students to raise funds to buy two boa constrictors for the science class-room. Before long they had a miniature menagerie—snakes, hamsters, gerbils, and other pets.

The wildlife program started by chance. A student brought an injured baby owl into class. Word of the students' efforts to cure the bird spread, and bit by bit students and people in the community began to bring injured or orphaned animals to the classroom. Students accepted more responsibility—cleaning cages and feeding the animals.

Today the entire science curriculum centers on the rehabilitation facility. In seventh-grade, Chattin teaches students primary care of the wildlife—stopping bleeding, cleaning wounds, suturing, and setting bones. In eighth-grade, students join the rehabilitation staff. Wildlife needs seven-day-a-week care. Students are in attendance during lunch hour, study halls, before and after school, and on weekends.

Chattin and his students are involved in 15 to 20 outreach programs and have presented in 47 states and seven foreign countries. They rescue about 80 animals each year and tend them at the school. Ninety-five percent of the program's annual budget of $10,000 is raised by recycling.

Students also travel to neighboring schools and communities to teach others how to care for wild animals. Concern for wildlife has led these students to pile up an impressive record as advocates. This includes:

- Initiating the prosecution in the first Indiana case involving the killing of a protected species of wildlife
- Playing a role in the passage of the first ordinance in Indiana banning the possession and sale of wild or exotic animals
- Helping to block the construction of a controversial hazardous/toxic waste treatment facility in their community
- Challenging the discrepancies in a renowned chemical company's report of the results of a chemical spill, which did not agree with the students' independent research

• Conducting a six-month investigation of a biological supply house accused of animal cruelty during preparation of animals for dissection, and thus helping to define new laws for the humane treatment of such animals.

Scottsburg is a rural town of about 5,000 in the middle of Scott County, Indiana. It has one of the highest unemployment rates and the largest number of people receiving food stamps. After involvement with the wildlife program, however, the National Science Teachers Association study of science programs nationwide placed the Scottsburg students in the top 97th percentile in science knowledge, the 95th percentile in ability to apply scientific knowledge, and the 100th percentile in attitude toward science—every one of Chattin's students selected science as his or her favorite subject.

Note

1. For information, contact:
   World Wildlife Federation, 1250 24th Street, N.W., Washington, DC 20037
   Environmental Defense Fund, 257 Park Avenue South, New York, NY 10010

CHAPTER 7

Environmental Science: Reduce, Reuse, Recycle

"The Earth may still have a chance because of kids."
— Michael, seventh-grade student, Robert Wagner Junior High School, New York City

"The younger generation is bullying America into changing its polluting ways," states an article in the *New York Times Magazine*.[1] Students of all ages are tackling pollution, monitoring waters, cleaning streams, challenging corporations to become environmentally aware, and insisting on recycling and conservation. They have been remarkably effective.

Environmental activities are no longer the domain of science courses alone. They have permeated the entire curriculum. Kids Against Pollution, an environmental group with chapters throughout the country, was organized in a social studies class. *One Voice for Wetlands*, a book of poetry that received a national environmental award, was written in a language arts class. A math class plotted the areas of the rain forests around the world and then raised money to save some of the acreage. Middle school teachers are finding the environment a particularly apt theme for an integrated curriculum.

Nor are environmental studies limited to specific grades. All kids starting with kindergarten are involved. It is not unusual for five- or six-year-olds to chastise parents for not turning out lights when leaving a room. Schools frequently team with community residents to celebrate environmental holidays: planting trees on Arbor Day and a host of activities on Earth Day or Earth Month. Together they engage in neighborhood cleanups, spring plantings, conservation days, and often a special lunch with foods from rain forests.

Teachers who wish to introduce a service activity in their curriculum might consider a topic related to the environment. It has many advantages. It can be related to almost any subject. It can be a short-term activity, such as planting bulbs, or a full semester's involvement, such as monitoring a stream. And it is of particular interest to students.

Environmental Activities

The activities in this chapter are categorized under the following headings:

- Organizing for Environmental Activities

- Cleanup and Beautification
- Waste and Recycling
- Water Pollution
- Air Pollution
- Ecosystems: Rain Forests, Wetlands

ORGANIZING FOR ENVIRONMENTAL ACTIVITIES

Ungraded Activities

Form an Action Group

To build awareness of environmental concerns, start by suggesting to the kids that they organize themselves into an action group. It may focus on a local concern, as in Southampton, New York. There kids in an elementary school were distressed by the erosion of the ocean shores on Long Island. They organized a campaign with the acronym S.O.S. ("Save Our Shoreline"), and undertook to teach every child in the school, from kindergarten through fourth grade, about the problems of erosion. The kids sold T-shirts to finance the purchase of beach grass to be planted to prevent further erosion. Groups may also address a variety of local and national concerns, as did the one formed in Closter, New Jersey, Kids against Pollution.

Projects can be selected that are less time-consuming than these. Students can encourage recycling in school, at home, or in the community. For example, two fourth-grade classes at the Schuylkill Elementary School in Phoenixville, Pennsylvania, conducted a successful drive to recycle old telephone books.

Kids against Pollution (KAP)

Tenakill School, Closter, New Jersey

"Save the Earth Not Just for Us But for Future Generations"

—KAP Motto

No one could have predicted the outcome of the homework assignment that teacher Nicholas Byrne gave to his fifth-grade social studies class back in April 1987. During a discussion of the Bill of Rights, Byrne asked the students to exercise their right of free speech by speaking out on an issue. Coincidentally, Earth Day had just been celebrated, and stories of medical dumping on the Jersey beaches were featured in the media. These influenced the students to concentrate on the environment.

They formed an organization, Kids against Pollution. They selected a logo and a motto and created a button and T-shirt to raise funds. They wrote to legislators, editors, and public officials to express their concern about topics such as beach, water, and air pollution; inadequate recycling; and sewage disposal. To have more impact, they invited other schools to establish KAP chapters. At one point, there were as many as 1,000 chapters, including many across the United States as well as in New Zealand, the Bahamas, Germany, the Netherlands, Mexico, Canada, Great Britain, Norway, Guatemala, Australia, and Russia.

KAP publishes a magazine, writes and distributes environmental brochures, and conducts workshops. Thousands of letters have been sent to newspaper and magazine editors, and to public officials. Their list of accomplishments would make any adult group proud.

Before pressing an issue, the group researches it carefully. It is to this detailed preparation that Byrne attributes their accomplishments. These include: banning the use of polystyrene cups, trays, and plates in favor of biodegradable paper products in school and most town functions; increasing use of recycled paper; publicizing the failure of towns to enforce local environmental laws; lobbying for a collection area for disposal of toxic substances, eliminating the use of helium balloons that might float into waters and, when ingested, choke marine animals; and conducting periodic town, beach, and water cleanups. They also participated in a drive that succeeded in convincing McDonald's to eliminate polystyrene packaging in its stores. In the process, they have educated their local community about the environment.

KAP's efforts have been recognized nationally and internationally, gaining them numerous awards and extensive media coverage. A KAP member, together with 80 students from all over the world and a dozen Nobel Prize winners, was invited to the Peace Child Conference in Holland in 1990. Others have been invited to environmental conferences throughout the United States, testified before state legislatures, the United Nations, and agencies in Washington, D.C., and been videotaped for the Earth Summit conference in France.

Perhaps their most impressive achievement has been the introduction of an Environmental Bill of Rights in the New Jersey state legislature. Arguing that the U.S. Constitution guarantees "life, liberty and the pursuit of happiness," the introduction to the Bill reads "we believe we are entitled, by law, to clean, air, land and water," and ends with a provision that environmental education should be taught at least one month each year from kindergarten through the twelfth grade.

The impact on the participants has been marked. "These students are engaged in real-life issues," Byrne explains. "They have become expert letter writers and poised speakers. Not only has their social studies curriculum been enriched, but all their subjects. They undertook difficult math computations to prove to the community they could save money by refining their recycling efforts...."

"Most important," Byrne adds, "they have become knowledgeable not only about the environment but about participatory citizenship."

CLEANUP AND BEAUTIFICATION

In schoolyards and parks, around public buildings and senior centers, kids are planting bulbs and gardens, beautifying their surroundings, frequently with the active cooperation of local botanical groups and parks departments.

Ungraded Activities

Plant, Plant, Plant...

In the community or around the school grounds, find a spot that can be beautified with bulbs or annuals. Plant bulbs in the fall, annuals in the spring. Germinate seedlings and pot them as gifts for seniors.

Plant Bulbs as Part of an Interdisciplinary Project

Sixth- and seventh-grade students at the Robert Wagner Junior High School in Manhattan planted 500 tulips and daffodils at a local park. This was only one aspect of their interdisciplinary project, which resulted from a collaboration between the National Center for Service Learning in Early Adolescence; the Wagner School's program coordinator, Sara-Jane Hardman; and other teachers at the school.

The project was initiated with the development and distribution of an environmental questionnaire. Three hundred responses were received expressing concerns about global issues such as the ozone layer, rain forest, endangered species , and animal experimentation. Closer to home was also concern about the disregard of some residents for the immediate neighborhood. The students decided to tackle this latter issue by beautifying a nearby park, the Jonathan Jay Park. The local Parks Department personnel were enthusiastic participants. They supplied tools, material, and know-how.

The project became part of the curriculum of all the classes. Hardman reports that, "In addition to the pleasure derived from strenuous physical work such as shoveling, digging and planting," the students gained immeasurably in self-confidence, poise, and academic skills. They wrote constantly—an environmental newsletter, poetry, journals and creative stories with titles such as "Do Plants Have Emotion?" and imaginative pieces pretending the objects discovered in the park cleanup were ancient artifacts discovered while on an archaeological dig.

Science was involved when an environmental lab was established and students were trained to test local water, analyze soil samples, and study the effects of pollution on trees and plants. In social studies, the class researched the legal requirements for a project in a city park and became acquainted with some of the problems of the homeless people who used the park. They researched environmental issues throughout the world, such as at Chernobyl. In math, they graphed their results and measured areas to be covered by the bulbs.

Other follow-up activities included school cleanups, recycling programs, and planting a vegetable garden in front of the school. The students also published a coloring book for elementary school kids.

Their environmental activities continue. Earth Day celebrations, for example, involve the entire community. Students construct displays, create games, and raise funds to buy acres of rain forest. They have truly become caretakers of their environment.

Celebrate Arbor Day

Originated by J. Sterling Morton of Nebraska City in 1872, Arbor Day is now celebrated in every state and in many other countries, usually on the last Friday in April. (Some states observe Arbor Day on other dates to coincide with their best tree-planting time.) On the first Arbor Day, it was estimated that more than one million trees were planted.

Tree planting has been part of many cultures. Trees are planted to remember loved ones, to show support for a new country, and in some cultures to celebrate a marriage. Trees are the oldest and largest living things on earth. The bristlecone pines in the southwestern United States are over 4,000 years old; some Redwoods in California are over 300 feet tall.

Students can celebrate Arbor Day with a ceremony at school. They organize a poster or poetry contest explaining why trees are important and plant trees in the school or neighborhood. Some kids identify and graph the species of trees in the community. They try to locate the oldest tree in town.

Care for a Tree

"Remember that a tree is alive," read a poster prepared by one youngster. Another poster listed the contributions of trees to the environment: help clean the air and ground water; anchor the topsoil; take carbon dioxide from the air and release oxygen; cool the streets; serve as shelters and provide food for birds, insects, and small animals. There is also the aesthetic component—trees beautify communities.

Kids can care for trees in a park or area near the school and can water them regularly, particularly in periods of little rain. They can help keep dogs away and remove garbage from the soil, which may prevent water from reaching the roots. If trees appear to be "sick," with branches broken, leaves falling off, or holes in the bark, the responsible community agency should be notified.

Reclaim Vacant Lots

In many towns, vacant lots that were eyesores are being reclaimed by students. In the South Bronx, kids from Public School 59, with the help of the community, converted rubble-strewn, vacant lots into a community garden and playground. On one lot, kids planted vegetables that were distributed free to the community. The Bronx Botanical Garden donated the plants and seeds. The kids studied the foods as part of a unit on nutrition.

A nearby lot was converted into a ballfield and playground, with benches installed for the residents of a senior center. Close by, Public School 42, with the help of the Parks Department, built a greenhouse where seedlings are germinated and later planted in a previously littered area.

Cleanup Days

Spring cleaning has acquired an environmental cast. Students organize a community revitalization day—raking and sweeping leaves, wearing plastic gloves to pick up trash and clear trails of deadfall. Plants, shrubs, and bushes replace the litter. Local beaches, stream beds, shore and river banks are cleared of winter debris, too, and sea grass is planted to prevent further erosion. Cleanup days can be organized in the fall, as well.

Cleanup of the Housatonic River

An entire community can be involved in a cleanup project. Nearly 1,500 volunteers turned out on a Saturday for an all-day cleanup of the Housatonic River in Connecticut. Classes came with their science teachers. There was a sense of adventure as the students set out on mud flats to pick up debris, and also surprise at how much trash is casually tossed in the river. They found washing machines, old tires, broken lawnmowers, car seats, construction rubble, and much more, and wondered about people who would trash the river this way. The students insisted they would return and pledged to work with environmental groups in the area to help change attitudes.

Activities for Intermediate, Middle, and Junior High

Education through Reforestation

In New York City, the Parks Department program "Parklands Partnership: Education through Reforestation" has reached close to 2,000 students each year in elementary and secondary schools with its environmental activities. The department is committed to giving inner-city kids a sense of stewardship toward their parks. By assigning students a "piece of park," it fosters in them a personal responsibility toward maintaining the natural areas. The youngsters study their piece of park and perform valuable restoration work while also learning natural science. The program is made up of two parts: Forest Ecology and Forest Restoration.

Forest Ecology. Initially, students are introduced to the park—its food chains, webs, and layers of the forest, and the relationships among plants, animals, and fungi of the ecosystem.

Students survey the park and, as they witness the severe problems the woodlands are facing, appreciate the need to restore native shrubs and trees.

Forest Restoration. At this point, the youngsters research the appropriate plants for the area and help decide which should be used and where they should be planted. (Recommendations can be obtained from a local Parks Department or Botanical Society.) Finally, the youngsters actually restore their "piece of the park."

Note: Middle school students are expected to conduct a more detailed site analysis of the park and also draw a landscape design before proceeding.

Study the Park. The Park Rangers recommend that teachers return to the park with the students after the restoration has been completed. They believe this inculcates a sense of responsibility toward the parks. The kids study pond life and urban botany, search for animal tracks in the winter, and continue to explore the forest ecology.

Explore a Compost Heap

Compost heaps can be mysterious; they are both fun and educational to explore. Under the direction of an Urban Park Ranger, a group of fifth graders explored a compost heap in Central Park in New York City. They could hardly contain their excitement at their discoveries. "I saw a scorpion," one fifth grader shouted. "Oh yeah, I saw a mole," another added. "Hey, here's some orange mold. Wow, we found orange mold!" "Why is there steam coming up?"

Earlier each child in the class from the local public school had been given a map with directions to the compost heap. When they reached it, the Urban Park Ranger explained the composition of the compost heap and then encouraged the youngsters to examine it and analyze their observations.

Create Nature Centers

Students have selected unused areas near their school grounds to create natural centers with wild flowers and special plants to attract butterflies and birds. Others have undertaken more ambitious projects, such as constructing a nature trail through a large nearby park.

Ralph Sloman Sensory Nature Trail

Public School 213, Queens, New York

"If we can instill in young children a real feeling for nature and for each other, they will be prepared for the decisions they will have to face as adults...decisions that will eventually bring humans and nature into harmony."

—Judy Intraub, ecology teacher

The trail runs for about a mile through a corner of Alley Pond Park in Queens, New York, directly across from Public School 213, and meanders through a variety of trees, plant life, and wild berry bushes leading to two ponds. It has a solid base of wood chips, plastic markers to prevent anyone from becoming lost, and a number of stations to highlight its unique features. A written guide explains the geology and history of the area and a description of the stations.

What's special about this trail is that it was built by third and fifth graders from P.S. 213 with the help of students from a neighboring high school. It is an extension of the elementary school's ecology program, which has long "used the park as a learning laboratory where students can study the environment while working towards saving it." Students organized Project SOAPP (Save Our Alley Pond Park) and secured a grant of $2,000 from the New York City Consortium, which made the plan for a trail feasible. It was dedicated to Ralph Sloman, an environmentalist and community activist.

Judy Intraub, the ecology teacher at P.S. 213, joined forces with a conservation teacher at Martin Van Buren High School, whose students acted as mentors to the younger kids. The result was not only a heightened respect for nature, but also for each other's cultural diversity. Van Buren is predominantly African-American and Latino, whereas P.S. 213 is more ethnically diverse.

Intraub provides lessons to students from neighboring schools using the trail to illustrate how animals adapt to the environment, and to conduct a series of experiments—examining leaf litter, taking the temperature of soil under the trees and outside of it, and studying pond water with hand-held microscopes. Students also learn to identify trees, plants, and insects.

Many integrated activities have been inspired by the trail, including a book of poetry expressing the reactions of the students as they walked silently through the trail. (See Chapter 4 for an example of such a poem.)

WASTE AND RECYCLING

Valuable materials are rotting in our garbage dumps. Metals are a particularly apt example. The United States now imports more than half of its metals—nickel, tin, aluminum, chromium, tungsten, lead, iron, manganese, and platinum. Yet recycling could save about 30 percent of these. Recycling metals saves energy, too. For example, it requires about 25 percent more energy to produce aluminum from ore than from scrap, eight times more energy to mine and produce copper than to recycle it.

Our forests are being denuded, yet paper can be recycled. Every ton of recycled paper saves approximately seventeen trees. Most of the oil that is regularly changed in cars is discarded; in Europe, by contrast, 50 percent is recycled.

In the past, the waste consisted chiefly of natural materials, which, when buried, were decomposed by bacteria in the soil and recycled into nutrients that enriched the soil. This can best be illustrated by preparing a compost heap.

Ungraded Activities

Construct a School Compost Heap

In a previous activity, kids explored a compost heap in a park. Students also can construct compost heaps on school grounds. Grass cuttings, fruit and vegetable leftovers, coffee grounds can all be collected and turned into rich natural fertilizer for soil and plants.

Set aside a small area in the schoolyard for a compost heap. You will need to build a wooden enclosure about 4 feet high by 4 feet deep by 6 feet wide.

Pack the material firmly, and moisten the layers with water. Cover with plastic. Continue to moisten and also mix the material at regular intervals.

Students study the heap over a period of time and check the temperature at different levels. They record their observations and determine when the material is ready to be used as a natural fertilizer.

Classroom Worm Composting

Don't say "Ugh!" yet. At a number of schools, including the Issaquah Middle School in Washington State, a number of classes have successfully started indoor composting bins, which produce rich soil for classroom or house plants. The experience is surprisingly satisfying.

You will need a large wooden box or heavy plastic bin, about a pound of worms, some garbage (banana peels, apples, lettuce, tea leaves), and newspaper.

Full instructions are contained in the book *Worms Eat My Garbage*.[2]

What Happens to the Solid Wastes?

The three most common methods of disposing of solid wastes are the following:

- *Dumps:* Tossing it into dumps
- *Landfills:* Packing it closely, covering it with soil and reusing the new earth
- *Incinerators:* Burning it

Students investigate how waste is disposed of in school, at home and in the community.

- Where is the disposal site?
- How is waste transported to the site?
- Are there any disposal problems?
- Any pollution problems?
- What is the cost of waste disposal to the school, community, city?
- How much of the trash is recycled? Where?

They interview the school custodian and local sanitation officials to find the answers to these questions. Are there any problems with disposal. Are any further inquiries suggested?

The Cost of Waste Disposal

In conjunction with their environmental studies, students at the Robert Wagner Junior High School in New York secured figures from the New York City Sanitation Department on the cost of garbage disposal, the amount of trash, and the disposal sites. They also researched how waste is disposed of in other countries.

Activities for Grades K–2

Is It Biodegradable?

To illustrate a reason for the continued accumulation of waste, distinguish between substances that are naturally broken down in the soil, as in the compost heap, and those that do not decompose but clutter the ground indefinitely. The first are considered biodegradable whereas those that do not decompose are nonbiodegradable. This is why concerned kids are asking that biodegradable products, such as paper cups, be substituted for nonbiodegradable polystyrene cups.

To test which are biodegradable, compare what happens to different products. For example, fill two equal containers with soil, and "plant" equal-sized pieces of newspaper in one and plastic wrap in the other. Keep the containers moist. Dig up your "plants" after a month and compare.

Plant a Waste Garden

A more involved method of testing for biodegradability is to select an out-of-the way plot at school. Kids dig holes about one foot deep, and plant natural and also synthetic products. Include pieces of fruit and vegetables, cotton, rayon, polyester, Styrofoam and plastic containers, and aluminum foil. Water regularly.

Every two weeks, they dig up the plants and check their conditions, chart the data, and issue a report indicating which products are nonbiodegradable and how they clutter the earth.

Play a Biogradeable Game

To reinforce the distinction between biodegradable and nonbiodegradable products, prepare a board game. It will contain a path leading to "clean earth." On the path should be boxes listing different items, some biodegradable and others not. To play, toss a die and advance the number of boxes indicated. If students land on a nonbiodegradable item, they must return to the beginning. The first person to reach "clean earth" wins.

Recycle Aluminum Cans

Teach kids to separate aluminum cans for recycling by testing cans with a magnet. Magnets attract steel cans but not aluminum.

Activities for Intermediate, Middle, and Junior High

How Much Trash?

Some of these activities require mathematical calculations and should be integrated with mathematics.

At Home. Have students compile an inventory of the trash that is discarded at home in one week using the Solid Waste Inventory.

In Class. Examine the class wastebasket at the end of the day. Could any items have been used further? For example, look at the discarded paper. Were both sides used? Could parts have been cut off and stapled to make a memorandum pad? Summarize the data and draw conclusions.

In the Cafeteria. Organize teams of students to note the trays of children as they finish their lunches. List all the uneaten food. *Estimate:* If all the discarded food was combined, how many sandwiches, pieces of fruit, and containers of milk would they be altogether?

At School. Ask the school custodian to estimate the pounds of trash generated in one day. Extend this to a week. How about a month?

Figure 7.1 illustrates a form kids can use to inventory the amount of solid waste discarded.

Publicize Your Findings

In a special "waste alert" bulletin, kids inform the community of the findings by making posters and charts and writing letters to residents and local newspapers. They research and report on the growing shortage of sites for safe disposal of waste.

Too Much Trash

As part of a National Geographic Kids Network telecommunications unit, "Too Much Trash," fifth-grade classes at the Shelter Rock Elementary School in Manhasset, Long Island, invited town officials including the supervisor, recycling coordinator, and president of the carting company, to school. They organized a news conference and invited the media. Questions were prepared in advance on major topics: amount of trash, disposal methods, recycled trash, and community concerns.

Data were sent to participants throughout the United States, Canada, and England.

Trash into Art and Toys

Collect rolls from paper towels and toilet tissue, plastic bottles, pieces of fabric, and other trash. Kids can turn these items into musical instruments, puppets, constructions, collages, and much more. Award a prize for the most original use of "junk." Display these at the school.

Use Trash to Construct a Miniature Golf Course

A creative way to recycle trash was discovered by Project CREATE (Children, Recycling, Educating, Acting to (save the) Environment, organized by seventh-grade students at the Solomon Schecter Day School in Commack, New York, with the help of science/math teacher Fran Greenspan. Utilizing material found in waste bins, such as newspapers, wood, carpeting, cardboard, and discarded toys, they built an indoor, reusable eighteen hole miniature golf course appropriately titled "Trashland." The course was donated to the local "Y."

Other CREATE activities include a school recycling program, planting fifty white pine seedlings around the grounds of the Y, recycling jeans by patching them and then donating them to shelters, educating the public on environmental activities with posters and displays at the library, and making an alphabet coloring book. The group has received numerous awards, including one from the president in 1992 that included a VIP tour of the White House.

Solid Waste Inventory

Place collected _____ Date _____

	Number Found of Each	Total Found	Those with Further Use
Item			
Glass:			
Newspaper			
Other paper			
Metal			
Cans			
Plastic			
Aluminum			
Cardboard			
Food			
Miscellaneous (specify)			

1. Add the totals from the students' lists.
2. How much is thrown away by all families together in one week?
3. Extend this amount by computing the total per month, per year.

Which of these items could have been recycled?

FIGURE 7.1 Solid Waste Inventory

Review Recycling Practices

Students should become familiar with recycling regulations. Does your town have special garbage cans for newspapers, bottles, plastics? Many kids are leading the fight for recycling—at home, in the community, and at school. They urge residents to obey town rules and separate their waste. If the town's recycling efforts are not adequate, students can lobby for ordinances to improve them.

In the Community. Check local restaurants. Do they recycle their garbage? What happens to unused food? Is there a project to send the food to the homeless as in the Rescue Food activity described in Chapter 12. If not, suggest one be organized.

At School. Kids have improvised creative ways to improve their school's recycling program:

- At the Issaquah Middle School in Washington, with parents' help, students have established *waste stations* with receptacles for soda cans, milk containers, drink boxes, paper, aluminum, and food. Some of the food scraps are given to classes that have worm bins for composting.
- Many more cans were recycled when fifth-grade students in Pam Lawrence's class at the Shelter Rock Elementary School in Manhasset, New York, placed signs next to soda machines saying, "Don't throw the can away. Recycle it."
- In another activity, the students at this school collected and made a pile of all the Styrofoam cups that had been used in a week. This helped convince teachers to substitute mugs or paper cups for coffee and other drinks.

Recycle Newspapers

There is more recycled paper on hand than is bought. Encourage the use of recycled paper in school, at home, in public offices, and by businesses.

Kids against Pollution in Closter, New Jersey organized a campaign to separate junk mail from newspapers, making it less expensive to recycle the newspapers.

Turn Newspapers into Logs

First and third graders at the Willow Elementary School in Alaska formed the Kid Log Company. They recycled newspapers into hand-rolled logs to be used for heating purposes. These were provided free to low-income households and sold to others with profits reinvested in the school and community. The program received a President's Environmental Youth Award.

Recycle Christmas Trees

Discarded Christmas trees clog up dumps. Contact your local Sanitation Department or Environmental Protection Agency urging them to provide dropoff sites or curbside collection of the trees, and to join Vermont and other states that grind the trees into mulch to be used for parks and private gardens.

Is That Plastic Recyclable?

Communities are beginning to recycle some plastic. Its recyclability depends on the amount of resin in the product. Some plastic products have a number stamped on the bottom; the lower the number, the greater the possibility that it can be recycled. Check plastic products before they are discarded. What is the policy on recycling plastic in your community? Students should be familiar with the policy and investigate whether they can encourage increased recycling of plastics.

Recycle Aluminum: "Great Balls of Foil"

Foil sculptures? Humongous balls of aluminum foil? Students have found the "Great Balls of Foil" contests sponsored by Reynolds an enjoyable way to recycle aluminum. Over one million students in thirty-five states have entered the contests, which award prizes for the heaviest weight of foil collected, either in one ball or in many, and for the most creative entry.

Here's how it's done. Ask students to collect used aluminum foil and foil products such as pie plates, muffin trays, and roasting pans. (Do not include aluminum cans.) Clean them and store them either at home or in school. If you have a place at school to store the foil, the students can keep a daily or weekly chart of the weight of the foil collected. Have students estimate what the total will be.

Now have the kids build the aluminum ball or balls. They should not use tape or glue to hold the foil together because it will contaminate the recycling process. If the foil doesn't stick to the ball, here are two suggestions from Reynolds Wrap:

1. Take flat pieces of foil and crimp the ends together to make a long ribbon of foil. Wrap this around the foil.
2. Roll the foil into a cylinder like a big foil cigar. Then crimp the ends together to make a chain and wrap this around the foil ball.

Try also to build sculptures from the foil. Students can make weird monsters or robots, as well as animals and even headbands. The fifth grade kids at the Shelter Rock Elementary School in Manhasset, Long Island, made chains from the foil, then weighed and measured them. To correlate this activity with their social studies, they arranged the chains in the schoolyard to form the shape of the perimeter of Long Island. They called their display "Shelter Rock Links to Long Island."

Encourage students to think of other creative ideas for the recycled aluminum.

WATER POLLUTION

Water is a finite resource, circulating in an endless cycle of evaporation and condensation, from the surface of the earth to the atmosphere and back to the surface in the form of rain. About 70 percent of the earth's surface is covered with water; without it, the earth would be unable to sustain life. But 97 percent of the water lies in the oceans, which because of their saltiness cannot be used for drinking or irrigation, and 2 percent is frozen, leaving only 1 percent fresh water, which must be shared by an ever-increasing population.

We are squandering this natural resource. Each person in the United States uses about 180 gallons of water per day for drinking, washing, bathing, growing and preparing food, and flushing toilets. Our lakes, rivers, and even oceans are being contaminated—treated as open sewers into which are dumped every type of pollutant.

Major Sources of Water Pollution

As students become familiar with the various causes of water pollution described here, they research evidences of effects on their community. They help institute a campaign to lessen the pollution of water?

Chemical and Metal. Lead, zinc, mercury, nickel, and over fifty potentially dangerous industrial agents are routinely discarded into water. Their effects have not been completely documented, although some, such as mercury, have created known problems. Mercury is absorbed by the plants and tiny animals in water, which are later eaten by small fish, which in turn are eaten by larger fish such as tuna and swordfish. The mercury accumulates in the tissues of the larger fish; people who eat them are susceptible to mercury poisoning.

Add to these common household detergents that contain an array of chemicals, particularly phosphates. Phosphates stimulate the growth of algae in water; as they decay, they deplete the oxygen supply. The suds in detergents create problems, too. They are decomposed by bacteria in the water that compete with the fish for oxygen. As oxygen is exhausted, fish suffocate.

Thermal: Varying the Temperature of the Water. Factories, particularly nuclear-powered ones, use large quantities of water for cooling and then return the heated water to the source, disturbing the natural environment of the fish. It is interesting that a rise in water temperature of just 5 degrees can kill off trout and salmon. The salmon population in the northwestern—United States already is threatened.

Organic. Agricultural wastes, runoffs from pesticides and fertilizers, and animal remains also pollute the waters.

A serious pollution problem facing Long Island Sound is hypoxia, caused by a chain reaction from nitrogen pollution from storm water runoff and from the more than one billion gallons of treated sewage dumped into the Sound every day. The nitrogen interacts with sunlight and warm water, causing algae blooms. The algae sink to the bottom, absorbing underwater oxygen. Some fish can swim to more oxygenated waters, but others die, particularly lobsters and other less mobile marine life.

Activities for Grades K–2

The following activities are intended to familiarize young children with some of the origins of water pollution and what they can do to publicize these.

How Scraps of Food Pollute

The effects of throwing garbage or bits of food into ponds or lakes can be demonstrated.

Accumulate scraps of leftover fruit or vegetables—skins, cores of fruits, banana peels. Place these in a jar with some water.

Seal the jar. After about a week, open the jar and observe the contents. Smell them, too. What happens to bodies of water when debris is thrown into them?

Suffocated Fish—a Sign of Pollution

Streams, rivers, and ponds contain bacteria, which are nature's sanitary engineers. They decompose the wastes in water, keeping it clean, but they require oxygen for their work.

When there are too many pollutants in the water, the bacteria multiply, exhausting the oxygen in the water faster than it can be replaced. Without oxygen, fish suffocate.

Kids who are aware of the effects of pollution on fish have made posters for the local library depicting fish saying, "If people keep polluting the water, I won't be able to breathe." Or they have posted signs near a local pond asking that people stop throwing waste into it.

Impurities in Water

Students collect water from different areas in the community: a stream, a lake, a puddle. Place each in a separate dish. Permit the water to evaporate. Is there any residue left? They compare the samples and repeat the experiment at different times. Keep careful records.

Activities For Grades 3–5

How Fertilizers Pollute

Students place equal amounts of soil in two containers. Plant a few seeds in each. Place both in a sunny spot and water equally. Add fertilizer to one of the plants. Which grows faster?

What could happen to plants if large amounts of fertilizer run off into the water? Why might this be a problem?

Disposing of Toxic Substances

Pesticides and insecticides, paints, solvents, drain and oven cleaners, and wood preservatives—all are toxic substances which, if dumped into the regular garbage or poured into storm sewers, may pollute the groundwater.

Many towns have instituted special collection programs for these hazardous household wastes. Encourage students to find out the regulations in your town. If there is no program, they can contact the town government, explain the problem, and urge that a program be instituted.

A group of kids organized "STOP (Stop Throwing Out Pollutants)" and distributed a recipe for homemade cleaning products that could be substituted for detergents.

Recipe for All-Purpose Cleansers

Unlike some commercial detergents, this cleanser will not pollute. It's a lot cheaper, too.

> 1 gallon hot water
> ¼ cup sudsy ammonia
> ¼ cup vinegar
> 1 tablespoon baking soda

For a stronger cleanser, double the amount of ammonia. Use gloves when handling it, and be careful not to mix ammonia with bleach; a toxic fume may result.

For a glass cleanser, mix 1 tablespoon white vinegar with 1 quart of water. It will usually do the job.

Test these recipes. Then publicize them. Students may wish to write an advertisement for them.

Research and Market More Alternative Cleansers

Kids from the Backer Elementary School in Austin, Texas, researched environmentally safe nontoxic cleaning products, packaged them in recycled containers, and sold them to the community. (This project received a President's Award.)

Kids can interview older people in the community. They may know of homemade cleansers they once used.

Activities for Middle and Junior High

Monitoring Waterways

The waterways can serve as a science lab for students, enabling them to conduct significant chemical tests and collect needed data. By performing tasks associated with scientists, the students are also recognizing the potential of science as a career. They monitor the water quality of rivers, lakes, ponds, and creeks; analyze their findings; seek evidence of pollution; check the animal and plant life; and examine the banks of the waterways. In many cases, the students report their findings to the appropriate state or local department. Their contributions are valued. Most states would not be able to study all their waterways without the kids' help.

Find out if there is a student monitoring program in your area. If not, contact the local water department or Environmental Protection Agency to ascertain if they would be interested in your data.

Two examples of effective monitoring programs follow.

Monitoring the St. Louis River

St. Louis River Watch
Minnesota Pollution Control Agency, Duluth, Minnesota

"There's no better way to teach young people about pollution than to take them down to the water to sample life in the river."

—St. Louis River Watch, Jill Jacoby, director

Seventeen schools with students from elementary through high school participate in the St. Louis River Watch program. Each has an assigned program and site on the river.

Several times a year, students, such as those from Barb Akre's Life Science class in the Morgan Park Middle School in Duluth, Minnesota, monitor the river from their site. They collect water samples and "critters," which they net from the bottom of the river. They conduct water chemistry tests, measure temperature and total dissolved solids in the water, and survey for benthic macroinvertebrates. They examine them to note the effect of water pollution on the river population. The results are sent to Jacoby, who accumulates the data.

One student participant, Todd Rustad, explained his feelings about the program: "The St. Louis River has been around for a long time, and we are the ones who have to take care of it. We need to learn how to do so."[3]

Reports of the worldwide decline in the frog population have led the River Watch Program to request that students also locate and monitor wetland areas along the river that are habitats of frogs. "Because frogs spend so much of their life in the water...and because their skin is permeable, they're more vulnerable to chemicals in the water," explains Jacoby. "That's why they make good indicators of what's happening. If we see a rapid decline [in the frog population] it would be a red flag. We'd know that something is obviously happening to the population."

The student volunteers learn frog songs from a tape recording, become adept at identifying different frogs, and tabulate data about frog populations in the river. Frog calls are easy to learn, according to Larry Weber, a biology teacher: "You can learn them in fifteen minutes."[4]

Monitoring the Ohio River

Kentucky Water Watch
Henderson County South Junior High School, Henderson, Kentucky

"It's an incentive for the students to actually experience science."

—Louis Smith, Jr., science teacher

An observer might wonder what those kids are doing wading in the Ohio River filling jugs of water. This is part of the science course at the junior high school. Henderson students participate in the Water Watch program of the Kentucky Division of Water. The purpose of this program is to develop a database about pollution in the various waters in Kentucky. A testing kit, which is quite expensive, was provided by the League of Women Voters.

Twice a month, groups of students go to assigned testing sites along the Ohio River and a nearby creek, Canoe Creek. They collect samples of water and water sediment and search for visual evidence of pollutants. They analyze pH level, temperature, dissolved oxygen, and, in the science lab, chemical content: nitrates, chlorides, and iron. Results are graphed and sent to the water division for its annual report. If, during the year, the testing reveals any problems, students retest for two months. If there is still concern, the division follows up.

Originally initiated as a project for gifted sixth graders, the program is now open to all students, including special education kids. Participating students are expected to make up any classwork they miss during their outings to the waters.

The program has received a President's Environmental Award, has been mentioned in the *Wall Street Journal,* and has been featured on local television and radio. Smith points out its value to the community and students: "The state gets information, while the students get field experiences and learn the relationship between life science and chemistry." He has been instrumental in building a pond and a life science study area behind the school building. His classes have also raised funds to conserve over fifty acres of rain forests.

Xeriscape Gardening

After researching xeriscape (drought-tolerant) plants, students in an eighth-grade class in the Suzanne Middle School in Walnut, California,[5] created and maintained a xeriscape garden, with plants adapted for growth under dry conditions. They contacted newspapers and officials in state government and water districts to urge the use of more drought-resistant plants. As a result of their efforts, a bill was passed in California that has saved the residents millions of dollars and countless gallons of water.

AIR POLLUTION

Hundreds of pollutants pour into the air at a rate that leads environmentalists to charge that we are treating our atmosphere as a garbage dump. Automobiles are among the worst offenders. Their exhaust fills the air with carbon monoxide, a poison that even in small amounts can cause nausea, headaches, and blurred vision. They spew out hydrocarbons and lead particles—both damaging to the nervous system. Automobile control equipment cuts down on these emissions but does not completely eliminate them. Furthermore, control equipment needs to be checked regularly to ensure that its effectiveness is maintained.

Other sources of air pollutants include incinerators, factories that manufacture fertilizers and explosives, and aerosol sprays. One of the most serious pollutants is sulfur dioxide, which is released from the burning of coal and oil. Particularly disturbing is the fact that powerful chemicals like sulfur and nitrogen oxides can be carried in the air for hundreds of miles and then fall as so-called acid rain, polluting land and water.

Also of concern is the buildup of carbon dioxide in the atmosphere, which results primarily from cutting the world's forests and burning fossil fuels. It is postulated that this will lead to global warming, an increase in the world's temperature, as a result of the "greenhouse effect." Activities in this section are directed to building students' awareness of air pollution.

Activities for Grades K–2

Can We See Gases That Pollute the Air?

Gases that pollute our air are released by cars, planes, factories, and people. Like the natural gases in the air, they are invisible, but we breathe them. The following experiments illustrate the presence of gases in the air that cannot be seen. Unlike the substances used in the experiment, however, most pollutants cannot be detected by odor.

Ask a kid to leave the room. Open a bottle of vinegar or perfume or spray some hairspray into a far corner of the room. When the kid returns, inquire whether he or she can see anything. Then have the kid walk to the corner of the room and detect that something was indeed added to the air.

Is the Air Dirty?

To determine this, kids can place a piece of white cardboard outdoors. Cover half of it with a piece of wood. After a few days, they remove the covering and compare both parts. Is there any evidence of dirt in the air?

How Does Pollution Affect Plants?

Kids tie plastic bags around two plants of similar size. In one they insert a pollutant from an aerosol spray or a cigarette. The other is left untouched.

As they observe the plants, do they detect any difference between the two? What conclusions can they draw?

Activities for Grades 3–5

Can Air Pollution Affect Clothing?

To note the effect of pollution on nylon, students can do the following:

1. Cut a discarded nylon stocking (not the stretch or mesh type) into equal pieces about 9" × 9". Staple onto two sticks so that the nylon is stretched between them and will stay in place. Do not stretch the nylon too tightly.
2. Prepare a number of such sticks and place them in different locations on busy streets, in garages, gas stations, and parks. Keep one indoors as a control.
3. Inspect and compare the sticks regularly for any broken thread, holes, runs.

Summarize the findings.

Examine Particles in the Air

You will need vaseline, waxed paper, heavy cardboard or wood, and a covered jar.

To proceed, students:

1. Spread a thin layer of vaseline on a few sheets of waxed paper, about 2" x 5."
2. Place one piece in a covered jar. This is the control.
3. Staple the other papers to the cardboard or wood. Place them outdoors in various locations where they will remain undisturbed.
4. Retrieve the papers in a week.

What has adhered to them? How do they compare with the control? Use a magnifying glass to look closer. Are there common particles on each? In which placement was there more evidence of pollution?

Activities for Middle and Junior High

Pollution from Aerosol Sprays

The earth is surrounded by an ozone layer that protects us from the ultraviolet rays of the son. Some aerosol spray cans contain a chemical called freon, which, when released in the atmosphere, destroys the ozone layer, as do chlorofluorocarbons (CFCs) released by leaky home and car air conditioners and refrigerators. Deterioration of the ozone layer has been associated with an increase in cancer and with damage to trees, fish, and the phytoplankton in the oceans. This last is the key to the ocean's food chain.

Students can publicize these facts and urge people to discontinue the use of aerosol sprays, whenever possible. They organize a campaign titled, "Aerosol Sprays Pollute (ASP)." Which products can be bought in non-aerosol cans? Make a display of these in class.

Cigarettes Pollute

Smoking cigarettes is harmful not only for smokers, but for nonsmokers as well. Smoke from cigarettes pollutes the atmosphere.

Cigarettes can cause lung cancer, heart disease, emphysema, high blood pressure, nose and throat irritations, and a host of other problems that shorten life span.

Mount an antismoking campaign in class. A group of kids organized a campaign against "Joe Camel," an advertising figure meant to entice people to smoke. Others interviewed adult former smokers asking them why they stopped smoking. They circulate this information to young people urging them never to start smoking (see also Chapter 8).

Signs of Air Pollution in the Community

Students walk through the community and observe indications of pollution: smoke from factories or chimneys, car exhausts, incinerators, trucks, open burning of leaves.

They photograph these, post them at the school and send the photos to the local environmental agency inquiring whether any laws are being violated.

Fight Air Pollution

After researching the laws on air pollution by contacting health officers and environmental agencies, students take the following actions:

They invite a local environmental officer to class to discuss the legislation and how the class can help.

They also encourage classmates to walk or bike instead of requesting a car ride. If their families own cars, they urge that they be kept tuned up and pollution-control equipment maintained.

They write to local officials requesting that certain streets be closed to traffic during weekends.

ECOSYSTEMS: RAIN FORESTS

"If you could attach earphones to the loggers and make them listen to the trees as they cut into them, I don't think they would cut them."
—Lumni Native American, living in a northwest United States rain forest, interviewed on Earth Day, 1993

Two hundred years ago, tropical rain forests covered about 20 percent of the earth's land surface. Today, they represent less than 7 percent, with over one-half in three areas—Brazil (33 percent), Zaire (10 percent) and Indonesia (10 percent). It is estimated that 50 to 125 acres of forest, the equivalent of 100 football fields, are destroyed each minute.

Why is this a concern? The Lumni Native American quoted above explained: "There are not unlimited resources on the earth. The earth is a finite resource; we must protect it. Already the buffalo, much of the salmon habitats, old timber, coal, minerals, migrating fowl are gone; and trees and metals are stripped."

And there are additional problems. Scientists have estimated that there are 5 to 30 million different species on earth, but less than half have been identified. The majority live in tropical rain forests. People are destroying the habitats of species so rapidly that up to one quarter of the world's plant and animal species could be extinct within fifty years.

Because many species are endemic to the rain forests, they may never be known and their potential may remain unrealized. Drugs for ailments such as leukemia, high blood pressure, and malaria originated from plants in the rain forest. So far, less than 1 percent of the plants in the forests have been tested for medical uses. Could we be destroying a possible cure for cancer or immune disorders? Could we also be destroying potential foods? Today, rain forests are a source of food and raw materials, such as cacao, peanuts, coffee, nuts, spices, fruits and vegetable, oils and perfumes, and wood.

And there is more. An acre of tropical trees absorbs four tons of carbon from carbon dioxide in the atmosphere, slowing global warming. On the other hand, when rain forests are destroyed to clear the land, the carbon dioxide released intensifies the greenhouse effect, leading to the warming of the world. The Amazon rain forests produce 40 percent of the world's oxygen. Consider also that trees recycle water.

About 50 million people live in the rain forests. Over the centuries, they have learned to coexist with the air, water, and plants with whom they share their ecosystem. An attack on any one part of this system may destroy it all. Unfortunately, people currently moving into the forests are unfamiliar with this delicate balance and are causing widespread damage by cutting and burning huge areas. It is not surprising that young people the world over have organized to help save the forests.

Ungraded Activities

Locate the Rain Forests

Using a map of the world, students pinpoint the location of the forests, indicating the areas covered and the types of forest.

Who Lives in the Rain Forests?

Research the people who live in the forests. How long have they lived there? In the past, little was known about them, but with the increased interest in rain forests, there may be some media reports available in the library. Students also contact embassies of the countries where the forests are located.

What can they discover about the trees, birds, and animals that inhabit the forests?

Publicize the Importance of Rain Forests

Serve Rain Forest Snacks. To illustrate the diversity of foods found in the forests, a class can collect as many of the following items as possible. Then arrange a snack for the school.

- *Fruits:* avocado, banana, grapefruit, lemon, lime, orange, pineapple, tangerine
- *Spices:* pepper, cardamom, cayenne, cinnamon, cloves, ginger, nutmeg, paprika, turmeric, vanilla, chocolate or cocoa
- *Other products:* Brazil nuts, cashew nuts, coconut, coffee, macadamia nuts, tapioca, tea.

Research Medicinal Products. Many drugs come from rain forest plants. Class members can speak to a scientist at a local university or to a pharmaceutical company representative for specific information.

Over the years, people native to the forests have used alternative forms of medicine that are only now being recognized. Find out about these.

Take Action

Students write letters to federal representatives telling of their concern over the destruction of rain forests and asking them to support laws that help to preserve them.

Organize a Debate

A logging company has been cutting trees in the forests and providing employment for lumbermen. Environmental groups want them to be prohibited from continuing, but the loggers say this will lead to the loss of their jobs and will destroy the economy of the area.

How should this be decided? (This problem is similar to the one confronting preservation of endangered species.)

Buy an Acre of Rain Forest

Throughout the country, students have been raising funds to buy a piece of a rain forest to ensure its preservation and protect it from development (For information, see the Notes section).[6]

ECOSYSTEMS: WETLANDS

Wetlands are areas that are submerged in shallow water all or part of the time—swamps, marshes, bogs, and wet meadows. They provide food and feeding stops for a variety of invertebrates—fish, birds, and waterfowl. They prevent flooding and loss of topsoil, and they filter pollutants from our water. Some of the plants and animals on endangered species lists live in wetlands.

Almost half the wetlands that once existed in the United States have been destroyed, drained to build shopping malls and other developments.

Locate United States Wetlands

Where are they in the United States? Are there any close by? If so, study them. What wildlife inhabit them? What function do they serve. Where are the largest wetland areas?

Students can interview an environmentalist to learn why wetlands should be preserved. They can research the legislation protecting wetlands and urge that it be enforced. Students have saved wetlands by organizing campaigns against threats to fill them in and build developments.

Protect the Wetlands

Students at the Georgia Middle School in Vermont eulogized the wetlands in a trilingual poetry book and then took concrete steps to protect the destruction of wetlands.

"One Voice for Wetlands"

Georgia Middle School, St. Albans, Vermont

"Our students have learned that hard work has its rewards: knowledge, pride, and a better future."
—Claire A. Delaney, language arts teacher

Sixth-grade students in Delaney's class, who live near wetland areas, "wanted to change the impression that wetlands are mosquito-breeding wastelands to be drained for developments and malls" and to explain the importance of preserving them. Having previously written poems about the environment, they were accustomed to expressing their environmental concerns in verse. However, this project was their most ambitious yet.

They decided to publish a trilingual poetry book, in English, Spanish, and French, to commemorate the treaty between the United States, Mexico, and Canada dedicated to preserving the waterfowl populations and their wetland habitats. Titled "One Voice for Wetlands," the book, in addition to the English section, contains poems in Spanish from the Tobin School in Roxbury, Massachusetts, and in French from the Holy Rosary School in Quebec. More than one hundred children participated in the project.

The St. Albans community was enthusiastic about the project. Professional artists came to the classes to teach the kids techniques of wildlife art. A wildlife biologist gave a demonstration on duck populations. Local businesses made donations for a publication dinner attended by Senator Patrick Leahy, and a special wetlands puzzle was created by a commercial company in Norwich, Vermont. Announcing that "Walt Whitman would be proud of the book," Amway/Newsweek awarded the project their national "Class Act" environmental prize.

The students went further. Putting their words into action, they built three huge duckhouses and donated them to the Missiquoi National Refuge, Vermont's only national wildlife refuge. Delaney asserted: "The experience has added to each child's view of the world and how they must preserve it. We are raising a generation which will look more closely at where and how to develop our land. Our farm children will not drain or fill in the wetland sections of their farms, and they know that they can even get help in reclaiming wetland areas."

Notes

1. Nancy Marx Better, "Green Teens," *New York Times Magazine,* March 8, 1992, p. 44.
2. Mary Appelhof, *Worms Eat My Garbage.* (Kalamazoo: Flower Press, 1984). This book explains the entire procedure for building a worm composting bin. The book and worms are available from Flowerfield Enterprises, 10332, Shaver Road, Kalamazoo, MI 49002.
3. Quoted in the *St. Louis River Watch Newsletter,* "Upstream," Summer 1993, p. 2.
4. Quoted by Chuck Frederick, "Croaks of Frogs Tell River's Story," *Duluth News Tribune,* March 15, 1993.
5. Further descriptions of the Suzanne Middle School program appear in Chapters 5 and 13.
6. A number of organizations have information on buying rain forest acreage. These include:
   • Rain Forest Alliance, 65 Bleecker Street, New York, NY 10012-2420 (212-677-1900)
   • The Nature Conservancy, 1815 North Lynn Street, Arlington, VA 22209 (800-628-6860)
   • Rain Forest Action Network, San Francisco, CA 94111 (415-398-4404)

CHAPTER 8

Health and Safety

"Are you going to give me a shot?" asked the litte boy with a tear in his eye. I said, "No, I'm just going to see if your ears are working." The little boy smiled. That smile made my day. I felt that I was doing something important."

—Randolph, eighth-grade student, Mott Hall School

Side by side with kids who seem to subsist on hot dogs, pizza, and fast food are others who are becoming more and more health and safety conscious and ready to help educate others about nutritious eating and safety procedures. In this chapter, service learning projects related to the health curriculum include health education, safety practices, and first aid.

HEALTH EDUCATION

Youngsters can help educate younger kids and the community to improve their health practices and to be aware of the dangers of substance abuse.

Ungraded Activities

Healthful Snacks

Encourage kids to eat more healthful snacks. One school planned an "incredible edible" day when each younger kid brought a tasty healthful snack to class. For another approach, have an older class prepare snacks and invite younger kids. Have the older students distribute a list of recommended snacks to each youngster.

Suggestions for healthful snacks include: carrots, celery, edible pea pods, juices, popcorn, fruits, raisins, green pepper strips, pretzels (instead of potato chips), yogurt, and bread with apple butter or peanut butter.

Good Health Habits

Underscore the need for kids to cover their mouths when coughing, and noses when sneezing, and to protect themselves from disease by washing hands before eating and after using the toilet, keeping foreign objects out of their mouths, getting enough rest, and eating nutritious food.

Students can create a "Good Health" book illustrating these habits for distribution to kindergarten classes.

Don't Be a "Couch Potato"

Surveys indicate that many kids engage in less physical activity and tend to be heavier than kids a few decades ago. It's easy to find the villain—television. The inordinate amounts of time that kids spend watching TV is time that in the past might well have been devoted to sports or other outdoor activities. Regular exercise is essential for well-being and optimal health.

Survey the TV viewing schedules of kids in your class. Publicize the importance of physical activity for children. Suggest the kids record the time they spend watching television, daily and weekly, then encourage the class to schedule a day, week, or other period without any television. Brainstorm alternatives for such a day: a sports instead of television weekend, a read-in, biking for health and so forth.

Perhaps other classes will join the effort.

Activities for Middle and Junior High

Perform Hearing and Vision Tests

In a number of middle schools, students are being trained to perform these tests regularly on their peers as well as on elementary school kids. Without the students' help, many problems might remain undetected.

Educate Kids and Peers about HIV/AIDS Prevention and Substance Abuse

Older kids are effectively teaching their peers and younger kids about unsafe health practices and the dangers of substance abuse. Kids are frequently more accepting of information that comes from other kids.

Ask students to research each of the topics listed in this section. Share the findings with the community, and take the steps described. In addition to the activities indicated here, consider newsletters, teach-ins, and forums with outside speakers.

HIV/AIDS Prevention

In a unique project in the Mott Hall School in New York, eighth graders are trained by the Upper Manhattan Task Force on AIDS to present AIDS prevention programs to their peers. Augmenting the basic information, the students also perform skits in the classes depicting the pressures, such as the desire to be popular, that lead students to use drugs or consent to sex. They then discuss how to handle these pressures.

One of the participating students, Kilsi, explains: "We tell them how you get AIDS and how to prevent it by cleaning needles and using contraceptions. We can help more than parents. Parents can't talk to kids the way we can. They just tell them to abstain, but we know some kids won't do that. We can save lives."[1]

"Drugs Not!"

Unfortunately, statistics show that drug use among schoolchildren is increasing. Kids will have to play an active part in combating this trend. Here is what some schools are doing.

One junior high school, taking off on the "Just Say No!" slogan, adopted "Drugs Not!" for their campaign. They researched different drugs and their effects on the body. Then, once a week, went into an upper elementary or middle school class to discuss the dangers of drugs and related problems, such as sniffing glue. At the end of the presentation, each kid received a brochure summarizing the information.

Fifth graders in Plano, Texas, wanted to teach younger kids about the dangers of drugs. To present the information, they decided to stage a carnival with booths for each topic. Some kids produced puppet shows, others skits. Local agencies helped with materials and volunteers. Parents and the mayor and police department pitched in. The entire community was invited.

Smoking

No-smoking campaigns should begin in elementary schools. The American Cancer Society has revealed that many kids are starting to smoke at a younger age. Although smoking has generally declined in the recent decades, it is disturbing to note that young women are smoking more heavily now than ever before. Among teenage girls who smoke, 60 percent reported that they started before the age of thirteen.

Cigarette smoking can shorten life by leading to cancer, heart disease, emphysema, and irritation of the bronchial passages. It affects almost all organs. Recently, the serious effects of secondhand tobacco smoke on nonsmokers has been documented. It too can cause respiratory disease, heart disease, and cancer. Most restaurants have established smoking and nonsmoking areas, and steps have been taken to ban smoking on airplanes and in many public places.

Advertising has been identified as a culprit in enticing young people to smoke. Some people believe cartoon figures such as "Joe Camel" appeal to adolescents.

Students can monitor their communities. Have restaurants established adequate nonsmoking areas? Are they sufficiently separated from smoking areas? Are there public places where smoking should be banned? How about your school? Has your school been designated a smokefree facility?

Smokefree Educational Services, a nonprofit advocacy group, recommends the following legislation:[2]

1. Require all indoor public places to be 100 percent smoke free.
2. Move warning labels to the top, front, and back of cigarette packs and enlarge them to 25 percent of pack surface areas (as Canada has done).
3. End the distribution of cigarettes through vending machines.
4. End the free distribution of cigarettes.
5. End the use of tobacco products in public schools or on public school property.
6. End tobacco company sponsorship of youth-oriented events.
7. End federal subsidies for growing tobacco.
8. Raise cigarette excise taxes to cover smoking-caused health care costs.
9. Require health warnings on U.S. cigarettes sold abroad.

Write to your legislators, town, and state officials urging them to support these measures.

Alcohol

Kids also are beginning to drink at an earlier age. They need to realize that alcohol is a drug that when abused, can have as serious effects on the body as any other drug. Urge students not to start drinking. A major cause of accidents among teenagers is driving while drunk. Help kids plan parties without beer or other alcohol.

In art class, make "Don't Drink and Drive" posters to be displayed at a local car wash or auto repair shop.

Publicize the Importance of Inoculations

Students are asked to find out where free inoculations for young children are available in the community. They then distribute this information and urge parents to have their children inoculated. The U.S. Public Health Service recommends that by the age of six, children should be immunized against polio, diphtheria, whooping cough, tetanus, and measles. Many school districts insist that kids be immunized before they are admitted to school.

Organize a Community Health Fair

Students set up booths with information on nutrition, diseases, inoculations, first aid, safety, and substance abuse.

They become familiar with organizations that focus on these topics as well as on others, such as child abuse. They can interview personnel from these organizations inviting them to class and soliciting material for the fair.

Try to arrange for a qualified person to screen blood pressure and cholesterol levels or perform other health-related tests at the fair.

Vials of Life

In Fort Myers, Florida, the Southwest Regional Medical Center distributes "Vials of Life" to the community. These are small tubes containing a form with vital medical information about illnesses such as heart disease or diabetes. The vials are placed in a person's home in a conspicuous spot. Then, in an emergency in which patients are unable to communicate medical information, paramedics or others called to the scene have it readily available.

Bilingual students at the Lee Middle School in Fort Myers, Florida, were concerned that non-English speakers might be unable to complete these forms. They received 500 Vials of Life from the Medical Center and went door to door in the Spanish-speaking community, distributing the vials, helping the residents complete the information and suggesting where the vials should be placed to be readily accessible.

Aid for the Visually Impaired

Students can tape books for visually impaired seniors or kids in hospitals. Suzanne Middle School youngsters in Walnut, California, prepared an audio tape of their interdisciplinary project which they distributed to the visually impaired.

Aid for the Hearing Impaired

Learning that an organization called Hear Now in Denver, Colorado, reconditions and repairs used hearing aids for needy individuals, students combed their community and set up a receiving bank for old or unused aids. These are then donated to the National Hearing Aid Bank or Hear Now.

The Great American Munchout

Seventh graders in New York City schools participated in the Great American Munchout, sponsored by the American Cancer Society. The students solicited ethnic recipes from their parents or other community residents. These were submitted to top New York chefs, who modified them to make them more healthful by eliminating some fat or other less healthful ingredients. The Cancer Society then prepared an ethnic cookbook with both the original and the modified recipes. Students who submitted the recipes were treated to a "munchout" where seven dishes were prepared for them.

Health as an Interdisciplinary Theme

At the Turner Middle School, health is not just another subject. It is the heart of the curriculum, providing the community with a wide array of health services and giving students considerable knowledge of health topics and health-related careers.

Health as the Focus of the Curriculum

Dr. John P. Turner Middle School, Philadelphia, Pennsylvania

"It's kids doing things they never thought possible. It helps erase feelings of helplessness and hopelessness."

—Marie Bogle, director, School-Within-a-School

The enthusiasm and excitement in Marie Bogle's voice as she describes the Turner Middle School is contagious. By any measure, it is evident that the school is unique, a true community school—open six days a week, year round, and functioning as the hub of education and other services for students, their parents, and other community residents. The wide array of programs includes Wednesday evening classes for adults; Saturday classes for students and adults; and after-school enrichment, remediation, and help with homework. All are remarkably well attended.

Key to the Turner program is its partnership with the West Philadelphia Improvement Corps (WEPIC), which coordinates the program together with faculty and students from the University of Pennsylvania and other community organizations. WEPIC is in other schools in Philadelphia, but its most developed unit is at Turner, which serves as the pilot for the entire effort.

At the Turner school, WEPIC operates the House, a school-within-a-school for grades 6–8, which focuses on service learning. The House consists of about 360 students, with 12 teachers in three teams. Each team includes English, social studies, science, and math teachers responsible for the basic curriculum as well as service learning projects. Block scheduling provides three periods weekly for service learning: researching, planning, executing, and reflecting on projects. It also enables team teachers to arrange time to meet and plan.

Seeking to identify a unifying theme for the curriculum that would benefit the community, it was no accident that the House selected "community health" and declared as its goal "to improve the health of the community through a thematic curriculum that incorporates job training and peer teaching." The intention is for kids to research and study health topics and then teach them to other kids and community residents.

Thus, seventh graders teach elementary school kids about health and, with participation from the other grades, arrange three Health Watches for the community each year, reporting on a topic they have studied. Topics have included hypertension, nutrition, injury prevention, cancer, HIV/AIDS, and substance abuse. At the Health Watches, eighth graders provide brochures on each of the topics, written in nontechnical language, and professionals are available for screening and advice.

A summer institute trains students in basic health procedures, such as how to take pulse and temperature, and on health subjects, such as specifics of various diseases. This information is then presented to the community at a Health Fair.

Participants in the summer institute are assigned to alert parents to the importance of kids receiving inoculations. They fan out into the community distributing leaflets and going door to door to urge parents to bring their kids to the Turner School for free shots.

In eighth grade, students intern in career sites such as the Misericordia Hospital in Philadelphia, where they work in a number of departments and also observe the jobs of hospital personnel. Bogle describes the pride of the youngsters as they walk through the hallways in their white coats. At the same time, the students continue to study more advanced health topics and procedures, such as measuring blood pressure.

The curriculum for the House also specifies that each grade complete an integrated unit. The themes for these are innovative and related to students' familiar experiences. For example, the entire House completed a unit on "Hoagies," a popular item in the kids' diet. Other topics included "The Breakfast Project" and "Community History: Past and Present."

There is no doubt that the Middle School health program has had a strong impact on the community. Bogle quotes a parent whose daughter had just taken a blood pressure reading as saying, "I never thought my daughter could do this. I will treat her differently from now on."

A letter from a community resident to the Turner staff reads: "I want to express my thanks for the awareness your students have awakened in me about the danger of hypertension and diabetes. Before your students came, I knew virtually nothing of these diseases, but today I have a good knowledge of how I can live a healthier and happier life. Thank you so much for all that you have done. May God bless you."

SAFETY

Ungraded Activities

How to Get Help in an Emergency

All children should be briefed on emergency procedures. In some schools, upper grade children review and practice these with younger kids, as follows:

- Teach the kids when to dial 911 or zero (operator).
- Instruct them to say, "This is an emergency."
- Rehearse the information to be given to the operator:
  1. Describe the nature of the emergency.
  2. Give the address.
  3. Learn how to answer the operator's questions succinctly.
  4. Don't hang up until instructed to do so.
- In the event of a fire, if it is at nighttime:
  1. Quickly wake other family members and leave the building.
  2. Call the fire department from a neighboring phone. If you don't know the number, dial the operator.
  3. Speak slowly and clearly: "I want to report a fire at [address]."
  4. Say, my name is [name]." Then wait for any questions.
  5. Do not go back into the building.
  6. DON'T PANIC!

Safety Tips

A group of sixth-grade students wrote booklets on summer safety for younger kids briefing them on water behavior, what to do about insect bites, preventing injuries, and bicycle safety.

FIRST AID

Children of all ages need to know basic first aid. There are many recorded instances of young children saving lives as a result of such information. Kristen, a five-year-old kindergartner in Bellmore, Long Island, saved her two-year-old brother from choking on a candy wrapper by performing the Heimlich maneuver: "I just put my hands together and squeezed his stomach, and the wrapper came out." Kristen was imitating what she had seen in a movie.

She then calmly dialed 911. "I learned to do that at school," Kristen reported.

The American Red Cross is an excellent resource for teachers. It has programs for all age groups, which include:

- FACT (First Aid for Children Today), "for kids K–3: ways for kids to help themselves and others to be aware of dangers, to prevent injuries and harm, and respond when injuries do happen."
- BAT (Basic Aid Training) especially for fourth-grade children, although it can be used for some third graders, designed to teach children the basic first aid and safety skills and knowledge they need to recognize dangers, treat common injuries and respond in emergencies."
- AIDS prevention program for youth, information for teachers and leaders.

Many branches of the Red Cross conduct training programs for students. They can also be used as service sites for middle and junior high students, who in turn can instruct their peers and other kids in first aid.

The activities that follow include many suggested by the Red Cross. The grade designations have been adapted to conform with the materials available from the Red Cross.

Activities for Grades K–3

Caring for Minor Injuries

Young children can learn simple first aid procedures to be initiated until an adult can be reached.

- *Mild bleeding:* To stop or slow mild bleeding. Hold or tie a clean cloth over the area and press hard. Don't pull off the first cloth if blood seeps through. This stops coagulation.
- *Animal bite:* Remember what the animal looked like. Try to stop the bleeding. Be sure to tell an adult even if the wound is minimal.
- *Mild burn:* Put the burned part in cold water, or use a cloth wet with cold water or ice cubes wrapped in cloth.
- *Fall:* Stay calm. Don't move the child.
- *Bruise:* If the bruise starts to swell, apply a cold wet cloth or ice cubes.

Activities for Grades 4–8

Caring for More Serious Injuries

In addition to the procedures described above, older children can handle the following:

- *Broken arm:* Make a sling from a shirt or rag. Steady the arm.
- *Broken bones:* Don't move the child. The broken bones should be kept stationary. If the child must be moved, improvise a splint on either side of the break.
- *Wounds:* Wash with soap and water. If outdoors, use water from a fountain if available. Stop bleeding. Apply bandage.
- *Nosebleed:* Sit down. Lean forward and stop the bleeding by pinching the nose shut.
- *Choking:* If the child is unable to breathe, cough, or speak, make a fist. Place the fist with the thumb just above the navel. Grab the fist with the other hand and place it against the person's abdomen. Apply thrusts by pushing in and up, pressing the abdomen with quick upward thrusts.
- *Artificial respiration:* Turn the person's head to the side and open the airway by removing anything from the mouth that might prevent air from getting through.

  Tilt the head back as far as it will go by placing one hand on the forehead and the other under the neck. Check for breathing for at least five seconds. Then proceed. Pinch the nose closed.

  Open your mouth and take a deep breath. Set your mouth tightly around the person's mouth. Give four quick, full breaths to fill lungs.

The chest should rise. Listen for breathing. If there is no breath and no pulse, repeat: for an adult, every five seconds; for a child, a breath every four seconds; for an infant, gentle breaths every three seconds.

- *Shock:* Treat the injury, then treat for shock. Have the person lie down, keep calm, and keep normal body temperature. Cover to keep warm if necessary.
- *Bee stings.* If possible, remove the stinger with fingernails or a stiff card, such as a credit card. Apply ice with a towel or cloth but not directly on the wound.

Practicing First Aid Procedures

Teachers can organize stations in their classrooms that include instructions for each of the procedures above. Dolls and other materials can be provided so that kids can practice the procedures.

Older children can be enlisted to visit the class during recess and work with small groups to help them practice.

Notes

1. Also quoted in Chapter 2.
2. Smokefree Educational Services is located at 375 South End Avenue, New York, NY 10280.

CHAPTER 9

Mathematics

"What I liked is that we helped reduce the national debt."
—fifth-grade student, Hillside School, Montclair, New Jersey

"A major reason for the high priority given to mathematics in school programs is its great usefulness in solving problems," according to a New York State Education Department guide.[1] Yet achievement tests indicate that this is the domain where students are least successful. "When it comes to mathematical problem-solving, most American students just don't get it," states a study reported in the *New York Times*.[2]

Significantly, it is precisely in the area of problem solving that service activities are most effective. Students working in the community confront real problems instead of the often irrelevant ones included in textbooks. They create charts, graphs, and statistical profiles to illustrate their findings. Math is a component of myriad service activities, frequently correlated with other subjects. For example, environmental projects, such as water monitoring, necessitate detailed computations. For other activities, as well, mathematics provides a means of organizing data. It is a key facet of interdisciplinary studies.

Ungraded Activities

Students as Math Tutors

Just as in language arts, students make excellent math tutors. In classes of younger children or in after-school programs, they help with homework and can reinforce and teach math skills. They can give the younger children individual attention, frequently playing math games to practice computations.

Math and Environmental Studies

Add a math component to your environmental activities. When planting gardens, bulbs, or trees, measure the area to be covered, estimate, and then compute the number required. Also measure the height of different plants over a period of time. Compare the growth of leaves of different species.

Math will also be part of reclaiming a vacant lot or constructing a trail. Note, too, the environmental activities related to waste and water pollution in Chapter 7, many of which will require detailed statistical data gathering and computations.

113

Keep Math Journals

Recently developed tests for assessing math progress require students to show reasoning skills and to use "drawings, words and numbers" to explain answers. Mary Lindquist, president of the National Council of Teachers of Mathematics, attributes the poor showing of students on these tests to the fact that "students are not used to writing about what they do."[3]

By keeping math journals, students reflect on the math processes they employ to solve problems and, in the process, refine their reasoning skills.

War on Want

Here's an enjoyable way to raise money for a needy cause. If, one million children gave one penny every week—

How much would this amount to each week?
How much would this amount to in a year?

Since we can't contact a million children, how many can you enlist? Suppose everyone in your school, every day, dropped a penny into a large jar on the way to class—how much would you raise in a week? A month? A year? The kids will enjoy deciding where to donate the funds.

Activities for Grades K–2

Pennies for Love

Aware of the presence of homeless people in a shelter in their neighborhood, first graders at the Harrif Elementary School in Baltimore wanted to help. The director of a local facility came up with a great idea. She suggested they present personal articles to the children in the shelter. But because most previous donations had been secondhand, she proposed that the first graders raise funds to buy *new* personal items. The outcome of that conversation was "Pennies for Love."

Pennies for Love

Dr. Bernard Harrif, Sr. Elementary School, Baltimore, Maryland

"The project strengthened the entire curriculum."

—Irma Brown, Principal

The kids decided to try to collect 10,000 pennies, a number that seemed ambitious. Youngsters accumulated pennies by reading to parents and friends at a set amount of pennies per page, by running errands, and by soliciting spare pennies. Parents enthusiastically supported the idea and secured special boxes to hold the pennies as they started to add up. The pennies were carefully counted and totals recorded on large "thermometers" mounted around the school.

Day after day, the thermometers rose until the original goal was far surpassed. A total of $300 was collected, three times the goal. The kids were delighted. They personally went to the shopping center to select underwear, socks, hair barrettes, toothbrushes, and other items, and then made the presentation.

It is evident that this was an effective way of reinforcing math skills: the kids counted the pennies, graphed them, totaled them, and recognized how many pennies add up to $300 dollars. Finally, their trip to the shopping center taught them what $300 could buy. It was not only math that was enhanced but many other subjects as well. Kids learned about social living, families, and the community—part of the social studies curriculum. Every child documented the project by writing in a journal; and they were motivated to read to earn pennies.

Pennies for...

Other schools have initiated penny drives for causes. In Springfield, Massachusetts, for example, schools have had drives for leukemia and for "people." Others have collected pennies to "save the rain forest," for the Red Cross, and for a host of other service projects.

Math skills, closely related to the K–2 math curriculum, can be reinforced by this activity, as follows:

- *Money:* Children identify coins and exchange pennies for other denominations: nickels, dimes, quarters. They learn one-to-one correspondence by counting pennies and wrapping them in fifty-cent packages.
- *Sorting and classifying:* Children sort pennies by year. The class then tabulates and graphs the frequency of different years.
- *Estimation:* Kids estimate items, such as the amount of pennies in a box, the total collected in a day or week, and the period of time required to accumulate a set amount.
- *Probability:* Working in groups, each child tosses a penny predicting the probability of it landing *heads* or *tails.* (In a more advanced probability exercise, two or three pennies are tossed.) Results are tabulated, leading to conclusions about probability.
- *Problem-solving:* One group of kids was confronted with an intriguing problem when they were asked to estimate the amount of pennies in a jar. They decided to weigh ten pennies on a postal scale. The ten weighed one ounce. They then emptied all the pennies from the jar, weighed the empty jar, returned the pennies, and weighed the full jar. By subtracting the weight of the jar, they were able to compute the total weight of the pennies alone as fifteen ounces. Multiplying by ten, they confidently concluded that there were 150 pennies in the jar.

At least that's what they thought, until they tried to verify their results by actually counting the pennies. To their surprise, there were only 132 pennies. For the next few weeks the entire class was absorbed in finding the "missing" pennies. The problem was not solved until one of the children thought of weighing different groups of ten pennies and discovered differences between the weights of new and old pennies.

Survey...

Acquaint young children with methods of collecting, organizing, and graphing data. Have them suggest questions. These might include:

- What do you do after school?
- Which is your favorite toy or game?
- Which is your favorite subject?

Tabulate the results. Parents may be interested in comparing their children's answers to the class mean.

Activities for Grades 3–5

Sell Cookies—Donate Profits

U.S. Senator Bill Bradley was at the Hillside School in Montclair, New Jersey, to receive a free tray of cookies and a donation of $100 toward the national debt, part of the profits earned by the Kids Cookie Corporation. An additional $200 went to a local agency that provides emergency food to needy residents.

Kids Cookie Corporation

Hillside School, Montclair, New Jersey

"Students learned a lot more than baking cookies."

—Michael Chiles, principal

The Kids Cookie Corporation was designed by a mathematics and home economics teacher, who shared a two-period fifth-grade instructional block. To raise funds for contributions, they decided to form a corporation to market cookies.

The math class had the assignment of organizing the corporation. Primed by corporate leaders from the community, the youngsters investigated how to set up a small business, estimate costs, and raise start-up funds by issuing stock in the corporation. Stock certificates, one to a student, were sold for fifty cents apiece.

In the home economics class, students baked the cookies. First they tested recipes and checked temperatures, textures, and cookie sizes to determine how many cookies they would need to cover the cost of the cookies and the stockholders' investments. They computed necessary ingredients. Local stores helped by contributing flour and sugar.

About 2,000 cookies were sold during lunch periods—large ones for 30 cents a piece, most for 25 cents, and broken ones for 15 cents. The corporation was so successful that stockholders saw their money doubled and enough additional profits accumulated to make donations.

More Ways to Raise Funds

First, have students identify a cause to which they would like to contribute. It may be a natural disaster like a hurricane, flood, or tornado; a needy family; a homeless shelter or a residence like Ronald McDonald house. They need to set a realistic goal, and be certain to keep careful records of receipts.

The kids at the Hillside School sold cookies. Here are some other ideas:

Construct a Game. Students at the Wantagh Junior High School on Long Island made a variation on Monopoly using names of actual stores and other businesses in their community. They sold the game to raise funds.

Sell Lemonade. First, prepare a budget. Buy paper cups. Then use frozen juice to prepare the lemonade, determine how much lemonade will be needed to fill each cup. How much will you charge? How many cups of lemonade must be sold to reach your goal?

Hold a White Elephant Sale. Students solicit the community for toys, games, books, and clothing that youngsters have outgrown. They ask the contributors to suggest a price—it should be low. The students tag the items and arrange for the sale—before school, or during lunch. If there are enough objects, consider a weekend sale involving the community. Record each sale.

Write and Sell Books of Interest to the Community. Students at the Schuylkill School in Pheonixville, Pennsylvania, raised funds by selling a history of their town. At the Schecter School on Long Island, students profitably sold an environmental coloring book.

Stage a Carnival. Select a theme. Organize games, solicit donations, and offer raffle prizes.

La Petite Academy in Fort Myers, Florida, has an annual Halloween carnival, with two purposes: to provide the community with a safe environment to celebrate Halloween and to raise funds for a local children's hospital. Youngsters, school staff, and parents are invited to come in costume. The Lee Middle School in town donates a piñata each year to La Petite Academy.

Graph School Attendance

Maintain a graph of daily school attendance. What percentage of students are absent each day? Can the kids identify any patterns?

Examine Food Contributions

If your class or school is participating in a food drive, there are many opportunities for reinforcing math and other curriculum skills.

Maintain a chart indicating the total items collected daily by food group. Read the labels. Compare calories, fat content, and cholesterol. If the price is on the item, compute the unit price.

Activities for Middle and Junior High

And More Pennies...

Not to be outdone by the younger kids, students at the Ethical Culture Fieldston Schools in New York raised $10,000 over a three-year period with the "Million Penny" project. They decided to make the Partnership for the Homeless the primary beneficiary.

In expressing appreciation for the donation, Joel Sesser, executive vice president/CEO of the Partnership, stated: "The value of their gift goes beyond the cash they bring to our work—it's their energy, optimism, fairness, and the hope it gives us that we can make the difference we all want to make."

Design Wheelchair Ramps

Middle schoolers noted that some entrances to the school buildings were not properly equipped for wheelchairs. They undertook to measure the spaces and design ramps to assure accessibility. The technology class constructed the ramps.

Selling Services

Older students can raise funds by offering services, such as arranging birthday parties for preschool and elementary school kids. They prepare the invitations, plan games, and make favors.

They can walk dogs for people in the community at a set rate, or take care of plants when owners are on vacation.

The Price of Vandalism

Is vandalism a problem in your community? Students can interview the principal and district business officer and compute the cost to the school district of vandalism.

What positive things could be done with that money? Students can organize a poster campaign showing the cost of vandalism by illustrating what the money spent could buy. A prize could be awarded to the student with the best suggestion for eliminating vandalism.

More Coordination of Math with Other Subjects

- A study of birds and migration patterns led seventh graders to compute the number of miles/kilometers different birds travel when they migrate.
- To demonstrate the destruction of rain forests, a Minnesota class, studying square units in math, computed the areas that had been destroyed by fire in rain forests in a given period and compared the total with the area of their state.
- Bolster the health curriculum campaign against smoking by computing the cost of smoking one or two packs of cigarettes daily, weekly, monthly, yearly. Suggest some other uses for the money.
- Integrating math with science leads to a more sophisticated level of science. For example, if students analyze water for pollutants, they can use math to determine the degree of pollution and set this figure as a baseline for later tests.
- Students can calculate the amount of food needed to feed an average family of four for a week and use this information to set goals for a food drive.

Math as Part of Interdisciplinary Units

Math is an integral component of interdisciplinary units. The following examples illustrate the imaginative use of statistics in such units. (A complete description of the units is included in Chapter 13.)

- The math component of the interdisciplinary unit on Dickens' *A Christmas Carol* by students at the Waseca Middle School in Minnesota called for a detailed statistical profile of the homeless population, both in Minnesota and nationwide.

     A purchasing plan was also a part of the unit. To demonstrate the problems of the Cratchets in *A Christmas Carol,* groups were given varying amounts of "money" to prepare a holiday feast. Those who received smaller amounts struggled to make a meal and could identify with the problems of the Cratchets and the poor generally.

- To call attention to the high cost of graffiti to the town, eighth-grade students in Alan Haskvitz's social studies class at the Suzanne Middle School in Walnut, California, as part of their unit on Graffiti Reduction, not only computed the cost to the town of removing graffiti, but prepared word problems directed to the cost per square foot and per household.

     Haskvitz's classes incorporate math in many of their award-winning service activities. An important factor in the success of their projects is the students' ability to calculate the dollar savings from their activities. By proving, for example, that the use of water displacement bags in city toilets would save the city 23 million gallons of water each year, they secured a donation of bags and permission to install them.

OTHER MATH SERVICE PROJECTS

Two other service projects are most often part of the mathematics curriculum: "Educating the Consumer" and "Kids in Business." These activities also can be integrated with Home and Career and Life Skills courses in middle and junior high schools.

EDUCATING THE CONSUMER

Ungraded Activities

Are You a Smart Shopper?

Students can become smart shoppers by examining packages, analyzing prices, evaluating purchases, testing products, and scrutinizing labels. In turn, they can help adults to be smart shoppers, too, by sharing the results of their tests in regular reports to the community, culminating in a community fair.

Institute a Product-Testing Laboratory.

Start with paper products. Working in groups, determine which brand of the following is most absorbent: napkins, tissues, paper towels.
Try this test:

Place five pieces of the paper product in an aluminum pie plate. Pour two teaspoons of water on the paper. After three seconds, remove the paper and pour the remaining water into a millimeter cylinder or narrow tube. Record the amount. Repeat this with each brand, being certain that the pie plate is dry after each use. Rate the products according to absorbency.

It is also interesting to compare the price and popularity of an item with its test rating. Devise tests for other products: cleansers, plastic wrap, and so on.

Try Taste Tests

Bring in samples of different brands of the same products: peanut butter, apple juice, cereals, cola drinks.
Set up a tasting panel of five students for each product. Put an equal quantity of each brand into unmarked paper cups, and have students rate which taste the best.
Compare the ratings with prices. Do they correlate?

How Accurate Are Product Claims?

Duplicate some of the claims made on television. Does a particular paper towel really absorb more? Do most people select a certain product in a blindfold test? Does a particular cleaning product remove stains more effectively?

Establish a Coupon Service

Clip coupons from the newspapers, and invite parents to contribute coupons or box tops that they do not need. File these by category—cereals, coffee, cleaning products, and so on.
Post a list of coupons on hand. Make them available to parents, senior citizens, and other residents. Total the dollar amounts.

Monitor Television Commercials

Older children can help younger children to evaluate advertisements aimed at them, particularly on cartoon shows.
Assign students to monitor cartoons on different channels on a weekend and note the advertisements. Examine some of the following:

- Does the product look larger on television than it actually is?
- Does the ad imply that children will be better or more popular if they own a particular product?
- Are children using the product in ways that the average child cannot? (For example, a basketball may be thrown into the hoop repeatedly in the commercial, implying that a child will be able do this.)

- Are there only boys playing with action toys? Girls with housekeeping ones?

What other conclusions can be reached from watching the kids' fare?

Activities for Grades K–2

How Many Raisins?

Kids count the number of raisins in a box of raisin bran. Raisins are a significant source of iron. A consumer advocate did this and discovered that private-label brands actually had more raisins than the advertised national brands and were about $1.00 per pound cheaper. Duplicate this test. Check for taste, too.

Does Packaging Influence Purchasing?

You will need three containers of different shapes: a tall and narrow jar, a wide squat jar, and a paper bag. Fill each with the same amount of a dry ingredient (sand, salt, or a cereal).

Now line up the three containers next to each other. Ask a kid who is not aware that each package contains the same amount which one has the most of the ingredient and which the least. Record your results. Can you draw conclusions about packaging from this?

Does Packaging Add to Price?

Kids examine boxes of toys. How much room is actually taken by the contents? Remove the contents and place in a paper bag. Compare the bag to the box. Would people pay as much for the toy if it were in the bag?

Activities for Grades 3–5

Compare Packages

Accumulate empty containers of cereal boxes. Ask kids to sort them by product, size, and weight. Now compare similar products. Note the size of the box and the weight. Does the larger box always have the most cereal?

How about price? Does the smallest amount always cost the least? How much difference in price is there for the same product depending on brand?

Does the outside of the box show the cereal with fruit? If so, is the fruit included?

Does Advertising Affect Prices?

Students will need to research the prices of store or generic brands of products compared to advertised brands. For the purpose of this experiment, assume that the brands are equal in quality. This is not necessarily true.

Secure samples of food products or cosmetics that are regularly advertised. Compare the unit prices of these products with those of similar brands that are rarely advertised. Is there a relationship between the price of a product and whether it is advertised?

Check Unit Prices

The unit price is the price of each item in a package. For example, a container of orange juice may hold 32 ounces and cost 99 cents, whereas another may hold 64 ounces and cost $2.29. It would actually be cheaper to buy two of the smaller containers.

Price per Serving

Another way of comparing prices is to compute the price per serving. Most items indicate the number of servings in a package. The price per serving is the price of the item divided by the number of servings.

(A word to the wary consumer! Some serving sizes are deliberately calculated to be unrealistically small. This makes the food appear to be inexpensive per serving. For example, a popular brand of salsa, usually served with chips, shows serving size as one tablespoon. This would only be enough to cover one or two chips.)

Activities for Middle and Junior High

Read Labels

Labels can be misleading. For example, foods like peanut butter and vegetable oil labeled as containing no cholesterol may derive most of their calories from fat.

Check the labels carefully for all contents. For example, colas and other sodas may contain caffeine, a stimulant. Parents may be unaware of this when they permit young children to drink them.

Juices and Juice Drinks

Distinguish between these. A *juice* must be 100 percent fruit juice, Whereas *juice drinks, nectar, punch,* and *juice cocktails* contain water in varying amounts. A juice drink may contain only 10 to 33 percent juice, with the balance water.

Another method of analyzing juices is to see which ingredient is listed first. Ingredients are listed in descending order, with the largest ingredient shown first. What does it tell you if water is listed first?

Analyze Instructions on Products or Clothes

Some instructions are written so obliquely that they are almost impossible to follow. If students see an example of this, they can write to the manufacturer and suggest that the instructions be simplified.

Some care instructions are difficult to find or are on inserts that are easily lost. Again, notify the manufacturer. Solicit examples of confusing instructions.

Are Companies in Compliance?

The Food and Drug Administration has issued rules on labeling of foods, both in supermarkets and on restaurant menus. Under these rules, labels or menus can no longer state that a food is "low-fat," "low-sodium," or "low-cholesterol," unless the claim can be backed up. Invite a representative from your local Office of Consumer Affairs to your class to discuss how you can help monitor this type of labeling for the community.

Guarantees and Warranties

These, too, can be misleading. Some are for parts only, others for parts and repairs. Some may not include the cost of returning the product. Students acting as consumer advocates have succeeded in convincing companies to include costs that are not specifically excluded in the warranty.

A Consumer Fair

After completing some of the activities described here, invite members of the community to a fair at which findings will be reported. Students create displays, charts, filmstrips, and posters illustrating the activities. They set up work tables where visitors can replicate the product and taste tests. Consider inviting a representative from the local Office of Consumer Affairs to make a presentation.

KIDS IN BUSINESS

When a fire destroyed a house and all the belongings of a family in one community, sixth-grade classmates decided to help. First, they organized Saturday car washes. Parents contributed supplies, such as soap and rags, and student volunteers turned out every Saturday for a month. The pleasure derived from helping someone inspired them to seek a more consistent way of raising money. Their solution was to organize a business, a cooperative enterprise that would provide a product to be sold.

Kids have frequently raised funds by running car washes, lemonade sales, white elephant sales, flea markets, or sales of books and toys. These are usually isolated efforts for a specific purpose, whereas "Kids in Business" is a more involved activity of longer duration. It may operate through most of a semester or just before Christmas. In this project, kids actually create a product to sell to other classes or to the community. In the process, they are exposed to basic skills involved in operating a small enterprise. These activities are appropriate for upper grade elementary or middle and junior high school students.

Careful consideration will need to be given to the following:

- Product to be sold
- Start-up funds
- Business organization and operation

Activities for Intermediate, Middle, and Junior High

Product to Be Sold

The first step is to identify products that people might wish to buy. Can students produce an object of high quality that is either useful or decorative? What talents do the kids in the class have that can be utilized?

The products should not be too costly or time-consuming to construct. Preferably, they should be items that can be manufactured during a lunch or free period.

Brainstorm possibilities. The school art teacher is an excellent resource.

Potential Products

- *Art objects:* Collect stones, paint them, and decorate them with eyes (from art stores) and woolen hair. They can be pretty or deliberately ugly.
- *Greeting cards:* Repeat a greeting such as "Happy Birthday" in different languages.
- *Pressed flower notepaper:* see Chapter 10 for instructions.
- *Cookbook:* Use recipes collected from the community.
- *Plants:* grown from seeds and pot them.
- *Papier-mache earrings or pins*
- *Paper-weights*
- *Place mats*

It is best to start with two or three products. Others can be added later. Make samples and judge how long each will take to produce.

Start-Up Funds

First, make a budget to determine how much money will be needed for raw materials. It may be necessary to conduct a number of fund-raising activities.

At the Hillside School in Montclair, New Jersey (described earlier in this chapter), students devised a novel way to raise funds. They organized a company, "The Cookie Company" and sold stocks to other students for 50 cents apiece. Students' investments were later returned with a 100 percent profit.

If the stock issue approach is selected, students will need to write a prospectus in advance to be distributed to investors. It should include information about the products to be produced, estimated expenses, and sales information. Numbered stock certificates should be given to each investor. Records of all transactions should be maintained.

Organization and Operation

Having determined the cost of the product, compute a fair price—one that will cover costs and permit enough of a profit to assure regular contributions to the *causes* that have been identified.

It will be necessary to delegate responsibilities. Which students will manufacture the items? When? Who will arrange the publicity and advertisements? Who will sell? Act as cashiers? Keep the books?

Organize committees for each task. Also pay attention to these six steps:

- Purchase supplies.
- Manufacture products.
- Find a site for the store and set hours of business.
- Advertise the products.
- Open for business.
- Maintain records.

Here are some tips.

- *Purchase supplies.* Start with a limited inventory until you can judge how well a product will sell.
- *Manufacture products.* A set time will have to be arranged so that it does not interfere with your other classwork.
- *Find a site for the store and set hours of business.* If only one or two products will be sold, it may be possible to secure a spot in the class-room. Otherwise, check to see if there is an available area elsewhere in the school. You will need a table to use as a counter and a place to arrange the stock. There must be sufficient space for customers to browse without interfering with those making purchases. Will the products be wrapped? If so, where?

  When will the store be open? Once a week at a preannounced time, during lunch periods, after school, or an afternoon are all possibilities.
- *Advertise the products.* Publicize the store widely. Design posters noting the features of the products, prices, and times of sale. Advertise the products in the school or local newspaper. Can a display of samples be placed in neighborhood stores or library?

  One group of sixth graders organized a Christmas Gift Shop. They made sample items: potholders, wall hangings, decorative pins, picture frames, and terraria. Items were priced and then listed in a catalog. Students took orders for the products and promised to deliver on a specified date.
- *Open for business.* The store is ready for business when a supply of products has been prepared and priced and students are clear about their roles.

  Numbered sales receipts should be prepared in duplicate, one for the customer and one for store records. This will facilitate balancing the cash at the end of the day.
- *Maintain records.* Pay meticulous attention to accounting. Books should be kept from the very beginning of the project, detailing:
  — Expenses and income at the start of the operation and for each transaction thereafter, noting dates.
  — For each period that the store is open, count the cash at the beginning and again at the end. The beginning cash plus the total of the sales receipts should constitute the cash at the end. Finally, review the business operation regularly.

Check the inventory. Some products may not sell. Are they overpriced? Not made well? Are the store hours realistic? Has there been sufficient publicity? Evaluate the practices and make necessary adjustments.

Good luck!

Notes

1. "Introduction to Mathematics K–6, a Recommended Program for Elementary Schools," New York State Education Department, 1991.
2. "Study Finds Most Students Lack Reasoning Skills in Mathematics," *New York Times,* September 3, 1993, p. A14.
3. Ibid.

CHAPTER 10

Creative Arts

"Art is frequently considered a secondary subject, but through art kids have had a significant impact on their communities and in the process enriched their entire curriculum."
—David Newton, art teacher, Midtown West Elementary

Throughout history, people have expressed themselves through various art forms. Primitive people designed jewelry, made and decorated water jugs, and painted pictures on cave walls. Art served to beautify their surroundings. Today, kids are still using art to beautify their environment.

Art educators today call for integration of the creative arts with other areas of the curriculum. This is consonant with the approach to art in service learning. Art is included in service projects in many subjects. Kids use artistic expression to illustrate, celebrate, and reflect on their service. Projects, such as community beautification and museum participation, may originate in art classes.

It is difficult to assign a grade level to these activities. In one elementary school, pre-K and kindergarten kids displayed their work in the lobby of a corporate building, yet an exhibit by middle school youngsters would have been equally valid.

Ungraded Activities

Display Artwork

Many senior centers and nursing homes for the elderly would be cheered by students' artwork. Residents may enjoy having a painting in their rooms. Offer to vary these at frequent intervals.

Also offer paintings throughout the community: to homeless shelters or shelters for women and children, libraries, hospitals, office lobbies, and vacant stores.

Produce an Art Book

Coloring books with an environmental theme are popular. For example, students from the Robert Wagner Junior High School in New York produced a book titled *Color Me Green* for younger kids. It had pages with copy and drawings to color. Some pages read, "Clean up the garbage or the world will look like your room." Another was, "We have to keep the oceans clean so fish can swim." A Spanish version is planned.

Concoct "Junk Art"

Reuse paper bags, rolls from paper towels, toilet tissues, boxes, fabric scraps, old socks, and more. Turn them into musical instruments, puppets, constructions, collages, and mosaics. Older students can make these with kids in after-school programs.

Create Murals

Celebrate diverse cultures. For example, when studying Latin America, students made murals depicting the history of the various Latin American countries. They displayed these in the lobby of their school and at a Latino center in the community.

Students worked jointly with seniors at the Star Senior Center in New York City to paint a mural, which was hung in the entrance.

Design Posters

Relate these to your studies. Posters are frequently prepared as part of service projects, either to illustrate a subject or to express a point of view. Place these in the school and in the community.

On the Environment. Develop posters to further an environmental concern, such as endangered species, pollution of a waterway, litter or recycling. A class in Carle Place, Long Island, drew posters of fish protesting the pollution of their "home". Another posted "Please Don't Litter" signs near a lake.

On Health Issues. Discourage driving after drinking. One class placed "Do Not Drink and Drive" posters in local car washes.

Take a stand against smoking. A poster might depict a person smoking and have a caption explaining that the person is more likely to develop cancer, heart disease, emphysema, and other health problems.

Posters might also be developed on the dangers of drug and alcohol abuse.

On History. When studying a past presidential election, suggest students make campaign posters for the candidates. For example, propose that students design posters that Herbert Hoover and Franklin D. Roosevelt might have employed in their 1932 campaign.

Photograph Your Community

Select one aspect of your community for a subject—for example, doors. Have students photograph doors in the community; search for examples of different periods from old to modern. Look at hospital doors, bank doors, car doors, swinging doors, house doors, school doors, and others.

This project can inspire a language arts activity. Suggest that kids write how they view the doors: as protection, invitation, works of art.

Teach Arts and Crafts

Teach younger kids in the school an art activity. Many students also teach arts and crafts to kids in after-school programs, or teach senior citizens, kids in shelters, hospitals, or other facilities.

Produce Pressed-Flower Notepaper

These notepapers are decorative and make a welcome gift for seniors or shut-ins. To create them, fold a piece of white or colored paper in half, and then paste one or more pressed flowers on the front. They add a delicate touch. Make the pressed flowers as follows:

1. Gather petals or single blossoms, preferably on a sunny day when the flowers are dry.
2. Arrange the petals, as you wish them to look when dry, between eight thicknesses of newspaper—four above and four below.
3. Place the newspaper into the middle of a heavy book.
4. Check daily. If the newspaper is damp, gently move the plant to a dry spot.
5. The flowers should be dry in about a week.
6. Carefully glue each flower onto the card. Handle carefully.

Fashion Quilts

Working together, parents, grandparents, teachers, administrators, and students at the Mary O. Pottenger School in Springfield, Massachusetts, made 23 quilts for a medical center clinic that addresses the needs of children born with the HIV virus. Each child attending the clinic was given a quilt.

Two fourth-grade students, reflecting on the project, wrote, "We hoped to ease their pain."

Make Over a Shelter

Students at the Ben Franklin Intermediate School in Chantilly, Virginia, transformed a shelter for battered women. They made curtains, planted flowers, painted and carpeted, and, with parents, helped build benches, (See Chapter 12 for a more complete description of this project.)

Present Gifts to Seniors

When creating gifts for Mother's or Father's Day in art classes, have each student make an extra one to be presented to residents of nursing homes.

Maintain Drawing Journals

These are utilized in a variety of ways. They can be a means of reflection—a substitute for or addition to writing journals, and a bonus for kids who can more easily express themselves through art than language.

They may act as a catalyst for a project. Children take a walk through the community. On their return, they draw an aspect that was of most interest. The class later discusses these.

The next activity indicates another use of drawing journals.

Art in a Multicultural Project

A social studies project on the theme "What Do Native Americans Teach Us about Living in Harmony with Nature," in a fourth-grade class in P.S. 161 in Brooklyn, New York, was enriched and expanded by the incorporation of art activities. Two artists, Jennifer Zitron and Margaret Petee, volunteered to work with the kids twice weekly and organized numerous activities.

- They accompanied the children on field trips to anthropological and natural history museums to sketch.
- Pueblo architecture was discussed as a demonstration of how Native Americans used natural materials in their buildings.
- Children kept individual drawing journals, which were critiqued by the class weekly and later made up the imagery for a mural.
- The artists explained the fundamental principles of impressionist painting and pointillism and illustrated these by having the kids make paper mosaics.
- A jazz pianist, part Cherokee, visited the class to speak of his childhood and musical influences.
- A legend-like Native American story was written and dramatized by the children.

The culmination of the unit was the design and construction of an 8' × 6' mosaic mural made from recycled, donated, and surplus materials, which was exhibited at the Brooklyn Children's Museum for three months, along with the kids's journals and other artwork.[1] After the exhibition, the mural was given a permanent home on the auditorium wall of P.S. 161.

Art in the Community

Kids at Midtown West Elementary School use the community as their art laboratory. Under the tutelage of David Newton, an enthusiastic, dedicated teacher, they have undertaken a mind-boggling array of activities, which range from decorating a public bus that runs on a busy city street, to helping build a large cityscape mural.

Beautifying a Community

Midtown West Elementary School, New York City

"I discovered my heritage, and it made me proud."
—Sahara, fourth-grade student, Midtown West Elementary

Imagine discovering that the skeleton of your great-great-great grandmother had lain buried under the sidewalks of New York for about three hundred years under layers of dirt, landfill, and concrete. Then imagine that as a construction company started to build a foundation for a new skyscraper, the long forgotten African-American burial grounds where she had been buried were exposed. Now imagine once more that you and other fourth graders from the Midtown West School were asked to help decorate a mural around the sacred burial ground, now designated as a protected landmark. That is what happened to Sahara Walsh, a fourth-grade African-American student at Midtown West Elementary School, who discovered her heritage "and it made me proud."

Sahara's class was studying the history of New York and discovered that Black men, women, and children were among the earliest settlers in New Amsterdam, brought to America as slaves by the Dutch and later to New York by the British.

Discrimination against Blacks extended even to death. They were buried in segregated cemeteries. It was one of these, possibly the largest, that was exposed when the construction company started to excavate in lower Manhattan.

As the children in Midtown West studied this history, many of the African-American kids interviewed grandparents and great-grandparents to see if they could revive their links with their ancestors. It was Sahara's grandfather who informed her that her great-great-great grandmother had been a slave in New York.

Midtown West is a magnet public school with a diverse population, grades pre-K to 5. It has a collaborative arrangement with the Bank Street College of Education and close community ties. Volunteers from two law firms work with the children, as do professional artists, actors, and writers.

David Newton is in charge of art for the school. Through his efforts and connections with the New York City Housing Authority and others in the community, the entire school has proceeded to "beautify" the city. Even pre-K kids participate. Newton insists that all children are capable of producing worthwhile art. In addition to the mural around the gravesite, Midtown West kids were involved in the many projects described below, often in cooperation with neighborhood groups or other schools in the city.

- A series of murals of "people and the city" along Forty-First Street in New York as an effort to revive a beleaguered street that had become an eyesore
- Two large canvases for the lobby of a law firm whose employees volunteer in the school, created as a token of the kids' appreciation
- Set designs for local theater groups, including an 11' × 6' acrylic painting on canvas featuring images from the New York Youth Theater's play "Aesop in New York"
- An elaborate set at the Victory Theater on Forty-Second Street, where Houdini made an elephant disappear. The set was for a play, *It's a Mystery*. Kids wrote mysteries, and the editor of *Ghostwriter* selected five stories and combined them into a play in which the kids performed.
- The graduating fifth graders worked with two artists, John Ahearn and Robert Torres, to create five plaster busts for the school. Each of the busts was of a student of a different ethnic background: Asian, African-American, Latino, Native-American, and Caucasian. The busts were exhibited to illustrate the "Diversity of City Kids." The artists actually created the busts by covering the kids with vaseline and layering them with dental plaster and plaster gauze. When this was removed, a mold was available to be filled with plaster. Students painted their busts to reflect skin tones and other ethnic features. Other fifth graders' hands were cast in plastic.
- They decorated the interior of a neighborhood children's day care center showing kids in motion. The project was titled "Kids for Kids."
- They decorated a bus that runs along Ninth Avenue, a busy street. The New York City Transit Authority gave permission to remove the advertising on the side of the bus and replace it with scenes of Manhattan drawn by the kids.
- In cooperation with the New York Housing Authority and community businesses and residents, the kids were involved in an ongoing project to design a six-story high, block-long billboard around a housing project on Fifty-Fifth Street in New York.

Side by side with art projects at the school are multicultural activities. Kids are introduced to the artistic heritage and culture of Puerto Rico and other Hispanic countries through classes in classical ballet, Hispanic folkloric, and classical Spanish dance.

ACTIVITIES RELATED TO MUSEUMS

Students have organized school museums on topics related to social studies. These are described in Chapter 5. The activities here relate to community museums.

Display Children's Art in Museums

The Heckscher Museum in Huntington, Long Island features an annual display of the artwork of fifth and eighth graders and selected high school students. The art is related to one of the exhibitions the children visited during the school year. These have included "The Edge of Childhood," "American Prints in Black and White, 1900 1950," and "In a New Light: Seven Artists in the Heckscher Collection."

An annual display of Nassau County elementary and junior high students is exhibited at the County Arts Center in East Norwich, Long Island.

Serve in a Museum

Many schools include museums as a setting for service activities. Students in Central Park East Secondary School in New York work in a number of different museums: the American Museum of Natural History, the Studio Museum of Harlem, the Museum of the City of New York, El Museo Del Barrio, and the Children's Museum of Manhattan. Their responsibilities vary. They conduct tours for schoolchildren, work in the office and on press releases, assist with minor administrative tasks and in the day-to-day operations—hanging art exhibitions and deinstallation.

In Fayetteville, Arkansas, Woodland Junior High School students help in the Sam Walton Art Center, shuttling elementary school kids on and off buses and guiding them through the museum.

Curate an Exhibit

In a major project that involved all the 1,250 youngsters in the Southampton School District, students mounted and curated an exhibit at the Parrish Art Museum in their town.

Assignment 1890s: Students Look at America

Southampton Public Schools, Southampton, Long Island

"The best part is that we were treated like colleagues instead of kids."

"The first time we went into the museum vaults to research the art collection, our teacher practically had a heart attack when one of us pulled out a pen to take notes. I guess he was afraid we'd draw a mustache on a painting or something."

"I'll never see a museum in the same way again. There's so much more to it than just looking at a picture on the wall."

—Quotes from Ria, Rachel, and Chris, students who participated in the project[2]

Both institutions, the Southampton School District and Parrish Art Museum, were celebrating their centennials. It was from a casual conversation about this coincidence, as Richard Malone, superintendent of Southampton Schools, recalls, that an exceptional collaborative project between the school and the museum developed—an exhibit at the museum focusing on the early years of both groups, the 1890s. What was most unusual was that it was to be a student-organized and -curated exhibit, with major responsibilities assigned to the students. They researched the period, collected materials, helped produce the catalog, mounted the exhibit, and acted as docents for the completed show.

Five themes were selected for investigation: history, aesthetics, childhood, science and industry, and gardens. The project took almost a year for planning and execution. During that year, it became the focal point of the schools' curriculum. Teachers developed curriculum plans integrating the art project with all subjects.

All grades in the district were involved in the research, even kindergartners who helped investigate toys of the past for the childhood theme. Older students found rich material in the history of the 1890s, including the birth of the women's suffrage movement, the growing nationalism, and the rise of the robber barons. The garden theme led to the construction of a replica of a formal nineteenth-century, eighteen-square-foot garden within the Parrish walls by twelfth-grade students.

Residents offered memorabilia from the 1890s: clothes, dolls, toys, books, cooking equipment, a sleigh, student desk, and farm implements. The local photography shop shared original photographic equipment. A panel of consultants from the Metropolitan Museum of Art, Northeastern University, the Southampton Historical Society, and a resident who was a museum exhibition designer all worked with the students.

The venture was highly successful; the exhibit well attended, staff and students enthusiastic, and the community most supportive. The students learned to view art from a more sophisticated perspective—analyzing paintings in order to gain insight into the period in which they were created. Malone states that the district will use the experience gained for other interdisciplinary themes, such as World War I.

It was evident that an art project had sparked an imaginative approach to curriculum and an appreciation of the potential for museums and school districts to collaborate to illuminate history, and it had left indelible impressions on the lives of the participants.

OTHER CREATIVE ACTIVITIES

Music and drama are also very much a part of service learning projects. Many examples of these have been reported elsewhere in this book as part of curriculum projects. One-shot activities in which students perform in senior centers, hospitals, or shelters during holiday seasons, though worthwhile, are limited as examples of service learning. The activities noted here are ongoing.

Music

The Hillside School in Montclair, New Jersey, has established a Traveling Troupe that regularly performs original scripts and music for the elderly throughout the state. The troupe has also given shows at the state Meadowlands Convention Center for the community and the governor.

In the Redlands Middle School in Grand Junction, Colorado, an intergenerational choir with preschool kids, sixth graders, and senior citizens, offers periodic performances.

Schools have established community bands inviting community members to join the kids in concerts.

The Lee Middle School in Fort Myers, Florida, features a multicultural choir, jazz band, strings group, and chorus.

Drama

The Bala Cynwyd Middle School in Pennsylvania uses life-size puppets to sensitize kids about disabilities (described in Chapter 16).

A number of schools use skits to teach kids about social problems, such as AIDS or substance abuse. Skits about the homeless were performed for elementary school kids by Carmody Middle School seventh graders in Lakewood, Colorado.

Notes

1. Also discussed in Chapter 15.
2. Quoted in Steve Parks "Hung Up on the 1890s," *Newsday,* February 26, 1993, p. 68.

PART III

Service Learning Themes in Interdisciplinary Units

An integrated curriculum is apt to stimulate students to reflect more deeply on the meaning of their experiences. From studying a subject through many different lenses, they develop a broader perspective. Students who visit a homeless shelter may ask why some people don't have homes. If, however, the visit is related to an interdisciplinary unit on homelessness, they ask that same question but within the context of a range of societal issues: the politics of low-cost housing, the ravages of drugs, the laws governing incarceration of mental patients, the role of institutions, and the consequences of unemployment. They may also analyze statistics describing the composition of the homeless population and where they tend to congregate.

Service learning meshes particularly well with an integrated curriculum. Many interdisciplinary projects include a service learning component. In some instances service, itself, is the unifying theme, with an interdisciplinary team selecting a service project around which a unit is built.

In elementary schools with one teacher primarily responsible for all subjects, integrated projects have not been unique. In the past, however, middle and junior high schools whose organization was patterned after the high school, with separate teachers for each subject, have been more resistant to an integrated approach.

In recent years, the middle school curriculum has come under review. Educators have recognized that early adolescence is a particular stage of life with distinct needs and concerns, that adolescents are not just "pre high schoolers." Middle schools have started to experiment with integrated core curricula. Many have reached out to interdisciplinary modes of teaching. The Carnegie Council's Recommendations for transforming middle schools was sprinkled with calls for interdisciplinary programs.[1]

The organization of interdisciplinary programs with team teaching and block and flexible scheduling is conducive to the incorporation of service activities.

In the chapters that follow, curriculum integration is viewed from a number of perspectives. Two themes that lend themselves to integration across the curriculum—"service to seniors" and "poverty, hunger and homelessness"—are discussed, each followed by suggestions for related activities in different subjects. The subject classifications can be utilized to design a flowchart for an interdisciplinary unit with a service component.

Reports of exemplary interdisciplinary and multidisciplinary programs complete this part.

Note

1. *Turning Points: Preparing American Youth for the 21st Century,* a report prepared by the Carnegie Council on Adolescent Development's Task Force on Education of Young Adolescents (abridged version). The Carnegie Council is a program of the Carnegie Corporation of New York.

CHAPTER 11

Service with Seniors

"Service learning experiences don't easily fade. Though a child may quickly forget some facts memorized for a test, years later he will remember the blind lady who finally got out of bed to hear him and his classmates sing Christmas carols."
—Winfred Pardo, administrative assistant, Shoreham-Wading River School

There is an affinity between the young and the old in our society. "Ironically, both young and old share a sense of uselessness...As our society disengages the aging, they, like adolescents, may have no meaningful work to do in a society where one's value is measured by work."[1]

Stereotypes frequently govern attitudes toward both groups, young and old. Reports about young people in the media tend to highlight the negative—crime, drugs, sexual promiscuity. It is therefore not surprising that older people may view youth as undisciplined, self-centered, and uncaring. Reports about the elderly are just as frequently distortions. To start with, although the term *elderly* may include a thirty-year age span, it often is used inclusively to cover the entire span, and all elderly are portrayed as complaining, forgetful, nonfunctioning people with severe physical and mental handicaps.

As the average life span increases, it is ever more crucial that young people have contacts with elders to establish realistic concepts of aging, to accept each stage of life as normal with pleasures as well as problems. Additionally, such contacts provide the young with an understanding of the past and of their heritage. Unfortunately, in our mobile society, many children have limited or even no contact with their grandparents.

Teaming young people with the elderly has been one of the most popular of the service activities, one that can be integrated with a particular subject or can be part of an interdisciplinary program reinforcing many curriculum areas. From the pleasure derived by students and elders alike from these activities, it is sometimes difficult to ascertain who are the *receivers* and who the *givers*.

In this chapter, grade levels have not been specified. Youngsters from kindergarten through high school have served in programs for seniors. Although the projects will obviously differ in practice, many can be adapted for diverse age groups. The conclusion of the chapter lists service with seniors by subjects, enabling teachers of any subject to engage in a project with seniors.

PLANNING FOR SERVICE WITH SENIORS

Settings for Service

Before establishing a project, the teacher will need to decide which setting is most appropriate: a senior citizen group or center or a resident facility. The latter include health-related facilities, nursing homes, and geriatric centers. The choice may rely on the proximity of the various facilities.

In some instances, the seniors may be able to visit the class. There may be an advantage to this, as transportation is frequently available to some senior groups.

Decide on a Schedule of Visits

The project may last an entire semester or even a year, or may be for a limited period; frequency of visits may be weekly, once a month, or even less often. In the latter case, there are usually written contacts during the month. The schedule also will be determined by whether you will be visiting the centers or the seniors will be coming to your classroom.

Orientation to Working with the Elderly

Students may have many misconceptions about the elderly. They wonder why people live in nursing homes. They question their mental faculties. Thus, a prior orientation for students is essential. It may be helpful to have a discussion of students' expectations and questions. If possible, schedule a visit by the director of the nursing home or other health care professional to discuss the physical, mental, and social abilities of the population to be served, as well as topics such as death and dying. Books on the topic as well as films or videos are helpful.

Efforts should be made to describe what the students will encounter. A teacher or service coordinator should visit the home first and, if possible, bring back photographs to the class. Regulations, schedules, and safety precautions, such as handling of wheelchairs, need to be explained.

From students' journals, it is clear that many initially face the experience with trepidation. Typical are the following comments: "I wasn't sure I would like it." "I thought older people were boring."

Ungraded Activities

Become Acquainted

Arrange for the students to visit the center. Tour the building, note the recreational facilities, and what residents are doing. What is the approximate age and physical condition of the participants?

When students meet the seniors in person, they can inquire about interests—games, hobbies, arts and crafts. If the site is not a residential center, do the seniors live alone or with someone? Do they have pets?

The "Me Bags" employed by the Schuylkill students and their senior visitors at the first contact of their "Fabulous Friday" programs is a useful icebreaker. Name tags also make it easier to become acquainted.

"Fabulous Fridays"

Schuylkill Elementary School, Phoenixville, Pennsylvania

"I think Fabulous Fridays are a great place to meet so many FABULOUS children."
—Sara Poinsett, senior participant in program

It was likely to be a difficult school year. Beverly Bonkoski and Florence Chapman, two fourth-grade teachers, were faced with classes containing a high number of at-risk kids. Senior citizens from the local Kiwanis Club had expressed an interest in working with the school. Welcoming the idea, the two teachers invited the seniors to their classrooms.

Kiwanis grandparents and a few other senior citizens from the community decided to meet with the children every Friday from 2:00 to 3:00 P.M., focusing on building the children's self-esteem. The program was titled "Fabulous Fridays."

For the first visit, the class met in small groups. Both the kids and seniors brought "Me-Bags," planned as icebreakers, sharing memorabilia that represented their personalities and hobbies. Seniors brought old pictures, sports objects such as golf clubs; kids included baseball cards and pictures of pets. Seniors recounted childhood experiences and described games of their youth; kids compared these to their own games. "The seniors quickly blended into our school environment," the teachers report, "accepting the title of 'adopted' grandparents."

Additional Fabulous Friday programs involved: children outlining grandparents' life-sized shapes and filling them with drawings representing highlights of the seniors' lives; grandparents creating profiles of the children as Valentine's Day gifts for the kids' parents; joint field trips, and collaboration on a host of environmental activities: cleanup of the Schuylkill canal and park, tour of a landfill, construction of an environmental graveyard on the school grounds for nonbiodegradable products, and collection and recycling of old phone books, with a visit by the kids to the paper mill where they were recycled.

In the following school year, the students prepared a Grandparent Yearbook containing a photograph of each grandparent, a biography, and interests. In the book, grandparents commented on how much they enjoyed the Fridays with remarks such as "I think the Fabulous Fridays are the best thing that I've ever done for children! I enjoy them and learn" (Stanley Rockey).

In the subsequent year, the collaborators undertook an even more ambitious project. Aided by the seniors' knowledge of the community, they produced a book on local history. The book was published, sold well, and received national recognition. (It is described in Chapter 4.)

Fabulous Fridays continued with other joint projects. To reinforce language arts further, they produced a community directory of service organizations. Students interviewed twenty-one representatives of local groups in their classrooms. As an additional environmental project, the kids, supported by the seniors, "adopted" a stream that flows on the property of a YMCA situated across from the school. A grandparent trained the kids to collect water samples, and the district high school science teachers opened their labs to the kids to permit them to test water samples and view them under microscopes.

At the conclusion of the academic year, the Kiwanis seniors hosted a dinner honoring the kids and their parents as well as the participating teachers and their parents. The program has been "magical," Bonkoski and Chapman reported enthusiastically.

Adopt a Grandparent

Programs may pair each student with a senior, one to one, or groups with one senior, or may decide not to pair at all. The "Grand Pals" program at the Redlands Middle School in Grand Junction, Colorado, seeks to pair every student with a senior. Grandparents include seniors in non residential centers and elderly in nursing homes, as well as Alzheimer's patients, disabled persons, and those suffering from brain trauma.

At Redlands, students work in groups to plan joint activities. The groups have different experiences. Nine kids who chose to work with Alzheimer's patients shadowed them for a full day to understand their problems better. Kids working with those with brain injuries were able to enjoy more frequent contacts, including parties at school, because this group has transportation available.

In addition to the group activities, Redlands conducts many multigenerational projects in which seniors participate including an intergenerational choir. (See Chapter 14 for a full description of the Redlands program.)

Plan Activities

After becoming acquainted, students will plan activities with the seniors. The seniors will have suggestions. If they come to the class, would they enjoy tutoring students, reading aloud, teaching a craft, sharing a meal, joining a choir, or just chatting with the class? If students visit them at the center, they will have an opportunity to explore their interests further and to determine which of the activities will be appropriate. Students should plan activities in advance for each contact.

Just Chat

If you visit a resident facility, there may be elders confined to their rooms. The director may suggest that you go from room to room introducing yourself. Many of the residents are lonely and appreciate an opportunity for conversation.

Just Listen

"To listen, when nobody else wants to listen, is a very beautiful thing."

—Mother Teresa

A touching story is related by a student who visited an elderly, bedridden woman in her room in a resident facility. The teenager had arrived with her class for its biweekly visit to the nursing home.

She entered the room of the resident and noticed that the woman was visibly upset. The woman explained that she had just received some sad news. The young girl stood quietly by the bedside listening as the woman related the details.

When it was time to leave, the elder turned to the young girl and asked, "What is your name? Then she added softly, "I'll never forget it."

Play Games

The most common break-the-ice activities are games: checkers, chess, bingo, or cards. The generations may play different games and can learn new ones from each other.

Collaborate on Projects

The joint projects on the environment and town history in the Schuylkill School, described earlier in this chapter and in Chapter 4, fostered a unique working relationship between Kiwanis seniors and youngsters. Other collaborative efforts with seniors are described next.

Organize Collective Actions

A small group of students from the Central Park East Secondary School in New York meet weekly with a group of senior citizens and an intern from Columbia University at the Ninety-second Street YM-YWHA in Manhattan. They form an intergenerational focus group that discusses current affairs, explores relevant issues, and researches and plans collective actions.

Before deciding on a project, they first become acquainted by questioning each other freely and by answering questions that have been prepared previously by the intern and are then randomly selected from a bag. They include: "What do you value more than anything else?" "What do you do to relax?" "What makes you happy?" "What do you like about yourself?" The discussion is frank and wide-ranging. Later, the group will select an action reflecting the joint interests of the participants.

Arrange Joint Trips

Invite seniors from neighborhood centers to join your class on a trip to a museum or other site of interest. Students at P. S. 59 in the South Bronx raised money to invite their "adopted grandparents" to a show at Radio City Music Hall and to the South Street Seaport.

Celebrate Together

Birthdays: Remember the birthdays of your senior friends. A birthday cake, cookies, cards, a bouquet of paper flowers, or a small gift made in class are much appreciated.

Holidays: Bringing joy to a senior by sharing a holiday celebration makes the occasion all the more memorable for the student. If the seniors are presenting gifts to friends or relatives for the holidays, offer to help wrap them.

- **Christmas** is the time for students to sing carols or perform at the centers. Encourage the seniors to join you in an intergenerational songfest. Put together inexpensive gift bags: hand or after-shave lotion, special calenders, a class book of poetry, or home-baked cookies.
- **For Chanukah** make and present dreidels and other symbols of the holiday. Include a special gift as described previously.

- **Valentine's Day** is another occasion for students to make greeting cards, poems, or presentations of bouquets of paper flowers or corsages.
- **Easter** lends itself to more than greetings. Jointly decorate Easter eggs or, if feasible, organize an Easter egg hunt. Create an Easter egg tree for the center. To do this, first blow out the contents of raw eggs by piercing holes in the tops and bottoms. The empty eggshells are more sturdy than the whole egg. Decorate the eggs. Select a few branches from a tree without leaves. Anchor them in a pot. Then carefully insert a pipe cleaner in the top hole of the egg, fold it, and hang it with the egg on a branch.
- **Halloween** means costumes. Perhaps students can visit the center in their costumes or invite the seniors to a class celebration. Is it feasible to have a joint costume party? Consider giving your senior friend a *treat* instead of a *trick*. Is there something special students can do on that day?

For Homebound Seniors

How can students help? The answer will vary with their ages. Some have been able to perform chores—shopping, raking leaves, shoveling snow, or simple repairs. Seniors who have pets may appreciate assistance with pet care or having a youngster walk the pet.

Third and fourth graders in the William Penn Elementary School in Indianapolis heard of an aged man who had always taken great pride in his garden but was ill and unable to plant it. The students volunteered to do this for him.

Also consider after-school visits by a small group of youngsters. They can cheer up a shut-in. Students may read aloud to the elders, interview them for an oral history project, play games, or just chat.

Telephone Seniors

Every morning, each of the third graders in Dian Wurst's class in the Polk-Hordville School in Polk, Nebraska, telephones members of the local senior center who are living alone. The program is titled, "Tele-Care." Conversations are brief, just a few inquiries: Are you all right? Do you need anything?

If after two calls the senior has not been reached, the student notifies Wurst, who contacts the center. The calls are reassuring to the seniors and their relatives. At the same time, the third graders improve their telephone skills and learn responsibility, and compassion for their "telephone friends."

It is an exhilarating event when both groups meet at an annual Halloween party and faces are attached to telephone voices.

Conduct Joint Physical Exercises

Students have joined with seniors in exercise programs during scheduled visits to the senior center. Low-impact aerobics or rhythmic exercises are fun and healthful for both groups. Your school physical education teacher can suggest specifics. However, no exercise program should be undertaken without consultation with the director of the center.

At the Bala Cynwyd Middle School, students participate in the "Magic Me" program under the direction of teachers Bobbi Wolf and Nancy Murphy.

"Magic Me"

Bala Cynwyd Middle School, Bala Cynwyd, Pennsylvania

"It is special to watch young people interact with people 80 to 90 years of age."
—Bobbi Wolf, co-director, "Magic Me"

This is a well-established national program that teams middle school students with geriatric residents. It is only one of Bala Cynwyd's many service activities. Originally, the program was slated for gifted kids, but currently it is open to all seventh and eighth graders. They visit the geriatric center every other week and participate in "getting to know you" activities, arts and crafts, and other projects. The goal is a one-to-one relationship between the young people and the elders.

Sports have become popular. Residents participate in baseball spring training with wheelchairs pushed around the bases. The students organized a Nurse Olympics for the residents that paralleled the official Olympics. It opened with the national anthem, a torch was carried around the stadium, and medals (made of paper) were awarded. Activities included balloon volleyball, basketball (hoops were improvised with arms circled), darts and Ping-Pong. Residents also engaged in disco dancing, waving their arms to the music.

"'Magic Me' affords kids an opportunity to be at their best," Wolf states. "It reveals a side of them you don't usually see." She quoted an eighth grader who, referring to the program, which was originally called a *Challenge* program, stated: "This program isn't only a challenge of the mind, it is a challenge of the heart."

A Long-Standing Program

The Shoreham Wading River Middle School on Long Island (grades 6–8) has had a highly successful service program for about twenty years. In addition to their work with the elderly, students work with preschoolers, elementary schools, and the disabled, completing a project in each of their three years at the school. They are responsible for planning each of their site experiences.

For their service with the elderly, they are assigned to adult homes or health-related facilities attached to nursing homes. Careful organization accounts for the continuing accomplishments of the program. It is fully integrated into the curriculum, part of a core program taught by teams of two teachers: one for English/social studies and the other for math/science. The teams are scheduled back to back for part of the week, enabling service to be slotted in at that time. Their unit on the elderly covers ten weeks. The last week is for a special event, such as a party. At the conclusion of the visits, follow-up activities are recommended, such as:

1. Write letters to seniors.
2. Invite seniors to school for lunch or performances.
3. Prepare articles for school or community newspapers about the experiences.
4. Make contact with active senior groups such as the Gray Panthers.

The value of the Shoreham Program is best described by these comments by the recreation director of the site the students visit:

The visits from the students are something special to look forward to. The men and women wonder what activity they will bring. The residents are a bit happier. They feel a bit better. It is a reason to come out of their rooms.

Aloha: A Report from Hawaii

The following letter, sent by student Sherelyn Medrano at the Waialua High and Intermediate School, Waialua, Hawaii, to First Lady Lynne Waihee, was reported in Star Serve.[3] It vividly portrays a visit of students to a senior center.

My classmates and I went to the Kupuna Housings in Waialua for our service project. Our program started with a game of charades for the senior citizens which was fun and filled with laughs. Next, two classmates performed a hula dance followed by our class singing three songs. While both young and old indulged in refreshments, some of us started conversations with the elders.

I was talking to an elder woman who said something that made me feel good about myself and my classmates. She said, "I've heard your winter vacation starts today (we got out of school at 11:30 and the program started at 12:15) and just coming here tells me that you have a lot of aloha *inside of yourselves." I've learned that spending just 30 minutes with a total stranger won't obligate you to anything but a new friend. ALOHA.*

ACTIVITIES BY SUBJECTS

Here are some suggestions for additional activities by students either in individual classes or as part of interdisciplinary units.

Language Arts

A relationship with seniors offers many opportunities for enriching the language arts curriculum. If seniors come to the classroom, they may listen to children read or tutor them. Kids, on the other hand, write to senior friends between visits, interview them, and compile oral histories, as suggested in a social studies activity below. Fascinated by tales of the past, the students gain an appreciation of history as they listen.

Correlated Literature

Read books about the elderly. Screen the books carefully to be certain that the older people are portrayed with dignity and depicted in a variety of roles: as active, prominent people enjoying meaningful work—paid or volunteer, as cherished grandparents, as founts of family and life history, as well as some who may be lonely or have physical problems.

Analyze books for stereotypes about the aged.

Book of Memories

Interview the seniors about their favorite memories. Help them write about these, then bind the pages and present them with the book.

Other Ways to Help

Students help seniors complete forms, read to elderly people whose sight may be impaired, and help with correspondence. Other seniors may feel strongly about a current issue—threats to Social Security, for example—and seek assistance in writing letters to editors of newspapers or magazines or to political figures.

Mathematics

Teach or Learn about Computers

Some retired seniors are computer whizzes. They may appreciate an opportunity to visit the school to teach young people. Others may enjoy learning about computers. If computers are available either at the center or at school, teach word processing or play computer games with your senior friends.

Compare Prices

Secure an old catalog or newspaper and compare the prices of food, clothing, and shelter when the older people were your age to the present. Another interesting comparison is with salaries. Check some want ads of the past and present. Compute percentage rises in beginning salaries for similar positions.

Changing Life Expectancy Statistics

There have been dramatic changes in the life expectancy of both men and women since the beginning of the century. Gather the statistics, graph them, and publicize them. It may be interesting to research the increase in the number of people who live to be 100 years old today as compared with periods in the past.

How Many Descendants?

Compute and chart statistics about all the descendants of the residents in the senior facility. How many children, grandchildren, great-grandchildren? Any great-great-grandchildren? What are their sexes? Ages? What other information is relevant? Find an interesting way to present your research.

Understand Social Security

Research information on Social Security. What percentage of payroll is paid into Social Security? How is the amount of benefits computed? What is the average paid? In which fund does the federal government accumulate payments? Are the funds solvent? This activity may be done in conjunction with social studies.

Help with Checkbooks

Some seniors may appreciate help with writing checks and balancing their checkbooks.

Art, Music, and Dance

It is fairly common for students to visit centers to perform a play or to sing carols at Christmas. The activities described here are of longer duration.

As part of the art curriculum, students undertake a wide range of activities with the elderly, from decorating centers to working together on art projects to learning new crafts from seniors. They make greeting cards and help the seniors make gifts for grandchildren. Stationery is frequently welcome. Students can design flower-pressed notepaper (see the instructions in Chapter 10).

In one center, students discovered a senior who had been a square dance caller. The students and seniors learned a repertoire of square dances from him.

Decorate Centers

Secure a space at a local senior center for the school's or your class's artwork. Change the display regularly. In some resident facilities, the elders may enjoy children's art in their rooms.

Collaborate with seniors on art projects. The Star Senior Center in Manhattan, for example, displays an impressive mural completed jointly by residents and youth.

Discover New Crafts

Many seniors are adept at crocheting, embroidery, knitting, or other crafts. Ask which they would be willing to teach. This is particularly applicable when seniors visit school classes. An art table can be included in the room with fabrics, wool, and thread. In some instances, the elders have helped younger children sew or knit doll clothes or make Halloween costumes.

"Project Patches"

Inner-city kids at the Dr. Bernard Harrif, Sr. Elementary School in Baltimore, Maryland, teamed with local senior citizens to make quilts for the elderly, the homeless, and babies with AIDS. The seniors came to the school once a week. Under their tutelage, kids learned to help the seniors cut, design, and sew the quilts. Three quilts were completed last year, and more are planned.

"The kids learned more than quilting," the Harrif teachers noted. "They realized that babies can be born with AIDS. And they learned to work together and experience the special joy of helping people."

Plan Sing-Alongs

Do any of the seniors or students play a musical instrument, such as the guitar or piano? Sing-alongs can be fun joint activities. Consider distributing song sheets.

Organize an Intergenerational Choir

Learn nostalgic songs—of the first half of the decade. Invite seniors to join with you in a choir performance.

Dance

Intergenerational dances or balls attended by students and senior citizens are popular. Frequently these are at the end of the year and are billed as "proms." Each group teaches the other some of the dances of their respective periods. Participants dress up and dance together.

The William Penn Elementary School in Indianapolis, for example, together with other schools in Project Service Leadership, sponsored a "Best Friends Ball" for seniors with whom they had been working.

Social Studies

The elderly are the repositories of our history. They have lived through the last decade, and their reminiscences are crucial to our understanding of the twentieth century. "If we don't gain the seniors' knowledge of our history now, we will lose it forever," warns Linda Epstein, principal of Crossand Elementary School in Philadelphia.

Learning History with Our Elders

Encourage seniors to reminisce about the past century with you. Your service will become an extension of your history courses.

Inquire about specific events: How did the Great Depression affect them?

Ask about the presidents. Which was their favorite? Do they recall the country's shock at Pearl Harbor, or the death of President Roosevelt? What was it like in the country then? How about when President Kennedy, Robert Kennedy, and Martin Luther King, Jr., were assassinated?

Discuss the civil rights struggle in the United States during the 1960s and 1970s. What were conditions in the South before those days?

Veterans of World War II and the Korean War will have personal experiences of those wars to relate. What other historical incidents do they recall?

Cultural Histories

Memories of the seniors' lives and families constitute a cultural history. Most seniors are pleased to share their experiences, to find someone interested in listening. In turn, the youth are enriched by the seniors' recollections. Record these on audiotape and, if possible, on videotape. Older students may be able to create a cultural journal in the "Foxfire" style.

Ask questions: Tell me about your family—your mother and father. Where were they from? Any siblings? Your position in the family? Where did you live? What kind of house? How was it heated? How was food cooked? Kept cold? What were your responsibilities? Did you have toys? Pets?

Which schools did you attend? How did you get there? How did they differ from schools today?

Was your clothing made or bought? Was food different? How did you shop for food?

What did you do for recreation? How did you travel? What was your first job? At what age? Tell about your friends, sports.

What jobs have you had? Which did you enjoy the most? Would you choose the same career again?

Were you married? How did you meet your spouse? What was his or her occupation? What do you recall about your engagement? Your wedding?

What do you recall about World War II (or other war years)? What do you consider the most amazing change you have witnessed through the years? What would be your counsel to future generations?

An Immigrant Geography Lesson

Question the seniors at your center to find out if any of them or their parents were immigrants. If so, from which countries? On a map of the world, note the countries. Can you research the historical reasons people tended to emigrate from those countries?

How does the pattern of immigration today compare with your data? Can you account for the differences?

Study Families

Link these activities with a social studies unit on families. With the help of the seniors, research how families have changed over the years. Do the seniors have memories of their grandparents?

How are the young and the elderly treated in other cultures? What are their roles? Responsibilities? Do these differ from those that are typical today?

Be an Advocate

Together with the seniors, kids can plan to improve some aspect of their community. Activities might range from contacting local politicians or relevant authorities, placing posters in the local library, or organizing a letter campaign.

Suggest also a roundtable discussion of issues affecting either the youth and/ or the elderly. Brainstorm with the seniors. Offer to help survey the neighborhood—are there facilities for the wheelchair-bound? Is there access to public buildings? Any other areas that require attention?

Can conditions for the elderly and for the homebound be improved? How about for youth? Are there recreational facilities? Would there be fewer kids just hanging out if there were more alternatives?

Science and Health

Recycle Used Eyeglasses and Hearing Aids

After reading about the cost of eyeglasses and hearing aids, students decided to collect used ones whose owners had outgrown the prescriptions and make them available to social service agencies.

Simulate Physical Problems

In an attempt to help youngsters empathize with some of the physical problems of the elderly, some teachers have suggested that they do the following:

- Smear vaseline on glasses to simulate distorted eyesight.
- Wrap a popsicle stick around an arm to simulate arthritis.
- Put on gloves and then try to pick up coins to simulate arthritis.
- Place cotton balls in ears and then whisper to simulate impaired hearing.
- Place rice in shoes to simulate the pain of walking on arthritis-wracked feet.

This exercise needs to be handled with understanding. Elderly people do not seek sympathy; most have learned to cope with their physical problems. They should be respected and admired for handling the adversities of aging with dignity.

Share Meals

Invite seniors to lunch, occasionally or on a regular basis. Prepare food for a meals-on-wheels program, or bring a lunch when visiting the centers.

Remember—standards for healthful eating have changed over the years. Be certain that your meals meet current dietary standards.

Consider collecting recipes for an intergenerational cookbook. Include comments from the contributors. Prepare a dish from the book for a shared meal.

Comments from Participants in Program for the Aged, Isabella Geriatric Center (Average Age of Residents: 86)

Comments by Students, Mott Hall Intermediate School, New York City

"I learned older people have a sense of humor. They tell us jokes. I tell them jokes. I like to see them laugh."

"When you get a job you count the hours, but when you are working with people, helping them, you don't notice the time."

"I thought older people don't know what they are saying, but now I know it's not true. I have learned a lot coming here."

"He told me different things about the war he was in."

"I have more patience now. At first when I asked them about their past, they said, 'I don't know.' But now they think about it, and it brings back happy memories."

"It doesn't matter if they are young or old. They have feelings.

"When people appreciate you, your being there means a lot."

"Before I came I thought old people were cranky and stubborn. Boy, was I wrong!"

Comment by Barbara Allan, head nurse at Geriatric Center

"I am grateful to have the students. The residents respond to them, and look forward to their visits. The students listen. Even the most quiet residents are drawn out."

Comments by Myrna Schiffman, Community Service Coordinator, Mott Hall Intermediate School

"The students have been wonderful. Some of them come to visit after the end of the program."
"The placement enables me to point out career possibilities in the health field to the students."

Notes

1. Winifred Pardo, administrative assistant, Shoreham-Wading River Middle School, New York.
2. "Star Serve Bulletin." Santa Monica, CA: Kraft General Foods Foundation, June 1992.

CHAPTER 12

Poverty, Hunger, and Homelessness

"We are all responsible for what amounts to a moral lapse of serious proportions in our civic life—that any of our families, our children, should be wandering around, unable to take for granted even the most basic of requirements, a place to sleep and find shelter, reliably and securely, day and night after day and night."

—Judith Berck, author[1]

VOICES OF HOMELESS CHILDREN

Judith Berck has interviewed homeless children in shelters. A few of their statements, excerpted here, are powerful indictments of the effect on kids of homelessness.

JIMMY: *Living in a hotel makes you feel low, because everybody knows it's a welfare hotel, and everybody knows that everyone in there is on welfare. It's degrading.*[2]

SHAMA: *I didn't want to tell my friends at school, because who wants to tell people that they live in such a bad place?*[3]

MARIA: *I must have changed schools five times in two years...*[4]

SERVICE WITH THE POOR AND HOMELESS

"I can't imagine not doing something. I think the kids get more out of something like this than the people they help."

—Judy Starr, special education teacher, Los Ranchos Elementary School, Albuquerque, New Mexico

When students engage in service for the poor and homeless, they become sensitized to the plight of the less fortunate in our society and gain insights that are not available in textbooks. Although such activities have generally been identified with the social studies curriculum, they can be relevant to all subjects.

For example, a language arts class can read and write about the homeless and then undertake to collect supplies for a nearby shelter. Similarly, a health class can investigate the food served in shelters from a nutritional point of view and then organize a food collection aimed at providing more balanced meals.

Activities related to the homeless vary from collections of food, clothing, blankets, bedding, personal items, and a host of other supplies to preparing meals, serving in soup kitchens, decorating shelters, or assisting children with arts and crafts. They may be one-shot experiences or more extended programs. They have been successfully practiced with all grade levels.

By reaching out, kids can make a difference. They show the homeless that someone cares. It is easy to become inured to the presence of homeless people in society. By their participation and reflection, children begin to recognize the homeless as individuals with aspirations similar to their own. One child summed it up: "I learned that the world is an awful place for poor people." Such an attitude may, in the long run, lead to a more compassionate society.

Ungraded Activities

Although some of the activities reported here originated in a particular grade, they are reported as "ungraded" because they are not necessarily limited to that grade.

"Adopt" a Shelter

Many classes "adopt" a particular shelter for an extended period.

Fourth graders at the Corrales Elementary School in New Mexico adopted the St. Martin's Hospitality Center, a day shelter for the homeless. They decided to seek donations of blankets, soap, socks, food, and other items. In a few months, they had collected twenty-one blankets and sleeping bags, which they delivered personally.

They realized, teacher Judy Starr recalls, "that a one-shot deal wasn't going to make a big enough difference." From then on, the shelter became an ongoing project as the kids advanced through the grades. They provided a steady stream of donated items, as well as student artwork, holiday cards, and gifts. A second facility, a day care shelter for homeless infants and children, was added. Students raised money to buy toys and also created puzzles for the youngsters.

Kids at Corrales Elementary organized a number of fund-raising activities: bake sales, car washes, flea markets, recycling, and fashioning ornaments. The project was integrated into the curriculum as kids wrote letters, read books, and studied the history of the homeless and the geographical areas where homelessness was most prevalent.

Starr subsequently transferred to the Los Ranchos Elementary School in Albuquerque, where she is in charge of eight special students—some learning disabled, others with communication or behavior disorders. She has inspired an interest in her students in helping the homeless and has found them eager to continue service with the shelters. (This project is described in detail in Chapter 16.)

Aiding Children in Shelters

Many classes focus on children who are living in shelters.

- Kids at the Dr. Bernard Harrif, Sr., Elementary School in Baltimore raised $300 to buy new underwear, socks, hair barrettes, toothbrushes, and other items for children in a family shelter. They went to the shelter to make the presentation. (See Chapter 9 for a more complete description of this project, titled "Pennies for Love.")
- Kindergartners collected clothing, books, school and art supplies, and toys, as well as bedding and diapers, for nursery children in shelters.

As described in Chapter 5, this project is part of the social studies curriculum of the Somerset School in Massachusetts.

- Students in third grade in a depressed neighborhood in New York City shared their outgrown warm clothing with kids in shelters. They solicited donations of jackets, caps, and gloves from all the families in their school.

Back-to-School Drive

At the beginning of the school year, more than two hundred school bags and supplies for disadvantaged kids were collected by students and distributed by the Yorkville Common Pantry, Bronx, New York. Many kids enclosed a personal letter in the bags.

Joy of Giving and Sharing

Kids can experience this special joy by participating in the following activities:

- On your birthday, select one new present to give to a homeless child. Have each kid in your class (school) do the same.
- Put a homeless child on your Christmas list.
- In the winter, decorate a "friendship" tree. Hang mittens, hats, and scarves on the tree. Place boots under it. Bring it to a shelter for homeless families.
- Schedule a sharing day in class. Have kids bring in items that are new or in good condition—a toy, stuffed animal, game, book, sporting equipment—and deliver it to a family shelter.

A Tradition of Service

The Ethical Culture Fieldston School in the Bronx, New York, has a long tradition of service "generated by the curriculum." Angela Vassos, coordinator of the Community Service Program, explained that this is in keeping with the Quaker philosophy: "You experience your own humanity through service to others."

The upper school has organized an extensive service program through SHOP (Students Helping Other People).

Students serve during an activity period once a week and also after school.

They have contributed to a number of shelters over the years and regularly participated in holiday parties in a neighborhood center that provides aid to residents from preschool to seniors. In addition, the entire school adopted the Yorkville Common Pantry (YCP), dedicated to feeding the hungry and serving as their advocate. The extent of their participation is evidenced by this letter received after a Thanksgiving drive: "We could never have made some 500 families happier at Thanksgiving without your help."

Be an Advocate

Kids at the Midtown Elementary School, an Ethical Culture School in Manhattan (pre-K to grade 6), learned the power of collective action.

Homeless men who had been raising money by collecting cans from waste bins or from residents for recycling were being treated badly when they attempted to redeem the cans. To provide a dignified process, a neighborhood resident organized a collection center in a vacant New York City lot and cashed in the cans for the homeless. After a while, this lot became the hub of services for the homeless.

When the Midtown kids heard that the city had decided to close down the collection center in order to build on the lot, they were indignant. They organized a "We Can" drive and bombarded the mayor and other city officials with letters of protest. They won their fight. The city provided a different, superior site for a collection center.

Serve a Meal

"I think the kids are great," one homeless man commented. "It's nice to have their company, and it gives them a chance to see that we're just like other people. We like to be treated the same."

Fourth graders at the Long Lots Elementary School in Westport, Connecticut, made several visits over a period of time to a local homeless center, where they served a meal that they had helped prepare at their school. The kids ate and chatted with the men. A lesson was brought home to the kids when one of the men revealed that he had undergone brain surgery as a result of a series of accidents. "I hope your teachers explain that this could happen to you if you do drugs," he told them. "That's how all my accidents happened."

Whole Elementary School Projects

At times, elementary schools select "aiding the homeless" as a schoolwide activity in which all students participate.

- When the local center for battered women was almost destroyed by fire, all students at the Harrif School in Baltimore cooperated to prepare sixty sandwiches for lunch for the residents and made a gift for each.
- The Tatnuck Magnet School, grades K–6, in Worcester, Massachusetts, participated in a month-long project titled "Friends Helping Friends" to help the Abby House, a shelter for homeless women and children. Different grades collected and stored specific items. For example, grades K–l: bathroom items; grades 2–3: kitchen and pantry; grade 4: leisure activities. Fifth- and sixth-grade students organized a snack sale to buy canned hams.

  The project became a real life educational experience, integrated throughout the curriculum. Kids graphed, weighed, sorted, categorized, and estimated costs of items received. They discussed health issues, created art, wrote stories and poems, and published a newsletter. Fifth and sixth graders teamed with a lower grade; they went into the younger kids' classes to talk with them about Abby House.

  In a culminating activity, students came to the Abby House. They had prepared a booklet containing original poems and stories, which they recited and also performed. Finally, they presented the director with a copy of the booklet together with a check for $230.57 that had been raised by selling snacks, flowers, and pussy willows.

- A cooperative effort by parents, grandparents, teachers, administrators, and students at the Mary O. Pottenger School in Springfield, Massachusetts, led to the completion of twenty-three quilts for a clinic that supports children who were born infected with the HIV virus.

- At the Alice B. Beal School in Springfield (grades K–4), the entire school addressed the service theme "Helping the Hungry and Homeless." The students collected 140 pounds of sneakers for children in Haiti.

Activities for Middle and Junior High

Citizenship Education Clearing House (CECH)

CECH is a nonprofit agency in St. Louis that involves students in educational programs.[5] One of the arms of CECH is the Metropolitan Issues Program, devoted to encouraging middle school students to participate in issues facing the St. Louis metropolitan area by providing support for action projects.

Math teacher John Shaughnessey developed the civic learning program at Nipher Middle School in Missouri with assistance from these groups.

CECH suggests specific procedures for service projects. As summarized by Shaughnessey, they include six steps:

1. Brainstorm, generate ideas, then select a topic.
2. Focus on the topic, study it through research, and then narrow it to a specific problem.
3. Investigate the problem through several means of research, such as newspaper articles, videos, and guest speakers.
4. Design an action program—a hands-on project to address an identified area of need.
5. Implement the designed plan of action.
6. Evaluate and reflect.

Civic Learning: Action through Community Service

Nipher Middle School, Kirkwood, Missouri

"This is why I enjoy teaching middle school. The amount of energy the students put into these projects is incredible."

—John Shaughnessey, math teacher

The Nipher Middle School includes grades 6 to 8 in a total population of about 480 students. About 25 percent are African-American, with 12 percent of this population bused into the district as part of a voluntary desegregation program.

Shaughnessey's service project is anchored in his sixth-grade contact (advisory) period. He was able to secure administration permission to substitute it for the existing contact curriculum. In most respects, Shaughnessey points out, the project is student-initiated and student-implemented.

Following the CECH procedures, the students selected "homelessness" as their topic. It is interesting, Shaughnessey reports, that for the past three years, this has been the topic students have chosen.

Research engaged the students for a five-week period. They viewed two videos, one in which actors portrayed homeless people, the second actual footage of the homeless with an eyewitness account by a local television news anchorperson.

During this period, the students reviewed news articles and magazine clippings and kept journals to capture any "personal thoughts, ideas, facts or concerns." They also designated a "Breakfast Cereal Day" on which boxes of the students' favorite cereals were collected for children in a local shelter.

The director of the shelter spoke to the class about homelessness and showed a video of the shelter. Another guest speaker explained the Missouri Education of Homeless Children Act, which is aimed at ensuring that homeless children attend the school that is in their best interest.

On the basis of research data they had collected, the youngsters wrote to newspapers citing facts and figures about the homeless. They also wrote to local and state representatives expressing their concerns.

The students were now ready to design and implement their own action plan. They determined to donate personal time at a shelter and serve meals in a food line. But first, they decided to eat lunch with the shelter residents.

"Shelter food was quite the experience," Shaughnessey recalls. "Reality was quick to set in when one student asked for a glass of water with his meal. The reply was simply that there was no drinking water."

Other activities included decorating the shelter for a Valentine's Day party, visiting other shelters and food lines, and preparing sandwiches for shelters for an entire week during all lunch periods at their school.

Reflection was embodied in the students' personal journals, poems, and slide shows and through actions such as letters to the editors, letters to legislators, and an all-school assembly. Documentation was through newspaper articles, photo albums, and collective writing. An examination on facts about the homeless and an interest survey evaluated the knowledge and attitudes generated by the students work on the project.

In May, all participating schools in the Metropolitan Issues Program came together in a fair to present their projects. At this inspiring event, students exchanged details about their service. They described projects on topics such as drugs, gangs, the homeless, child abuse, environmental awareness, and the elderly.

Oxfam America: A Program to Combat Hunger

Oxfam America is a nonprofit worldwide group working to fight hunger in partnership with poor people around the world.[6] Among its projects is one that helps students organize programs to raise consciousness about hunger. A number of schools have conducted Oxfam events. (See the Coppachuck School event in Chapter 13.)

Rescue Food

Concerned by the amount of freshly prepared, perishable food that is thrown away each day by restaurants, hotels, caterers, bakeries, and food stores, a group of Long Islanders organized to collect the food and deliver it to soup kitchens and homeless shelters. "These are not leftovers," a spokesperson for the group explained, "but food that would spoil if not used immediately. It's a program that sensibly combats two problems—waste and want."

Can students organize such a program in their community?

Remodel a Shelter

First initiated as a project for teacher Kathleen Klein's civics class, the plan to adopt a shelter for battered women, part of a study of homelessness, spread to include 550 more students and six teachers at the Ben Franklin Intermediate School in Chantilly, Virginia.

The students decided to transform the building from "bleak, old, and dirty" to a "special home," and that is exactly what they did. Each of the sixteen classes involved adopted one room for the makeover. They sent class representatives to take photographs and videos of the rooms at the shelter, then worked in teams to transform the building. Using only donated supplies or reused items, they made curtains, collected bed linens, organized meals, made welcome signs in English and Spanish, planted a garden and cared for the lawn. Parents helped by building benches, laying new carpeting, and painting walls.

Klein notes that the project became part of the curriculum. Students studied legislative bills, wrote letters, read and wrote articles about homelessness, and followed legislators' and candidates' views on related issues.[7]

Note: Interdisciplinary units related to poverty, hunger and homelessness are described in Chapter 13.

ACTIVITIES BY SUBJECT

The following activities by subject should facilitate incorporation of units on the homeless in all classes, either by one teacher or by two or more working collaboratively. Each of these describe what students can do.

Language Arts

Correlated Reading and Writing

Read books about the homeless. (See the bibliography in Appendix A.) Also follow newspaper articles related to the homeless.

What causes homelessness? Find out more about the homeless, particularly homeless children. In some instances, families are separated when they move into shelters. Many children look forward to the day when their mothers or fathers will have jobs and be able to afford apartments and reunite their families. Can you interview a child living in a shelter?

Write stories about homeless people—a family or a child. What is it like to be homeless? Describe a day, a week, an incident. Can you imagine what it is like to be homeless during holidays? How did your character become homeless?

Write fictional stories with a homeless child as the leading character, such as Jimmy or Shama quoted at the beginning of this chapter.

Mathematics

Collect Data

Who are the homeless? Collect data about their ages, ethnicity, former occupations. Are they from urban or rural communities? In which areas are the homeless most prevalent? Which states? Has the number increased during the past few years?

Analyze statistics on the number of families living below the poverty line in the United States. How are they determined? Have the numbers changed over the past years?

Find out how much it costs the government to keep a homeless family in a shelter.

Tabulate and graph food donated to your school, by day or week and also by food group.

Raise Funds

Schedule a walk-a-thon or bazaar. Research and sell books of math puzzles for different grades. Keep detailed records of the funds accumulated. (See Chapter 9 for additional fund-raising activities.)

Social Studies

Research the Homeless

Visit or write for information to agencies involved with helping the homeless. What are the issues? What plans have been proposed to alleviate some of the problems? Is there a need for more low-cost housing? Why hasn't it been built?

What has been the effect on the homeless population of plant closings and accelerated layoffs throughout the country?

How have revised regulations on institutionalizing the mentally ill contributed to a rise in the homeless population? Are there adequate facilities for caring for the mentally ill?

Take Action

Ask your library or local businesses to become collection drops for contributions of food or clothing.

Become familiar with your legislators' and candidates' views on these topics. Write to them for action on behalf of the homeless.

Science and Health

What Do the Homeless Eat?

Analyze a typical weekly diet in a soup kitchen or shelter from a nutritional standpoint. What conclusions do you draw? When collecting food, it may be advantageous to assign a different product to each grade to ensure that you will provide a more balanced diet.

Those not in shelters may subsist on leftovers or free items from lunch counters, such as saltines, packets of ketchup, overripe food, or leftover bread.

Health Problems

What are the most common health problems of homeless people? Are there adequate facilities for their treatment?

In the Waseka School unit on Dickens' *A Christmas Carol*, science students undertook to diagnose Tiny Tim's disease on the basis of symptoms described by Dickens. At a later date, a group of physicians were asked to do the same and expressed surprise at how close the kids had come to an accurate diagnosis.

Examine statistics on infant mortality and life expectancy. Are they the same for all ethnic groups? For all economic classes?

Creative Arts

Publicize

Design posters for libraries and neighborhood stores publicizing collection drops.
Create bookmarks listing names of agencies that accept contributions for the homeless. Distribute these through the local library.

Decorate

Decorate shelters with children's artwork. Design a mural. Invite residents of shelters to participate.

Create

Help homeless kids make artwork, holiday cards, and gifts for parents. Donate art supplies.
Send greeting cards to homeless kids.

Home and Life Skills

Cook and Bake

Donate food cooked in class to a shelter.
Once a week, bake bread and deliver to a shelter.
On a regular basis, cook an entire balanced meal, breakfast or lunch. Deliver and serve it to people in a shelter.

Sew

Prepare baby clothes or towelettes. Recycle jeans by adding decorative patches and donate them to a shelter for children.

Assemble

Compile "friendship" bags donating personal items, such as travel-size toothpaste, toothbrushes, soaps, shampoos, razors, and shaving cream.

Notes

1. Judith Berck, *No Place to Be: Voices of Homeless Children* (Boston: Houghton Mifflin, 1992), pp. 1–2
2. Ibid., p. 101.
3. Ibid., p. 103.
4. Ibid., p. 73.
5. Material for this section was provided by John A. Shaughnessy, Nipher Middle School, Kirkwood, Missouri.
6. Oxfam America is at 26 West Street, Boston, Massachusetts.
7. Reported in "Star Serve Bulletin" (Santa Monica, CA: Kraft General Foods Foundation, June 1992).

CHAPTER 13

Interdisciplinary Programs

"I learned that many people in the world go to bed hungry every night."
—Eighth-grade student, Coppachuck Middle School, Gig Harbor, Washington

This chapter highlights reports from schools that have participated in service learning through award-winning interdisciplinary programs.

Theme: Poverty, Hunger, and Homelessness

Waseka Middle School

An innovative approach to the theme of homelessness, the *Christmas Carol/ Homeless Unit* at the Waseka Middle School in Minnesota, was the product of a four-teacher interdisciplinary team made up of teachers of science, English, social studies, and math. Together they were responsible for about 115 students.

Teachers in the team have classes scheduled for the first four hours of the day. The fifth period is reserved for staff planning, which occurs at least three times weekly. The teachers coordinate their release study halls to provide meeting time. Flexible schedules enable the team to ignore bells and to group students in a variety of ways. Every five or six weeks the team undertakes an interdisciplinary project lasting two to two and a half weeks. For each unit, students conduct research, complete a reaction paper, keep a journal, and reflect.

Christmas Carol/Homeless Unit

Waseka Middle School, Waseka, Minnesota

"The kids realized that somewhere tonight people are sleeping out in the rain."
—Steve Dibb, science teacher

It was a cold, wet, snowy night just before Christmas. On the school's parking lot, about sixty seventh graders huddled in makeshift cardboard boxes for shelter, warmed their hands over coal fires in large barrels, lined up for a cup of chicken noodle soup, and reflected on what it was like to be cold, hungry, and homeless. This was the culminating activity of a seventh-grade interdisciplinary unit on the homeless sparked by the English class's reading of Dickens' *A Christmas Carol.* (The complete unit is presented here.)

The event was billed as "awareness night," intended to draw the students' and the community's awareness to the plight of the homeless. Although the weather was cold, rainy, and generally miserable, about 120 people turned out to support the kids. Each contributed a food shelf item for a neighborhood homeless center.

It was an emotional evening. Some students read personal accounts of homeless children in New York to the crowd. Others from the high school sang Christmas carols. Local television stations and area newspapers covered the event.

A formal evaluation of the unit by students and committee members gave it high scores on all items. Students deemed the unit "highly successful." "Most important," Dibb added, "from the formal evaluations and journal writing which students did in their classes, it was apparent that the participants gained an appreciation of the difficulty that being homeless presents. Many expressed a desire to do more for the homeless and want to extend the unit to include a visit to a homeless shelter in Minneapolis, fifty miles away, 'to help in some way.'"

Christmas Carol/Homeless Unit **Plan**

Waseka Middle School, Waseka, Minnesota

Prepared by: Gary Meurer (Math), Laura Krumwiede (Language Arts), Jim Gleason (Social Studies), Steve Dibb (Science)

Length: Two and a half weeks

Number of students involved: 114

Objectives

- To incorporate a service learning component (homelessness) into the existing seventh-grade curriculum, which includes Charles Dickens' *A Christmas Carol.*
- To create an awareness of the homeless, foster personal values, and promote action by our students.

Procedure

The English teacher on the team initiates the unit by assigning Dickens' *A Christmas Carol* to students.

Other team members, together with the school Youth Service and Leadership Coordinator, begin activities relating to the homeless in their classes. Meanwhile, the Coordinator creates a committee of students, team teachers, and community members to plan "Homeless Night."

Subject Activities

English

Students will read *A Christmas Carol* during a two-week period. They will note the British class system and the disparity in the distribution of wealth during this period.

Mathematics

Students will incorporate statistics on homelessness in their graphing unit by constructing three bar graphs, as follows:

- Racial and ethnic comparison of the homeless population of youths, ages 11 to 18, in the shelter for youths in that age range in all of Minnesota
- Analysis of placement history of homeless youth by sex in a variety of facilities: foster home, chemical dependency treatment, residential treatment, detention or correction center, halfway house, facility for persons with physical disabilities, hospitals for persons with mental health problems
- Statistics by sex on where homeless usually stay when they do not have regular housing: with friends, in shelters, with relatives, outdoors, in vacant buildings, in a car

In addition, data will be collected on states where homeless youth were reared and how long they had been homeless.

To emphasize the inequities in society, groups of students will be given a set amount of money to plan a holiday feast. Some will receive a very small amount (like the Cratchits in *A Christmas Carol*), others large allotments.

Social Studies/Civics

Students will investigate child labor laws or the lack thereof during the period of Dickens' book and compare data to present laws.

They will discuss why Tiny Tim did not have medical care: poverty and social conditions.

Science

During the early part of the unit, students will read the testimony of young homeless people from New York City to create an awareness of what it would be like to be a homeless teenager. These accounts will be read again on "Homeless Night."

As part of the science microbiology unit, students will be organized in cooperative groups to research and solve the problem of "What's Wrong with Tiny Tim?" They will first research various viral and bacterial diseases using journals, encyclopedias and a CD-ROM program on diseases. They will note the symptoms of these diseases and make a comparison to Tiny Tim's symptoms. On the basis of their findings, they will write a grammatically correct science news article documenting their data.

Finally, reports will be read to the class, and students must be prepared to support their conclusions.

Music

Students will research songs of the period.

Homeless Event

This will be the culminating activity of the unit. After the projects in all classes are completed, a videotape of *A Christmas Carol* will be shown to the entire team of students, with a cameo appearance by the Four Ghosts of Christmas who bear a striking resemblance to the team's teachers. On the following evening, December 15, from 7:00 P.M. to 9:00 P.M., the event will be presented.

Evaluation

Formal evaluation will consist of six items on a rating scale, including organization, rating of each event on homeless night, attitude toward homeless, and general reaction. All students and committee members will be polled.

Coppachuck Middle School

Interdisciplinary units are only one approach to service learning at the Coppachuck Middle School in Gig Harbor, Washington. Seven teachers—language arts, reading, social studies, science, health, computer technology and learning strategies—form a sixth-grade integrated team and provide a block of time for activities. In addition to in-class activities, this partnership has led to an after-school program titled SHARE (Students Helping and Respecting Everyone). Over one hundred kids volunteer to serve after school participating between one and four times weekly. In groups of six to eight, they serve in hospitals, homeless shelters (where they plan activities for the children), food banks, and a resident Alzheimer facility, as well as other areas as the need arises.

The community has been most supportive. Parents volunteer transportation, and local businesses sponsor twice-a-year celebrations for the students and parents in SHARE: a pizza party in the winter and a barbecue at a city park in the spring.

A Hunger Banquet was the culmination of an interdisciplinary social studies unit on Africa.

Hunger Banquet

Coppachuck Middle School, Gig Harbor, Washington

"Take something you have learned and act upon it."

—Jim Vaughan, sixth- and eighth-grade social studies teacher

It was like no other banquet. On this cold day in February, the town mayor and representatives of the media were present to observe about a hundred eighth-grade youngsters participating in an Oxfam "hunger banquet."[1] The students had been arranged in three groups. The 15 percent in the first group enjoyed a gourmet meal provided by a local restaurant, with parents and other volunteers acting as waiters and waitresses. A second group, about 25 percent, were eating a simple meal of rice and beans. The majority, about 60 percent were sitting on the floor subsisting only on rice.

The kids were following the Oxfam script designed to demonstrate the distribution of food resources around the world. A large meal is prepared and divided among the guests in proportions that represent the earnings of people who live in the world's high-, middle-, and low-income countries. Some of the students had decided to initiate their "banquet" with another Oxfam activity, Fast for a World Harvest. Accordingly, they had fasted for twenty-four hours prior to the meal.

Billed as an "awareness event," the banquet was part of the eighth-grade social studies unit on Africa. The students had studied hunger on the African continent, particularly in Somalia, Ethiopia, and Sudan. With Somalia in the news, current events were diligently followed. They had also worked closely with Oxfam, which supplied videos, and with the Red Cross, which supplied additional material.

The program had tangible impacts. Students volunteered at a local food bank and wrote stories on the theme of hunger. After the event, the kids undertook an enthusiastic campaign to raise funds to support Red Cross activities in Somalia. Canisters were placed in every classroom, announcements made, publicity arranged. In a short time, they had collected $600.

At this time, the students were confronted by a dilemma—how to allocate the funds. Originally, they had planned to donate them to the Red Cross, but the kids were introduced to an exchange student from Zaire who was living in Tacoma, a nearby town. She informed them that her sister had died of starvation in Zaire and that her family was still in difficulty. The youngsters voted to divide the money between the Red Cross and the family of the student from Zaire.

Their interactions with the African continent continue. A pen pal arrangement was forged with students in Zambia. The Coppachuck students were able to help their pen pals with English and also to send supplies to their schools.

Theme: Graffiti Reduction

Suzanne Middle School

> The unique social studies program of Alan Haskvitz' eighth-grade class at the Suzanne Middle School in East Walnut, California, has been described in previous chapters. In addition to their other service learning activities, Haskvitz's students complete interdisciplinary units on topics that they select, research, design, and execute. An example of a unit on a novel theme is presented here.

Tagging or Graffiti Reduction

Suzanne Middle School, Walnut, California

"The value of education is in its application."

—Alan Haskvitz, eighth-grade social studies teacher

"Everything you ever wanted to know about graffiti and more" might well be the title of the following unit. Evidences of mindless destruction in their neighborhood had originally led the kids to decide to research "vandalism." However, as they initiated their research, they learned that historically the word Vandal had other connotations. Because that could be confusing, they decided on a related topic, "tagging," derived from the acronym TAG, for Tough Artists Group. This was the process of carving one's initials into as many sites as possible, aiming for dangerous sites. Tagging was later identified with graffiti, the topic the kids settled on.

Their research began in the town library, but, to their surprise, there was practically no primary resource material. The few books merely reported laws passed by cities to control graffiti. Nor were there any helpful references in data banks. They decided they would have to create their own primary sources.

They looked at history going back to prehistoric people, and the walls of Pompeii, and analyzed messages that had been left by the Norsemen in Minnesota and by Columbus in the New World. Today, graffiti may still serve as messages, sometimes to and from gangs defining their turfs.

To gather more information, students interviewed the local sheriff and other law enforcement officers. They discovered that little was known about the extent of graffiti or attempts to prevent them. A sociologist was invited to Haskvitz's class to explain why people participated in graffiti. The explanations included peer pressure, the need to express oneself, and the need to build self-esteem.

Haskvitz's students are accustomed to call on all the disciplines in their research. Accordingly, they engaged in a comprehensive list of activities.

- To determine the magnitude of the practice, the youngsters wrote to all the embassies and many world leaders. They asked about local ordinances, the amount cities were spending for cleaning graffiti, and how offenders were handled. Sixteen countries responded, including the Fiji Islands, Czechoslovakia, and England, as did many leaders. Ordinances were checked with the town legal department, and expenditures of the cities were compared.
- Math skills were further utilized when the students examined the per capita cost of reducing graffiti in ten cities by calculating the population of the cities and the total spent on graffiti reduction. It was substantial! They graphed these statistics.
- A diffusion map indicating the incidents of graffiti reported in the community at a specified date was prepared. This map involved geography and could be used to compare any changes at a later date.
- Science was included with a discussion of aerosol cans and how they affected the ozone layer.
- The social studies piece stressed the history of graffiti and their societal implications.
- The students published four newsletters sharing facts they had learned in their research.
- They prepared a ten-minute cable television script shown in three cities which explained the history of graffiti and how they could lead to gang violence. The term slipping referred to spraying in an area considered the province of a neighboring gang. Violence, including gang killings, was frequently the result.
- A script was written for a play that described the dangers of "slipping."
- The students uncovered the fact that graffiti scrawlers tended to start in grade 6 and the practice escalated by grade 8. They concluded that if it was to be discouraged, education would have to be started no later than grade 5. With this in mind, they created an interdisciplinary unit for the fifth-grade. It included math activities: word problems posing the cost per square foot of removing graffiti, cost per household, and effects on town budgets.
- Art appreciation was involved. Their research had led them to believe that some graffiti painters thought they were creating signature masterpieces, works of art. The students prepared portfolios for the fifth graders that contained reproductions of great American artists and of graffiti urging the younger kids to compare graffiti with "real art."
- For younger children, the eighth graders created a coloring book titled "Is Tagging Cool?" and accompanied this with tapes in four different languages to

meet the needs of their minority populations: Mandarin, Japanese, Spanish, and Tagalog. The last page of the book was left blank for the kids to complete.

What continued to concern the students was that all the existing legislation was reactive, fines ranging from $5.00 to as much as $500 or $1,000, and penalties generally restricted to cleanup. It occurred to the students that these were largely ineffective. What's more, no town seemed to know what others were doing. A troubling factor was the general lack of concern from parents, who do not appear to consider graffiti a crime.

In a meeting with the Los Angeles Superior Court system, they proposed education instead of punishment. Youthful offenders, they suggested, should be sentenced to do research on graffiti. Finally, the youngsters assembled a kit including the material they had produced and summarizing their research and recommendations. It is being offered for sale to municipalities around the country.

One of the most satisfying consequences of the unit did not appear until months later. A routine check with the Los Angeles sheriff, who compiles monthly statistics on complaints about graffiti, revealed a startling fact. In January, when their unit was first completed, there had been 100 complaints. In the following May, there was just one. Six months later, the incidents were up to 48, still half of what had been reported before their work. It was evident their work had had an effect!

The students had called on all their subjects to investigate the topic and to educate their town residents, peers, and younger kids; they applied their knowledge to develop original material, suggest legislation, and perform a worthwhile community service validating Haskvitz's original statement: "The value of education is in its application."

Theme: Civic Education and Participation

City Youth L.A.[2]

Based on the theme "the role of the active individual in society," City Youth L.A. seeks to integrate civic education into an interdisciplinary core curriculum of selected middle schools in Los Angeles. Designed by the Constitutional Rights Foundation, the program helps students learn about their community—its institutions, resources, and problems—and apply this knowledge through service.

A Civic Participation Model for Middle Schools

City Youth L.A., Education and Community Action

"This program gives inner-city middle school youths a chance to make a difference in their communities through knowledge of the resources available to them."

—Keri Dowggett, project director

The objectives of the program are challenging: to harness the energy of middle school youth into positive community action and, in the process, help develop effective, active citizens. The methods are no less demanding: to restructure middle schools in Los Angeles by encouraging new models of teacher organization, team teaching, flexible scheduling, and an interdisciplinary core curriculum. The integrating factor is community service, designed to give students the knowledge, skills, and attitudes to function as effective citizens in their communities.

The framework for the program includes five steps:

1. Building an awareness of community
2. Exploring community problems and needs
3. Meeting community needs
4. Youth's role in the community
5. Citizen action

Civic education and participation are integrated in the core courses—social studies, math, science, and English—and taught by teams of four teachers, who share a common planning period and teach the same 160 students. The social studies course forms the foundation, but each member of the team establishes content-related objectives. The service experience is designed to reinforce the classroom teachings.

The plan is for each team to complete four interdisciplinary units of eight lessons each in a year, prepared by City Youth L.A. with teacher input. "Students explore concepts of change, growth, culture, and political and social action... "This is illustrated by one of the units, which investigates the community, past and present. This unit centers on a river system in Los Angeles, the problems that confronted the peoples who lived along the river at different times, and the impact of earlier decisions on later generations.

The students researched three communities who had lived on the site in the past—Native Americans, farm villagers, and a new city—and evaluated the effect their actions had had on future generations. They then examined the community currently on the site—a large metropolis. The predicament confronting the present inhabitants is portrayed by observing a young girl surfing on the river. The river is now heavily polluted. She sees dead fish and animals and evidences of toxic wastes flowing from the channel. Students are presented with a current problem. They note that there is no filtration system and that people are dumping waste into the rain drains. They are aware that their action or lack of action will affect future generations.

The youngsters decided to take action by publicizing the dangers of pollution, attending public hearings to urge new legislation to restrict dumping of toxic wastes, and stenciling "Do Not Dump in Drains" on the storm drains in the area.

Notes

1. Oxfam America is a group dedicated to fighting hunger around the world, located at 26 West Street, Boston, MA. One of its suggested activities is a Hunger Banquet.
2. Information for this section is from material by Ingrid Sausjord and Keri Dowggett, director, Civic Participation, Constitutional Rights Foundation, 601 Kingsley Drive, Los Angeles, CA, 90005.

   City Youth L.A. is supported by grants from the Carnegie Corporation of New York and the Ralph M. Parsons Foundation.

CHAPTER 14

Multidisciplinary Programs

"I felt really good that I did something for someone else instead of just thinking of me. I learned not to be afraid of people who are hungry, not to waste food, and how to cook."
—Seventh-grade student, Redlands Middle School, Grand Junction, Colorado

It's like that chip advertisement which challenged: "Bet you can't take only one." Service learning is habit-forming. Many schools find that, after initiating one service project, they soon adopt others. In some schools, community service is part of the school's mission. In others, community service itself is viewed as the theme uniting disparate disciplines.

There are now numerous examples of full-service schools, those with a wide range of service programs in which most students are involved at some time. In these schools, the projects are more often multidisciplinary; that is, they span many curriculum areas and themes, as contrasted with interdisciplinary projects, which tend to center on a particular theme.

The programs described here are but a few examples of schools with multidisciplinary programs. In fact, many of the service learning programs discussed previously can at times also be termed multidisciplinary.

Service in an Elementary School

P.S. 59, as part of the New York Community Schools Program, serves as the geographical site for extensive community services.

- The school is open to the community daily from 7:30 A.M. to 6:00 P.M., on Saturdays from 9:00 A.M. to 12:00 noon, and for six weeks during the summer, offering a roster of educational and cultural activities.
- A hospital van unit at the school provides on-site services to more than 100 families.
- A mental health center provides students with on-site therapeutic assistance during the school year.
- Pre-K classes have been established on a full-time basis year round, and educational enrichment is offered to all students.
- Several partnerships have been established with community-based organizations.

The school has also organized a service learning program, "GIVE."

GIVE (Getting into Volunteerism Educates)

Public School 59, The Bronx, New York

"The contributions the kids make can improve the quality of life for everyone."
—Salvatore Sclafani, principal

Situated in an impoverished area of the Bronx, P.S. 59 has an enrollment that is almost 100 percent minority, two-thirds Hispanic, and one-third African American. Nearly every student receives free or subsidized meals and is part of a family that is on public assistance. Sclafani reports that 75 percent of the students read below grade level. The building dates back to 1921 and is deteriorating. There is no gymnasium. (The former gymnasium was divided to make two additional classrooms.) The school backed onto two large littered areas, one now a garden and the other planned as a playground.

Commenting on low reading scores, Sclafani stated "these indicate low academic ability compounded by low self-esteem. Children and parents have a feeling of hopelessness because they are trapped in a community filled with violence, crime, and drug abuse. A need exists to create a community atmosphere and spirit of cooperation and caring to overturn these negative forces."

It was to counteract these negative conditions that Principal Sclafani, together with a dedicated faculty, had turned to Project GIVE, which infuses service learning into the entire curriculum. A host of service projects are scheduled for third, fourth and fifth graders including bilingual and special education students, to "strengthen existing ties to the community as well as focus student awareness on the many rewards of working together for the benefit of all people in the community."

Primary concentration of the curriculum is on reading. This is evident from the sign on Sclafani's door, which declares, "Reading brings us together."

"That's the mission of this school," he adds, "to have each child improve their reading and gain a greater understanding of themselves and human nature." In a tie-in with the New York City Volunteer Program, fifth graders meet regularly with the volunteers and with professionals from Literary Leaders, as well as with parents, to reinforce skills and discuss and analyze stories they have read.

But the emphasis of the school is not only on reading. Other programs include the following:

1. *Farm in the Bronx:* A vacant lot has been converted into community gardens. The school utilizes part of the lot to plant vegetables that are distributed free to the community. The Bronx Botanical Gardens donates the plants and seeds. This activity is part of a unit on nutrition in which the garden is viewed as a hands-on lab.
2. *Peer Tutoring:* Students also act as "teacher helpers" for pre-K youngsters. They assist teachers by educating four-year-olds in "good nutritional habits" and also by reading to them. They develop their own curriculum for these sessions.
3. *Neighborhood Cleanup and Beautification:* Nine hundred bulbs were planted around the school. The New York City Parks Council donated the bulbs.
4. *Earth Week Cleanup:* Wearing rubber gloves, kids and members of the community cleaned a vacant lot and the area around the school.
5. *Partnership with Neighborhood Hospital:* Kids made arts and crafts for patients: jewelry boxes, Christmas wreaths, and valentines. They also decorated hall-

ways, entertained, and performed for patients. Programs were carried to rooms from the hospital auditorium via a closed-monitor video system.

6. *Adopt-a-Senior:* Kids visited a neighborhood senior center, provided holiday decorations, and performed during holidays. They served luncheons or dinners on an ongoing basis, had a read-aloud hour, helped write letters, and played checkers and other games. They also took joint trips with seniors to Radio City Music Hall and South Street seaport. Kids raised money for the expenses.

7. *Family Night at the School:* Students conducted entertainment programs with dance and instrumental music. A movie was shown once a month. Evening activities are considered vital in a community that is often shut down after dark because of inner-city crime.

8. *Multicultural Festivals:* These are regularly held—for example, Apollo amateur night, with kids performing.

9. *Saturday Morning Reading Hours for Parents and Kids:* These are geared to helping parents learn to read to their children.

The school also participates in Project BASIC (Business and Students Improving Community), which offers a forum for local merchants and students to work together to improve their community. As part of this project, students created pictures and wrote compositions illustrating how they could make a difference in their community, at school and at home. Merchants awarded prizes for the best essay at a special assembly at which students and business leaders spoke.

All the programs have a reflection component. Students meet for one period each week to discuss their experiences and write in their journals. Sclafani theorizes that the kids' participation in these many programs "will develop a greater feeling of self-worth, accomplishment and responsibility, as well as develop communication and group collaborative skills, problem exploration, and a sense of positive interdependence and accountability."

Service as Part of a School's Mission

Situated in Mesa County in the valley, Redlands Middle School is a relatively new school, established in 1992.

Service learning is a key component of its mission statement. Determined to reach out to the valley people in its area, the school has organized a service program that involves the entire community. Its extent is truly remarkable.

Grand Vision

Redlands Middle School, Grand Junction, Colorado

"The Day of Caring was the best teaching day of my life. The teachers felt so good about what we had accomplished that we all went out to celebrate."

—Judy Jepson, service learning coordinator

The Redlands Middle School houses about 550 sixth through eighth graders divided into two or three interdisciplinary cores in each grade. Each middle-schooler as well as "special" kids and all ESL kids from the district who are housed at Redlands, participates in a minimum of three service activities during the year. To a large extent, activities are cross-graded, with one-third of the participants from each grade. Jepson states: "Our model is self-help. We tell kids, 'Think of what you can do; don't wait for others.'"

Appropriately titled Grand Vision, the service learning program of the school is extensive, including the following components:

- Grand PALS
- Grand RAP
- Grand Performance
- Grand Riverfront
- Grand Outdoor Center
- Grand Day of Caring

- *Grand PALS:* The goal of this program is to pair every student with a senior citizen or elderly resident of a nursing home, including Alzheimer's patients, disabled persons and those suffering from brain trauma.
- *Grand RAP (Redlands Advisory Program):* The Advisory is the locus of many service activities. Fifteen to seventeen students meet three times a week with a teacher for twenty-five minutes. In this period, each group plans a variety of service learning projects. Some are for the one advisory class, such as preparing corsages for residents of nursing homes; others involve the whole school— instituting a contest to collect the most books for patients in a local hospital.
- *Grand Performance:* A multigenerational choir consists of participants from four different groups: sixth-grade students, kids from Mesa State College pre-school, Head Start kids, and senior citizens from the community. For two months, each group rehearses separately with occasional participation of the school musical director. Meanwhile each youngster is paired with a "Pal," a participant from a different age group. They correspond and exchange pictures. Excitement runs high when they finally meet at a mass dress rehearsal, followed by a celebration, such as a picnic, before the performance. Admission to the performance is a can of food, later donated to a food bank. The choir gives two performances a year, in December and May.
- *Grand Riverfront:* Middle-schoolers work with an alternative high school and senior citizens to beautify the riverfronts of the Colorado River and the Grand River. This was also a project of the school's technical education class, which helped to lay foundations and install park river benches.
- *Grand Outdoor Center:* This is an ambitious ten-year plan to build an outdoor center on school grounds for use by the entire community. It will include nature trails, outdoor classrooms, an amphitheater, a compost center, and more. To date, a community garden, part of the seventh-grade science curriculum, has been completed. Head Start kids pick pumpkins for Halloween.
- *Grand Day of Caring:* This is a multigenerational culminating event. On this day, which coincides with Youth Service Learning Day in April, students, staff, seniors, and other community residents engage in a full day of service. Preparation commences in January. Students, faculty, and parents brainstorm a list of possible service mini courses. From this list, each advisory teacher develops a curriculum, lesson plans, outcome-based goals, and a culminating activity for one of the suggested courses. In a typical Day of Caring, 670 participants worked on seventeen different service projects, together contributing 4,500 service hours. The program received top evaluations. (See end of section for a description of the seventeen projects.)

Students were given an opportunity to indicate the project on which they wanted to work. Most, according to Jepson, received one of their top two choices.

Every student participates in the Day of Caring and is graded. For ten days prior to the actual day, students work on their projects during an extended advisory period. The additional advisory time is arranged by reducing each class for those two weeks by ten minutes. Activities culminate during the Day of Caring.

The highlight of one year's activities was an intergenerational "amazing mosaic." For one week, Redlands invited all in the community—preschoolers to retired citizens— to come to the art room, to purchase a tile and impress their hands on it. The Redlands youngsters then cut, glazed, and fired the tiles. The result was an "amazing mosaic" that was hung in the hall of the new Mesa State preschool building. "We try to contribute all we do to the community," Jepson explains.

On the day following the Day of Caring, students and staff reflect on the program, evaluate, and offer suggestions for the following year.

Service Learning Course Descriptions Culminating on the Day of Caring

1. *Helping Hands:* Students will be placed in several different community service agencies in the Grand Valley.
2. *Blazing Trails:* Design and construct a safe innovative walking route to school.
3. *Monumental Adventures:* With participation of Park Service, explore the Colorado National Monument and participate in various service projects within it.
4. *Amazing Mosaic:* Create a community artwork that will symbolize multiple generations working together.
5. *This Old Shed:* With help from an architect and concrete workers, students will assemble a garden shed near the community garden. They will also become familiar with a variety of architectural designs and careers in the architectural and construction fields.
6. *Babes of Broadway:* Students will present demonstrations at a local elementary school in science and in math manipulatives. They will also write, read, and present a book to their elementary school "buddies."
7. *For the Birds:* A representative from the Department of Wildlife will help students design a pamphlet on safe bird-feeding practices, to be distributed in the community along with bird feeders.
8. *Home Improvement:* Students will gain skills necessary to participate in the RSVP Handyman Program.
9. *Growin' of the Green:* This project is preparation for a community garden on the school campus. Kids prepare soil and start plant germination.
10. *Outdoor Classroom:* With the Colorado Division of Wildlife, Environmental Center, and RSVP, kids design an outdoor classroom and begin preliminary preparation for construction.
11. *Inquiring Minds Want to Know:* Kids produce a video on the Day of Caring to share with other schools and the community.
12. *That Was Then, This Is Now:* Kids interview senior citizens to create a living history. They prepare a book and present seniors with a copy.

13. *For Kids by Kids:* Kids research and prepare a brochure for visitors' centers, motels, restaurants, and the Chamber of Commerce on local attractions.
14. *See What I Wanna Be When I Grow Up:* Kids interview guests, view films which feature nontraditional career choices, visit career sites in the community, and write a short report about a possible career choice.
15. *Traveling Minstrels:* Kids entertain elementary school youngsters with theater and drama and produce a joint performance with them.
16. *Ballistic BLM:* Kids become familiar with the need for environmental management and job opportunities in the field.
17. *Museum Mania:* Kids work with curators and paleontologists to gain information about museums.

A Full-Service School

The service program THRIVES began as an effort to combat seemingly intractable school problems: a large at-risk population, the highest rate of suspension among district middle schools, poor attendance, low self-esteem, a lack of respect by kids for themselves and others, and a highly mobile population. THRIVES has had a widespread impact.

"Attitudes have changed," noted teacher Tommy O'Connell. "Attendance is up and suspensions are way down," confirms Principal Ron Davis.

A letter from Jack Bovee, the Social Studies Coordinator of the Lee County School District, summarized:

> *I did not expect Lee Middle School to approach anywhere near the level of success experienced by your staff and students. The program literally brought what is most probably the most diverse racial, ethnic, and socioeconomic groups of students together for the purpose of having them work cooperatively to accomplish several goals and objectives. Not the least of these goals was to have the students gain greater respect for one another and for the adults who serve them. In this respect, the program was an overwhelming success.*

THRIVES (Teaching Healthy Relationships, Individual Values, and Ethnic Sensitivity)

Lee Middle School, Fort Myers, Florida

"There is no problem with abstenteeism for students involved in community service. They want to come to school."

—Vivian Smith, assistant principal, THRIVES coordinator

THRIVES is a three-pronged program incorporating school and community service projects, multicultural education, and conflict resolution. It has received local, state, and national recognition. It is fully integrated into the instructional program; all faculty and students participate, as do volunteers from many segments of the community. Teachers work in teams creating interdisciplinary service projects with time found for service in the field by flexible scheduling. All students are given an opportunity to discuss, reflect, and write about their service.

Projects cover the gamut of imaginative service programs under the rubrics of substance abuse, violence prevention, child safety, intergenerational (pre-K to seniors), environmental, and additional ones titled "Projects for the Public Good." Examples of these include raising funds to buy a wheelchair for the school, food drives, making and donating toys, producing a video, and technology classes that design and build swing sets for toddlers at an adolescent mothers' program.

A number of school groups participate in special activities. Bilingual students are involved with the Spanish-speaking community through the Vials of Life campaign (described in Chapter 8), creating pinatas for neighborhood groups and organizing events for Hispanic Day. They also perform Hispanic dances in authentic costumes for school assemblies and in the community.

A bilingual specialist for the Lee County School District explained the special significance of service projects to economically disadvantaged non-English speakers. "These students traditionally find themselves in the role of recipients of services. What a boon to self-esteem when they can find they can also be givers!"

A Dropout Prevention Class of about 100 students from each of the grades has been among the most dedicated to service. Organized as PASS (Pupils Achieving School Success), the service program has helped improve their attendance and retention rate.

All students are given time to discuss, reflect, and write about their service activities.

One of the most imaginative of the projects at Lee is the school post office. Originally designed to accommodate the large number of letters written as a multicultural bridge, it has now become an important feature of the school, has been established as a regular class, and is integrated into the technology and language arts curriculum. The technology class created Lee Middle School stamps and stationery on the computer. Here's how the postal system works.

All students are grouped into PODS of nine students in a single grade level and a mixture by race and gender. The PODS remain the same throughout the school year and form the basis for all multicultural training and field trips. Friday afternoons are devoted to letter writing, with students writing to each member of his or her POD once each month. The school postal service processes and distributes the letters to the students' classrooms.

Lee's multicultural activities are equally impressive. These are described in the following chapter.

Service throughout the Community

The multidisciplinary service program at Central Park East Secondary School dates back to the establishment of the school in 1985. Each site is carefully selected to broaden students' horizons, expose them to adult occupations, and engender increasing responsibility.

Service in Over Eighty Sites

Central Park East Secondary School (CPESS), New York City

"Once you see it in action, you have to believe that service is going to make a difference to the kids. I'd never teach any other way."

—Anne Purdy, community service coordinator

When you enter the building, you understand why this school has been described as one of the best secondary schools in the country. It is not only that the building is well maintained, its hallway decorated with colorful murals, but the atmosphere is immediately friendly. A mural in the courtyard, a student service project, depicts the history of the area—its Italian, African-American, and Puerto Rican heritage. The students appear purposeful, helpful, and relaxed. It is not quite 9:00 A.M., the time school is supposed to start, but the community service office is bustling. Students have been at school since 8:00 A.M. studying Spanish and are now preparing to leave for their service—meeting their partners, securing tokens for the subway or bus, and signing in.

Signing in or out is what these kids do frequently: when they depart for their placements in the morning, when they arrive at and later leave from the sites, and once again when they return to school for lunch. Every student is constantly accounted for. "It takes a lot of energy to organize," Purdy admits. "But with about 270 students in 80 to 85 sites, it is that kind of careful organization which is necessary to assure that the program will run smoothly." In a few minutes, Purdy will be leaving to visit the students in the field.

Situated in East Harlem in an economically depressed area, with all its attendant problems, CPESS has about a 90 percent minority population with many kids who in other situations could well be described as at risk. Purdy notes: "The program is not only for high academic achievers. Sometimes kids who struggle the hardest in class have the greatest success in their service." As many as 90 percent of CPESS students go on to higher education.

Every student in eighth, ninth and tenth grade, together with a few seventh graders, participates in community service one morning each week. In case of absence, they notify the office promptly. They work in over 80 different sites which include a variety of settings, such as museums, schools, nonprofit community organizations, city agencies, the city ombudsman's office, Central Park, and senior centers. In none is the assignment simply make-work. Agencies requesting students must indicate the learning opportunities and the responsibilities that will be expected. Take this example from the Children's Museum of Manhattan: "Students involved in this program will be trained on environmental issues that relate to the Urban Tree House exhibit...and will then act as explainers to young visitors to the Museum."

A caring staff who make an effort to know each kid is aided by an organizational structure that helps break down the impersonal atmosphere found in many secondary schools. Two divisions have been established, one for seventh and eighth graders, the other for ninth and tenth. Each has its own faculty. Scheduling service for an entire Division at the same time provides an extended period for the faculty to meet together for planning. There is a core curriculum integrated around broad themes, such as Peopling of America, Culture and Children (with emphasis on South America, Asia, and Africa), and Justice. A block program—Math/Science and Humanities (literature, social studies, art/music)—provides for flexible scheduling.

Also key is the Advisory system. Up to fifteen students are assigned to a faculty member who remains as their Advisor from the seventh to the tenth grade. Advisories meet three to four times weekly. A special relationship develops among the Advisor, the student, and her or his family, and the other kids in the group. The Advisor coordinates all aspects of the students' progress in school—maintaining contacts with the home, keeping tabs on academic progress, service activities, attendance, and any special problems. Part of the curriculum, too, is covered in the Advisories, such as sex, health, and career education and journal writing. As an added bonus, Advisories engage in recreational activities and may take overnight trips together.

Advisors also help students prepare the service portion of their portfolios. As a requisite for graduation from the high school, all students must submit a detailed fourteen-item portfolio, which includes a yearly report of service activities in the form of a résumé with names of organizations, supervisors, evaluations, comments on work problems and issues, and an exhibit or essay summarizing the experience.

"These kids give quality service and do quality work," Purdy summarizes. "In service activities, they are with an adult who is neither a parent nor a teacher. They relate in an adult way, free from pressure of a peer group. Many become resources for their families because they are acquainted with the different agencies and opportunities in the area. What's more, they have helped the school develop allies in the community. The school is no longer just an autonomous building, but connected to the community because of the service our kids offer."

She concludes with an interesting piece of data: "A follow-up study of our students in their second year at Brown University revealed that many pointed to the service experiences as their most significant memory of secondary school."

PART IV

Related Practices

A number of practices that are frequently found in classes that incorporate service learning are reviewed in this part. They include multicultural activities, programs for students with special needs, conflict resolution, school partnerships, career education, and critical thinking. These span many curriculum areas. Each helps create a school environment in which service to others can flourish.

Although multicultural activities and those for students with special needs are often related to the curriculum of specific subjects, they are presented here in separate chapters to underscore the special relevance of these topics to service learning. Respect for all peoples and sensitivity to their diverse cultures is a basic premise of service learning. Similarly, the chapter on students with special needs is consonant with the service learning concept of **inclusion,** which emphasizes the potential of all kids to make valuable contributions to society.

Conflict resolution programs involve kids in service in their schools. These programs are flourishing as kids are recognized as effective in reaching their peers to identify together peaceful methods of resolving problems.

In school partnerships and career exploration, described in Chapters 18 and 19, the kids themselves do not engage in ser-

vice, but the programs are significant examples of community—school ties.

Chapter 20 examines the relationship of critical thinking to service learning and explores means of further augmenting critical-thinking skills.

The concluding chapter expresses the author's personal reflections.

CHAPTER 15

Multicultural Activities

"Prejudice is an awful thing. It made a lot of people suffer and still does."
—Katherine, seventh-grade student, Willets Road School, East Williston, New York

More than ever before, the U.S. population is characterized by cultural diversity. Currently, ethnic minorities constitute over 20 percent of the school population, and the majority of the enrollment of almost all of the largest cities. By the year 2000, it is projected that 40 percent of the public school population will be children of color.

It is therefore no longer a question of teachers including a sprinkling of multicultural activities in the classroom. Teachers will "need to have an attitude of respect for cultural differences, to know the cultural resources their students bring to class, and to be skilled at using students' cultural resources in the teaching–learning process."[1]

"Service learning has the potential to help those concerned with issues of race and culture to move beyond talk to specific action," Rich Cairn points out. By its very nature, service learning requires collaboration between schools and a diversity of communities. In fact, to organize service projects in any community without adequately involving leadership from that community is to add to rather than to help solve the root problem."[2]

The following guidelines have been outlined by the National Youth Leadership Council for planning service learning projects with people of diverse cultures and ensuring that each group has an adequate opportunity to participate.[3]

- Listen.
- Don't do service *for* anyone. Serve *with* people.
- Cultivate flexibility.
- Create an environment that fosters the contributions of all.
- Challenge your own prejudices—we all have them.
- Respect the cultures of all learners.
- Train yourselves to work effectively with culturally diverse students and communities.
- Foster co-responsibility for each other.

Ungraded Activities

Celebrate the Diversity of the Country

Get to know the cultures of the various ethnic groups in your community and nationwide by studying their art, poetry, history, food, language, and heroes. Join in commemorating their holidays.

Many holidays and festivals celebrate tales of brave individuals who struggled to bring freedom to their people. These tales become part of their cultural heritage. For example, Diwali, the Hindu Festival of Lights, is so called in honor of the legend of the brave Crown Prince Rama, who fought evil forces in his country. His wicked stepmother had him exiled. When he was permitted to return, the people were overjoyed and lit candles in every house to show him the way. This holiday is celebrated in October to mark the beginning of a New Year. Hanukkah, a Jewish holiday, also honors the struggles of people against destruction of their temple.

Kwanzaa, an African-American festival, celebrates the African cultural heritage of Black Americans and their contributions to the world. It lasts seven days, from December 26 to January 1. Started in 1966 by Maulana Karenga of the California State University in Long Beach, it refers to the Swahili phrase "first fruits of the harvest." Candles are lit on each of the seven days to honor the seven guiding principles: unity, self-determination, collective work and responsibility, cooperative economics, purpose, creativity, and faith. The last day is generally marked by a feast and gifts of toys for the children.

A Korean holiday, Chusok, known as the Harvest Moon Festival, is celebrated on the fifteenth day of the eighth month of the lunar calendar, usually in September when the moon is farthest from the earth. Families gather to share food delicacies, count their blessings, and honor the deceased. Towns have firework displays, and kids play special games.

Kids can research other holidays: the Moslem festival of Ramadan, the Native American celebration of the winter solstice, Mexican holidays of Cinco de Mayo and Three Kings' Day, as well as occasions such as the Japanese Children's Day, and the Chinese Dragon Boat Festival. They can celebrate Puerto Rico week in November, and find out how different groups celebrate the New Year.[4]

Holiday celebrations need to be handled sensitively and linked to curriculum wherever possible. Louise Sparks notes that some multicultural activities that "teach about cultures through celebrations and artifacts of the culture as food, traditional clothing and household implements" may deteriorate into a tourist curriculum, which is "patronizing, emphasizing the 'exotic' differences between cultures, and trivializing, dealing not with the real-life daily problems and experiences of different peoples but with surface aspects of their celebrations and modes of entertainment."[5]

Ingrid Sausjord adds a similar caveat: "Activities which expose students to the traditional dress, holiday foods, or other 'typical' features of a racial or ethnic group may not be helpful. Done in isolation, such activities can inadvertently bolster habits of steryotyping. Unless linked to the core curriculum, they also may reinforce the notion that the particular racial or ethnic group is not an integral part of American society."[6]

Day of the African Child

This day, which focuses on children of African descent, is a worldwide holiday promoted by the United Nations Children's Fund (UNICEF) and the Organization of African Nations. Wearing homemade African clothes and waving flags of African nations, students congregate at the United Nations on October 15. They sing African songs, observe presentations, and meet African children. The holiday is observed officially in many schools. It commemorates the 1976 uprising and massacre of students in Soweto, South Africa, when ten thousand Black students protested against a government regulation requiring the use of the Afrikaans language in the schools.

Martin Luther King Birthday

This holiday is now observed in over 100 nations around the world. Concerned that remembrance of Dr. King had become routine in some schools students have been organizing schoolwide celebrations that include the community. At one event a group enacted a skit depicting the bus boycott sparked by Rosa Parks. Others read from Dr. King's speech at the Washington memorial. They invited residents who had participated in the civil rights movement of the 1960s to tell of their experiences, and they prepared displays of Dr. King's work.

Coretta Scott King, Martin Luther King's widow, has initiated a drive to rededicate the holiday as a time of peace and unity for all Americans and a day when people engage in community service. Suggesting the slogan "service, not shopping," Mrs. King, speaking at the United Nations, stated: "We want the holiday to become a time for every American to make a contribution to alleviate homelessness...fight drugs and crime...to reach out to make a difference."

Encourage the kids in your class to organize a special service day in the spirit of Mrs. King's statement.

Thanksgiving Feast of Ideas

To counteract the stereotypes and misinformation associated with Native Americans and Thanksgiving Day, Barbara Bernard, a literacy consultant for the Anchorage School District in Alaska, worked with teachers to organize a Thanksgiving Feast of Ideas "as an opportunity for teachers to think critically about the topic of cultural encounters."

In workshops and after-school sessions, teachers prepared units for the Thanksgiving Feast of Ideas, which included ethical considerations of one people conquering another, lifestyles and traditions of different Native American peoples, the pilgrimage, a simulated invasion, and a comparison of the first Thanksgiving menu with a current one. Students were guided to separate facts about Thanksgiving from misinformation. Authentic Native American recipes were shared, as well as legends, an important part of Native American history.[7]

African-American Read-in-Chain

Over a two-day period, hundreds of thousands of Americans congregate in homes, schools, churches, libraries, bookstores, community groups, and even homeless shelters to read works by African-American writers. They are participating in the "African-American Read-in-Chain," scheduled on the first Sunday and Monday in February, as part of Black History Month.

Sponsored by the National Council of Teachers of English and its Black Caucus, the Read-in was started in 1990 to celebrate the African-American literary tradition. Dr. Jerrie Scott, director of the project, explains: "The contributions of African Americans to literature have sometimes been overshadowed by an image of illiteracy. This activity is an attempt to reverse that image."

During the two days, all Americans are encouraged to gather with family, friends, large groups, or organizations to read works at the same time by African-American authors and poets—novices and professionals. Sunday at 4:00 P.M. is reserved for community groups, Monday for schools and businesses. Volunteers from all ethnic groups are asked to host a Read-in in their communities and to document participation. The goal is to have one million readers by the year 2000.[8]

Reach Out to a School

As they study world communities, children become aware of the shortage of school supplies in many Third World countries. They can contact embassies or United Nations representatives for a school they might help.

Students collect school supplies—paper, pencils, pens, compasses, crayons—and send these regularly. Kids in these countries may be studying English, so texts and easy children's books are also helpful. Some students may wish to become pen pals with the foreign kids.

The Coppachuck Middle School in Gig Harbor, Washington, corresponds with kids from Zambia. The Coppachuck students help their pen pals with English and also send them school supplies.

Ethnic Cookbooks

Suggest that students collect ethnic recipes from community residents and organize them into a cookbook. They also solicit memories: How long have the recipes been in the family? How were they acquired? This information is included in the cookbook.

Prejudice Reduction through Literature

"We can be taught not to hate each other."

"I will not call anyone retarded again. I understand what it means."

—Student comments on evaluation of Prejudice Reduction Program

An annual interdisciplinary program to sensitize kids to the negative effects of prejudice has become part of the curriculum of the elementary and middle schools in the East Williston district on Long Island. Designed by Glenn Pribek, Curriculum Associate for Social Studies, the program involves students, parents, the entire staff of the school, and guest speakers.

The success of the program has led to its extension to the high school with a series of panel discussions and reports by educators who have experienced discrimination in their careers. Asked about the effect of the program, Pribek states: "I think it has made young people aware of the many ways people encounter prejudice and bias on a daily basis. Some kids don't realize how hurtful prejudice can be. The program is helping them to appreciate and respect people of diverse cultures and backgrounds."

Willets Road Middle School (Grades 5–7)

Pribek, together with the librarian and a committee of teachers, identifies a variety of children's literature on the theme of prejudice. These are annotated and copies distributed to faculty, administrators, and staff, who will later act as discussion leaders.

Guest speakers address each grade about their personal experiences with prejudice. One year, this included three Nazi Holocaust survivors, one of whom was a Catholic.

Students select their books with guidance from their English teachers. Letters are sent to parents informing them of the program and urging them "to take an interest in the book your children are reading and engage them in discussion."

Book discussion groups of children reading the same book are formed, preferably with no more than ten in a group and of mixed grade levels.

Group leaders are assigned from among the entire staff. They are briefed on leading discussions and are given questions to guide the talks. The questions relate both to the specific content of the book and to broader applications.

Two periods are set aside for group discussions. At the final one, students complete evaluation forms, and a follow-up bibliography is distributed. Group leaders are also asked to complete a program evaluation.

Northside School (Grades K–4)

A faculty committee, working with the school librarian, identifies appropriate children's literature dealing with a variety of groups that have encountered prejudice: the physically disabled, the elderly, and racial and ethnic minorities.

Guest speakers from the community and the student body visit each class and discuss their personal experiences with prejudice. About 35 students from the high school Intercultural Unity Club are assigned (one or two to a class) to read aloud to the kids and engage them in a carefully designed discussion.

Multiculturalism in the Elementary School Curriculum

In the Crossand Elementary School in Philadelphia (grades N–5), "multicultural understanding is the instructional curriculum," according to Principal Linda Epstein. With the school targeted for desegregation and kids bussed in, a primary goal is for the students to understand different cultures. A number of activities support this.

On United Nations Day in October, the school conducts a multicultural fair. Each class selects a country representative of the ethnic heritage of the school population, which now includes Polish, Greek, Irish, Russian, German, Latino, and African-American kids, and presents a program of that country's art, dance, and songs.

Members of foreign countries are invited to participatory assemblies where they involve the kids in hands-on activities. A speaker from Uganda, for example, brought implements and artifacts and presented a script based on a folktale with parts for the children to read. After the assembly, he continued activities with the first graders. A Native American speaker made a presentation to the whole school, then spent the rest of the time with fifth graders explaining the customs of his people.

Parents also participate. The school is accumulating multicultural books and hopes to buy instruments associated with different countries. Rounding out the program are cultural fairs with ethnic games and dances, and crosscultural visits with other schools.

Hispanics and Asian-Americans from the entire school population, including central administration, have been conscripted to conduct workshops for parents and teachers aimed at helping them understand each other's cultures. Epstein explains: "By stressing the importance of understanding other cultures at an early age, conflicts later in life are ameliorated."

Elementary School–High School Partnerships

An unusual partnership has been established between kids at the Bernard Harrif, Sr. Elementary School in Baltimore, Maryland, and the Francis Scott Key High School in Carroll County, a rural community outside of Baltimore. One Christmas, the young children wrote letters to Santa Claus. Students at the high school volunteered to respond, and a pen pal relationship resulted. The high school became involved with the kids, at one point preparing attendance banners for the school as an incentive for improved attendance.

Harrif's students are 99 percent African American, Key's mostly Caucasian. During Black History Month, the elementary school kids were invited to the high school to teach the older students about African-American history. This motivated the kids to do added research in order to be well informed.

Learning from Native Americans

Jeanne Damone's fourth-grade class of kids, primarily of Carribean descent, at P.S. 161 in Crown Heights, Brooklyn, selected "What Do Native Americans Teach Us about Living in Harmony with Nature?" as their social studies theme. A goal of the unit was to illustrate the respect with which Native Americans respond to their environment.

Two artists, Jennifer Zitron and Margaret Pettee, volunteered to work with the kids twice weekly to integrate art into the unit. They accompanied the children on field trips to different anthropological and natural history museums to sketch. In their science class, the kids discussed how Native Americans related to the environment.

Children learned to keep individual drawing journals to supplement their writing journals. A jazz pianist who was part Cherokee spoke to the class about his childhood and musical influences. A legend-like Native American story was written and dramatized by the children. The kids also established a pen pal relationship with fourth graders at the Zuni Reservation Middle School in New Mexico.

Culmination of the unit was the design and construction of an 8' × 6' mosaic mural made from recycled tiles and donated surplus materials. And the "most wonderful thing": the mural was exhibited at the Brooklyn Children's Museum for a three-month period, along with the kids' journals and other artwork. (Chapter 10 contains more details on the art component of this program.)

Activities for Intermediate, Middle, and Junior High

Combat Bias

Students in Commack, Long Island, were horrified when they returned to school after a weekend and found anti-Semitic slogans painted on the school track and football stands. This was one incident in a growing number of bias and racist incidents throughout the country. School districts are reacting.

The Commack district organized a "Face the Hate Week" with sensitivity groups to discuss discrimination and stereotypes, films, and a cross-cultural festival. Despite the recognition that one week can't change behavior, high school Principal Ron Vale stated: "We've got to keep chipping away at it. We're hoping that this will stimulate thinking among the kids and lead to other follow-up activities."[9]

Other districts have added anti-bias activities to their curricula in recognition that early intervention is essential. On Long Island, for example, the Rockville Centre Middle School has instituted a counseling program, PINK (Prejudice Is Not Kool); the Longwood Middle School features STAR (Students Together against Racism) and BUTY (Bring Unity to Youth).

Many educators believe that parent involvement is essential. They work with PTAs to organize anti-bias parent committees and multicultural activities. The East Williston book program, "Prejudice Reduction through Literature," discussed earlier in this chapter, encourages parents to engage children in discussion on books that relate instances of prejudice.[10]

Courses in Cultural Awareness

The Shoreham–Wading River Middle School presents a three-week course in Human Rights Education, specifically tailored to build cultural awareness; challenge stereotypes; and confront ageism, sexism, racism, and prejudice against kids who are different—the fat, the skinny, the exceptional.

The course includes sessions on kids' perceptions, rumors, media influence, stereotypes, discrimination, and slavery. Kids learn scientific explanations for differences in appearance and skin color. They discuss the discrimination against Asians during World War II. They applaud those who fought against hate by protecting Jews during the Nazi era, and those who battled for civil rights during the 1960s.

At the end of the course, they frankly share the prejudices they had or had observed and discuss steps that can be taken in school to eradicate prejudice. One they quickly agree on is that there will be "no more name-calling." A school club has been formed called: Bring Unity to Youth (BUTY) to stress "pride in what you are."

A number of partnerships have been established with schools of different ethnic backgrounds, some of which have a similar course: in Riverhead, Long Island; New York City; Bridgeport, Connecticut; and a Japanese school in Greenwich, Connecticut. Students exchange visits and field trips.

The course is taught by Joanne Urgess, the Service Learning Coordinator, who is enthusiastic about the reactions of the kids. "I see the best in the students," she explains.

Holocaust Tiles

Eighth-grade students in a number of schools, including those in Southhampton, Long Island, were invited to design tiles that became part of the Holocaust Museum in Washington, D.C. This followed a discussion of the Holocaust and *The Diary of Anne Frank.*

Translate Children's Books

Spanish language classes in the middle schools have undertaken to translate beginning children's readers for children of newly arrived Latino immigrants. Because Asian languages are not taught in most middle schools, however, this has rarely been done for children of Asian immigrants. If there is a large Asian immigrant population in your town, students can ask for help from a university professor or someone in the community fluent in the language to translate easy readers for Asian kids. Art students can illustrate them, and they can photocopy as many as needed. This activity can be extended to other ethnic populations too.

Multiculturalism in the Service Program

The Lee Middle School in Fort Myers, Florida, has a culturally diverse student, faculty, and staff population. Multiculturalism is one of the segments of their service program. This segment has three components: trust building, training, and communication.

Trust Building. Guidance counselors, teachers, administrators, parents, and students participate in six hours of activities devoted to building trust, developing decision-making skills, and cultivating respect for diversity.

Training. The participants form a core group to train the rest of the student body in the skills they acquired. There are about twenty five field trips to ensure that all students participate.

The school is also building a Project Adventure trail with a rope challenge course that will involve students, faculty, staff, and community residents in activities emphasizing teamwork, trust building, and decision making. It is viewed as a resource to prepare students and adults from diverse backgrounds to co-exist effectively and harmoniously.

Communication. All students in each grade level, mixed by race and gender, are clustered in PODS of nine. These remain constant throughout the school year and are the basis of all grouping for multicultural training and field trips. Each student writes to every member of her or his POD once each month as a means of becoming acquainted.

Students are also expected to read books with multicultural themes as part of their language arts curriculum.

Service in Native American Communities

Service has long been part of the ethic of Native American culture. Roger Buffalo Head, a Ponco elder, expressed this: "One of the things that has interested me over the years in terms of Native education is that what you call service learning is how Native people transmitted knowledge and culture in their own communities."[11]

Spearheaded by the National Indian Youth Leadership Project (NIYLP), service projects have proliferated in Native schools. McClellan Hall, director of the NIYLP, explains: "Service is a way to reconnect our youth with the community's traditional values that have been around for a thousand years. It is the common bond that holds our communities together."

It is interesting that terms exist in various Native American languages to describe a service ethic.

Native American Terms

- *Gadugi* is a Cherokee tradition. It is a call to bring people together to help one another.
- *Si-yuu-dze*, in the Pueblos' Keres language, translates to "everybody's work," referring to communal services such as cleaning irrigation ditches, planting corn, and preparing the plazas for ceremonies.
- *Yanse'lihanna* is a Zuni term similar in meaning to the one above.
- *Bik egho da iiani* is a Navaho concept that views compassion as "giving direction to life."
- *Yaa-joo-ba*, also Navaho, means "having compassion for others above all else." It was applied to Navajo leaders in the olden days.
- *Mitakuya owasin* is a Lakota term meaning "we are all as relatives."

Every summer, Hall runs camps for Indian youth, one for six- and seven-year-olds and another for kids seven and eight years-old. He describes the camps as "ignition experiences." The kids design and carry out a service project during their stay in camp and then use the skills acquired to plan year-round activities at their schools. They receive help from a mentor from the school or community to carry out the projects. A key objective of the camp is to instill a model of leadership. Hall describes a leader as "one who leads by helping and empowering others. Above all," he adds, "a leader is a servant of the people."

Native American youth have piled up an impressive record of service activities, such as the following.

Adopt a Highway

Acoma Sky City School seventh and eighth graders adopted one mile of a highway on their reservation to demonstrate their commitment to revitalizing their community. The entire school participated in an all-day trash clean-up.

The Acoma Pueblo is the oldest continuously inhabited city in the United States, dating back to 1140.

Buddy Works

A peer tutoring program teams Acoma Sky City middle schoolers with kindergarten kids. The older students meet with their "kinder-buddies" once a week preparing their own lesson plans and tutoring materials.

Prime Time

This programs builds partnerships between young people and adults in the Zuni Middle School through mentor relationships with Zuni staff.

Plant Trees

One hundred Zuni seventh and eighth graders planted trees at a Zuni forest to revitalize the area.

There is an interesting anecdote which inspired another tree planting project back in 1988. At that time, the entire NIYLP summer camp population, eighty in all, visited Canyon de Chelly, one of the most scenic locations on the Navaho reservation. Their Navaho guide told about the bloody history of the canyon. In 1860, Kit Carson and the U.S. Army rounded up Navahos, destroyed their homes and crops, and chopped down the fruit trees in a effort to drive the Navahos from the canyon. A youth with the camp group was so moved that he suggested that the youngsters replant peach trees in the canyon. They started in 1989 and have planted one every year since.

Service at Laguna

Elementary students at Laguna Elementary take part in a program called, SOS (Save Our Students), geared to helping students with special needs. Staff members trust that student participation in service programs will not only improve their academic skills but also prepare them to assume the role of a caring tribal leader in the future.

Unit at David Skeet Elementary

A thematic unit at Skeet celebrates Native American culture through studying Native American values. Service projects at David Skeet also include intergenerational learning, peer tutoring, and environmental awareness.

Help with a Pow-Wow

Junior high school students at Taos, New Mexico, were recognized by their tribe for helping with a pow-wow and raising money for local runners.

Adopt a Lake

Zuni Middle School students adopted Eustace Lake on a Zuni reservation in New Mexico. They cleaned the lake, built trails, stocked it with fish, and built a recreation and picnic area.

Build a Playground

Working together with their teachers, fifth- to eighth-grade kids from four tribes, Navaho at Ramah, Acoma, Zuni, and Laguna, built a playground for Laguna Elementary School.

Notes

1. Yvonne Rodriguez, Barbara Sjostrom, and Ana Maria Villegas, "Approaches to Cultural Diversity in the Classroom," Report, American Association of Colleges for Teacher Education. San Diego, California, February 25, 1993.
2. Rich Cairn, *Generator, Journal of Service-Learning and Youth Leadership* (Roseville, MN: National Youth Leadership Council, Spring 1993), p. 2.
3. Ibid., p. 15.
4. Dates celebrating holidays of different groups are included in the multicultural calendar in Pamela Tiedt and Iris Tiedt, *Multicultural Teaching* (Boston: Allyn and Bacon, 1990).

5. Louise Derman-Sparks and the ABC Task Force. *Anti-Bias Curriculum* (Washington, DC: National Association for the Education of Young Children, 1992), p. 7. This is an excellent resource for multicultural activities for young children.

6. Ingrid Sausjord, "Service Learning for a Diverse Society," *Network* (Los Angeles: Constitutional Rights Foundation, Fall 1993), p. 2.

7. Barbara A. Bernard, "If It's November, It Must Be Indians," *Teaching Tolerance* (Montgomery, AL: Southern Poverty Law Center, Fall 1993), pp. 54–56.

8. For more information on the Read-In, contact Dr. Jerrie Scott, National Coordinator, African-American Read-In Urban Literacy/Lower Library, Central State University, Wilberforce, OH 45384 (513-376-6715).

9. *New York Times*, Sunday, October, 17, 1993, p. 13.

10. Many national organizations, such as the NAACP, American Civil Liberties Union, Anti-Defamation League, and local human rights groups, have multicultural programs and materials available for schools.

11. Comment at the National Service Learning Conference, St. Paul, Minnesota, 1991.

CHAPTER 16

Students with Special Needs

"It teaches the special kids what it's like to be givers rather than receivers of services."
—Jill Eisner, special education teacher, Harper's Choice Middle School, Columbia, Maryland

Middle school students tutoring elementary school kids...planting marsh grass to prevent beach erosion...collecting and mending used clothing for children in shelters...sewing colorful patches on jeans...delivering food to the homeless. Elementary kids calling bingo games and leading physical exercises in senior centers...collecting toys for children in shelters.

All of these are fairly typical service activities. But what is special about these programs is that they are all being performed by kids in special education classes, some with severe mental retardation or other disorders. Service learning, as a program of inclusion, encourages these kids, frequently for the first time, to work alongside other kids. It eliminates the isolation many exceptional kids have previously felt. "Students with disabilities are breaking into the life of the school, and their prestige is beginning to soar within both the school and the community," reports Cathy Brill.[1]

In the process, the general population kids who work with them also are changing. By collaborating on projects with the exceptional kids, they confront their preconceived notions of these children. As they do so, they become more sensitive and empathetic, learning to look past the impairments to the persons, past the differences to the similarities among all kids. Gradually, their stereotypes about exceptional kids begin to break down.

The exceptional kids learn to be less self-conscious about their impairments. Patt Kells states, "service learning programs improve disabled students' self-images because they provide an avenue for interacting in the community with dignity where nondisabled peers see them as "not so different after all."[2]

Service learning projects benefit from the participation of the exceptional kids. With careful preparation and orientation, and frequent reinforcement, they can take part successfully in most activities. At the service site, personnel will need to be aware of the characteristics of the special group, to be briefed about specific problems, and to be assured that they will be adequately supervised and prepared for their responsibilities.

When projects team exceptional students with other classes in the school for service, both groups need to know what to anticipate. It is important that the general population view the exceptional kids realistically. That implies that they recognize their special problems but also recognize their capabilities, and that the kids will be assigned meaningful roles.

Like all kids, at the completion of each service experience, exceptional kids need opportunities to reflect. By sharing reactions in group discussions, they gain insight into their potentials for service as well as into aspects of their community with which they may have had little or no contact. Individual reflection should also be encouraged. Kids with language problems can do this through drawing journals or photographs.

In some of the activities cited here, special education classes work together with other classes in the school; in others, they initiate and carry out a project on their own. Also included in this chapter are examples of programs aimed at sensitizing all kids to the problems of exceptional children.

Where kids are mainstreamed, they are routinely included in the service activities of their classes. As a result, there are no separate reports of these activities.

Ungraded Activities

First-Grade Buddies

At the William Penn Elementary School in Indianopolis, first graders have a "buddy" relationship with special education preschool kids. They hold their buddies' hands while accompanying them to lunch, to the bathroom, or else-where in the school. They share books with their buddies. The first graders also have learned to push wheelchairs.

"The relationship benefits both groups," asserts Ginger Lentz, Service Learning Coordinator. The preschoolers have a first grader as a friend; and she adds, "Imagine the pride of the first graders at the responsibilities they have been assigned!"

Plan an Olympics

At the same school, William Penn fourth and sixth graders planned an Olympics program for the special pre-school kids. They organized relays, including relays in wheelchairs, ball games, races, and other activities.

Prepare Kids for Special Olympics

A number of schools have programs that help physically-challenged kids prepare for the Special Olympics. They train them for events, give them an opportunity to practice sport skills, and frequently accompany them to the games.

Multiple Projects

Friends Academy students in Locust Valley, New York, participate in a Halloween Fair with students at a local Helen Keller Institute. They also arrange for riding lessons for exceptional students at a nearby stable and help train kids for the Special Olympics.

Teaming in the Fresh Force Program

A districtwide Fresh Force service program at the Battle Creek Middle School in St. Paul, Minnesota, is enriched by integrating exceptional students. The other students act as buddies to the exceptional kids helping them engage in service-learning projects. Together they measure and pack food such as cornmeal, pasta, popcorn seeds, oranges, and onions to be distributed in the community. They also help them construct, stain, and paint wooden toys and flowers for kids in shelters.

Environmental Projects

Ten severely retarded kids at the Harper's Choice Middle School in Columbia, Maryland, participate with other students at the school in a number of environmental activities. They have planted marsh grass to prevent soil erosion along the Chesapeake Bay, planted trees, and painted storm drains. Special education teacher Jill Eisner pointed to the advantages of a joint project. Working together gives the general population an opportunity to recognize the capabilities of the retarded students. Because the exceptional kids' orientation is vocational, in some instances, such as projects related to horticulture, these students may be better informed than their partners.

The inclusion program at Harper's Choice was initiated by David Patterson, a teacher at the school. He also involves special kids on outdoor education trips.

Service with Seniors

The exceptional students at Harper's Choice also helped serve at a senior citizens' center. The service helped the kids learn appropriate behavior as they shared lunch with the seniors, joined in craft activities, and gradually expanded their activities throughout the year. Many seniors are particularly patient and helpful to kids with disorders, and kids in turn respond easily to them. At a party given for all volunteers, the exceptional kids were particularly pleased to be singled out for recognition.

At the Oakville Elementary School in Mechanicsville, Maryland, special education students in Sonia Thurmond's class teamed with a third-grade class for a project with seniors. Contact with seniors is especially important at this school because it draws its students from a community near a military base, and most of the kids do not have grandparents closeby.

The seniors came to the school once a month and made paper toys and art objects for the kids; the kids made chocolate kisses for the seniors on Valentine's Day. The kids interviewed the seniors, clipped grocery store coupons for them (great for fine motor control for the exceptional kids), and exchanged cards and notes.

At first there was concern that there might not be enough interested seniors, but after the first visit there were more than enough. The third graders and kids in the special education class are now more accepting of each other, Thurmond reports. All the students are more outgoing and communicate more easily with adults. This was evident when the group invited veterans from a nearby veterans' home to the class. The teachers were concerned because the veterans weren't very communicative, but the kids took over and, by talking to them, succeeded in getting them to answer questions and invited them back.

Serving the Homeless

When Judy Starr was a fourth-grade teacher at the Corrales Elementary School in New Mexico, she instituted an award-winning program for the homeless. Subsequently, she transferred to the Los Ranchos Elementary School in Albuquerque, where she is in charge of eight exceptional students, some learning disabled, others with severe communication or behavior disorders.

She has continued her activities for the homeless with her exceptional students and has found them very responsive. They are eager to help and solicit items for a homeless shelter throughout the school and community: blankets, sleeping bags, shoes, and personal items. They also raise money through bake sales or donations. Although some of the youngsters lack speaking or writing skills, Starr points out that they grasp the social situation and are proud to take part.

Starr ruminates, "It's interesting that those who have less, sometimes involve themselves more."

Relating to Exceptional Kids

"Kids on the Block"

A unique program at the Bala Cynwyd Middle School in Pennsylvania teaches young children about disabilities. Originated by parents, the program is based on a type of Japanese puppetry known as Bun Ra Ku and uses life-sized puppets to simulate children with various conditions, such as profound visual impairment, communication disorders, mental retardation, or physical challenges. The young kids learn about the puppets and then have to act as if they had the disabling condition.

Scripts are given to the young kids that summarizes the philosophy of the program: "We all have strengths; we all have weaknesses; we all learn but differently." "Just because I learn differently; just because I am in a wheelchair, I still can learn."

Learn to Sign

Students can learn a song in sign language. They then visit a school for the hard-of-hearing and sign the song while they sing it. Perhaps they can follow this by becoming pen pals with the other kids.

Wheelchair Ramps

Students in a middle school, incensed by the inaccessibility of spots in their community for wheelchairs, fanned out to check this. They discovered that, in some cases, required wheelchair ramps had not been installed; others were not in conformance with regulations. They reported this to authorities and also arranged for a project to build the ramps with aid from local carpenters, other members of the community, and technology students.

Notes

1. Quoted in "Serve America," Newsletter of the Commission on National and Community Service, Washington, D.C., August 1993, p. 6. Cathy Brill is director of special education for the Maryland Student Service Alliance, which has produced a manual and a curriculum for students with mental retardation.
2. Ibid., p. 6. Patt Kells is executive director of the Kansas Office for Community Service.

CHAPTER 17

Resolving Conflict

"I used to kick people when I was angry. But now I talk it out."

—Desiree, mediator, P.S. 40, New York City

As schools struggle with increasing instances of violence, programs for resolving conflict are mushrooming throughout the states. They have been described as teaching a basic skill: "emotional literacy." Their objective is to educate kids to solve problems without resorting to violence and to cope with a range of emotions—anger, frustration, jealousy, and fear. As Linda Lantieri, national director of the Resolving Conflict Creatively Program, puts it, "to show students that they have choices for dealing with conflict besides passivity or aggression."

Two of the programs frequently employed are Resolving Conflict Creatively and Educators for Social Responsibility.

Resolving Conflict Creatively (RCCP)[1]

The two fifth graders were wearing blue T-shirts with the word *mediator* printed on the front and back. They were monitoring the schoolyard during the lunch period. Suddenly, shouting erupted. Two girls were about to come to blows; each was pulling at a small leather pouch, each claiming ownership. The girl who was holding the pouch was emphatic: "I found it. Finders, keepers! Losers, weepers!" Just as emphatic was the other: "But it's mine, I dropped it!" The shouts were escalating. Quietly, the mediators interrupted: "Hi, I'm Sarah and she's Desiree. Would you like to try mediation?" The disputants hesitated. Finally there was a reluctant assent: "O.K." The group adjourned to a quiet area in the lunchroom.

The structured mediation commenced. First there was a statement of the rules. Mediators asked kids to agree to ground rules:

1. Help solve the problem.
2. No interrupting.
3. No name-calling.

When the girls acquiesced, the mediation proceeded step by step. The same questions were asked of each: "What happened?" "What could you have done differently?" "What can you do now to solve the problem."

Mediators are trained to listen actively, note body language, and paraphrase what each person is saying. In this case, it was the last question, "What can you do now to solve the problem?" that was thorny. Finally, the youngster who claimed that the purse had originally been hers suggested that she call her mother to affirm that it had been bought for her. This was accepted when the other youngster was given permission to place the call.

At this point a mediator turned to each: "Do you accept the solution?" They agreed. The purse was left with the mediators. The two girls were asked to shake hands. They walked out chatting amiably.

This incident was a typical peer mediation session at P.S. 40 in lower Manhattan. It lasted about fifteen minutes. All the kids at the school are familiar with the program. Mediators are viewed as neutral. They do not have the power to impose solutions. More and more often, kids seem to welcome an opportunity to resolve a dispute without losing face.

P.S. 40 is one of over two hundred schools in New York and in selected districts throughout the country in the Resolving Conflict Creatively Program. It is the largest such program in the country, a collaboration of the New York City Board of Education and Educators for Social Responsibility.

Twenty-four fifth graders are trained as mediators each year in half-day workshops over a period of about a week. Mediators are nominated and elected in their classes. Teachers can screen the lists, but there is no behavior or grade threshold. Kids in special education classes and kids who have themselves been in trouble frequently are selected as mediators.

Three volunteer teachers, who also attend workshops, participate as coaches. On a rotating schedule, four mediators are assigned to patrol the schoolyard and lunchroom each lunch period. A coach is also on duty. Mediators are instructed not to interfere in fist fights or drug-related incidents. These are reported to the coaches.

"Young kids live in a climate of violence from movies, television and even in their neighborhoods," Ben Dratel, a coach of the program, explains. Another coach, physical education teacher Andrew Bieber, adds: "We are not trying to eliminate conflict; that's not necessarily negative. What we want to do is show kids that there are alternatives for dealing with conflict."

Rules for "fighting fair" are posted:

1. Identify the problem.
2. Focus on the problem.
3. Attack the problem, not the person.
4. Listen with an open mind.
5. Treat a person's feeling with respect.
6. Take responsibility for your actions.

A key by-product of the program is that it "empowers kids," teaching them that they are capable of solving problems. "When kids have disputes," Jim Tobin, staff developer for RCCP, explains, "adults tend to be impatient, acting as the judge and jury, frequently imposing solutions." In this program, both sides can present their points of view; someone listens, and they are more apt to arrive at a fair solution.

Although some schools in the program focus only on peer mediation, this is but one aspect of the RCCP program, which also includes:

- Twenty-four-hour training courses for teachers
- Classroom instruction in creative conflict resolution, affirmation of self-esteem, bias awareness, and mediation skills. (Starting in kinder-

garten, situations are simulated and youngsters are taught to cooperate and come up with a "win-win" solution.)
- Classroom visits by consultants
- Monthly two-hour follow-up sessions with teachers

Before the program was put into effect in P.S. 40, coaches went into every class explaining the difference between "put-ups" and "put-downs." Laughs at the expense of others and "disses" hurt, they emphasized. The school integrated the program into the curriculum. A Conflict Resolution Month was proclaimed. Classes made banners and wrote poetry, skits, and songs that were presented at a special assembly. The yearbook theme was "peace and conflict resolution." Parents have been supportive. Sixteen volunteered for training as future coaches.

When the impact of the program was evaluated, there was testimony that the entire school climate had changed since the institution of the program. As proof, a coach noted that previously during any lunch period, kids were sent to the principal's office in droves for having committed some infraction. Now it is rare to see any there. Heather, one of the mediators, summed it up: "When we started we had more problems than we could mediate in a lunch hour. Now there are days when there are no problems."

The impact on the mediators themselves has been dramatic. Sarah explained: "I used to be a tattletale. As a mediator, I learned I can't talk about anybody else's problems." William looked for the program "to help me in the future." The coaches were even more explicit in praising the youngsters: "These kids are the leaders of tomorrow. Parents report that they have shown their entire families acceptable ways of dealing with conflict."

An end-of-the-year picnic was held in Valley Stream Park for the mediators, where they were presented with medals. "And you know, we were there from 8:45 A.M. to after 3:00 P.M. in this large park with twenty-four kids," Jim Tobin reported, "and there was not even one fight."

Educators for Social Responsibility (ESR)[2]

This program organizes workshops and training sessions for teachers nationwide to develop teaching strategies for multicultural education as well as conflict resolution. A relatively recent project, STOP (Schools Teaching Options for Peace), is directed at middle school students in New York City.

STOP includes an intensive three-day workshop to train parents and teachers, at which the forty-lesson STOP curriculum is introduced. It focuses on understanding the components of conflict resolution: communication, cooperation, affirmation, and intergroup relations. Teachers then present the curriculum in classes over a one-year period with help from staff developers from STOP.

Workshop participants, parents, and teachers go into the schools and train up to thirty-five students as peer mediators. In the middle schools, the peer mediators provide full-day coverage. Disputes are referred to them by teachers and guidance counselors, and they may be called out of class on a rotating basis when needed. STOP places considerable emphasis on parent participation. To reflect the diverse population of the schools, parent training is frequently conducted in Chinese or Spanish, with Russian and Haitian Creole to be added.

Changes in the climate of schools have already been noted, according to STOP director Bruce Gill, and are evident in the "language of students. They are more apt to talk to each other about conflicts." Increased parent participation is also apparent. Gill adds, "STOP respresents a potentially powerful intervention for changing the environment in schools."

Other Programs

There are other programs for conflict resolution, many with only minor variations from those discussed here. In St. Paul, Minnesota, the program of the Inner City Youth League, "preventing and resolving nonviolent conflict," includes strategies for culturally based approaches and extends from elementary school to high school. Mediators are selected by asking students in each class to "pick the person you trust the most, to whom you would turn with a problem." Disputes are referred and mediated twice a week in two-hour meetings. Disputes are not limited to lunch hours; they may be class-related. Mediators may also be taken out of class in an emergency.

In Chicago and Urbana, a three-tiered approach includes training students in violence prevention, teachers in positive classroom discipline, and parents in creating a threat- and violence-free atmosphere in the home. Over four thousand students in sixteen elementary schools are involved.

Many kids today arrive at school troubled and unable to handle their emotions, particularly anger and aggressive feelings. All the programs agree that early intervention is essential, that emotional education must teach children peaceful means of resolving conflicts if the increase in violence in the schools is to be halted.

Notes

1. RCCP is at 163 Third Avenue, #239, New York, New York.
2. National headquarters of Educators for Social Responsibility is at 23 Cambridge Street, Cambridge, MA 02138.

CHAPTER 18

School Partnerships

"Kids trail me through the halls asking for a lunch buddy."
—Janice Lacey, program coordinator, Oak Grove Elementary School, Richmond, Virginia

As students go into their communities for their service learning assignments, community organizations are reversing the process—going into schools to help educate youngsters. Corporations, government agencies, and local groups are forming partnerships with schools, releasing their employees to tutor kids, become "buddies" with them, and serve as role models. The adults introduce kids to the world of work and expose them to careers.

These partnerships are expanding rapidly, led by large corporations which, instead of complaining about inadequate education, are beginning to view themselves as part of the solution. In a period of shrinking resources for education, the partnerships provide extra help for the school and a boost for the kids, particularly for those who have had no previous exposure to the business community.

The National Association of Partners in Education, Inc. (NAPE), an organization devoted to encouraging the formation and growth of school partnerships nationwide, reported that there were close to three million volunteers involved in "the nation's partnership initiatives in local school districts."[1] A broad spectrum of community groups are included: parent organizations, businesses, health care agencies, universities, the media, labor unions, community clubs and organizations, foundations, and government.

NAPE defines education partnerships as a "collaborative effort between a school(s) or school district(s) and one or more community organizations with the purpose of improving the academic and personal growth of America's youth."

Examples of Partnership Programs

The programs are varied. A number of different patterns are described here.

Local Employees Working with Kids

In the Oak Grove Elementary School, the "Lunch Buddy," project pairs volunteers from businesses and city agencies with at-risk kids throughout Richmond public schools on a one-to-one basis. A similar program, "Business Partners in Education" in Indianapolis, Indiana, between the Chamber of Commerce and public schools, places ten to twenty volunteers per day in the schools. They act as individual mentors and "special friends," arrange for job shadowing by the students, and collaborate on a variety of projects.

"Lunch Buddy"

Oak Grove Elementary School, Richmond, Virginia

"This program is the most fantastic thing to come to the school since the invention of ice cream."
—Janice Lacey, program coordinator

No "buddy" would deny that Thursday is a special day. Every Thursday from 12:00 noon to 12:45 P.M., employees from the Richmond Department of Public Works, dressed in their work uniforms, sit down to lunch with their buddies in the relaxed environment of the school's media center, away from the hustle and bustle of the cafeteria. Thirty-five adults participate; about half on the first and third Thursday of the month, the other half on the second and fourth. Each employee has been paired with a kid from third to fifth grade who has been identified as at risk, needing support and perhaps a role model. Oak Grove has an enrollment of about 525 youngsters, pre-K to fifth grade, about 98 percent African-American.

At lunch, the adult buddy may tutor or just chat about school progress, personal problems, or any other topic. It is not long before a warm ongoing relationship is established. Some of the adults see the kids on weekends, meet their parents, or invite them to a ball game or family outing. Some continue to tutor outside of school, play educational games, or help kids with projects. It is not unusual for kids to be involved with their buddies even when they graduate to middle school.

Asked about the reaction to the program, Janice Lacey replied: "It seems that all the kids want to take part. Kids trail me through the halls asking for a lunch buddy. Moms send notes asking for a buddy for their child. Our goal is to increase the number of participants."

There has been no formal assessment. Informally, however, teachers, comparing the buddies with nonparticipants, speak of a noticeable growth of self-esteem and improved academic performance among the buddies.

Teaming with a Local Bank

Another partnership pattern is exemplified by the BEST project, which pairs a bank with a middle school in Wantagh, New York, for community ventures.

BEST: Business and Education Serving Together

Wantagh Middle School, Wantagh, New York

"We wanted to express our gratitude to the community. Community service seemed the ideal vehicle."
—Dr. Carl Bonuso, assistant superintendent, Wantagh Public Schools

It happened that two key anniversaries fell in the same year, 1988, the twenty-fifth anniversary of the Wantagh Middle School and the thirty-fifth of the Chemical Bank in the same town. As they speculated on the possibility of a joint celebration, Dr. Carl Bonuso, then principal of the middle school and Anthony DeTomasso, vice-president of the bank, agreed that they wanted to do something for the community. It was from this premise that the award-winning service partnership between the bank and schools, BEST, was launched in Wantagh, New York.

Community service was not a new concept for either group. Details were easily decided. The bank donated $6,000 in seed money as well as contacts with the business community; the school provided "people power." Student participation was to be voluntary, after school or on weekends. For the first year, the goal would be a minimum of 2,500 hours of service by the students, 10 hours for each of the 25 years of the middle school's existence.

A constitution was written establishing a fifteen-member executive board consisting of parents, teachers, students, and community representatives, each with one vote. The board drafted an application for students who wished to participate. The response was enthusiastic. By the end of 1989, a bar graph prominently displayed in the school showed that over 5,000 hours of service had been contributed, twice the original goal.

BEST's first activity was a free car wash. Visible in their gold T-shirts, which had been purchased with part of the bank's donation, students spent a Saturday at the Chemical Bank parking lot, washing residents' cars and refusing any payment, even tips. Later, on Halloween, they escorted younger trick or treaters through the community to ensure their safety. On the Saturday following Halloween, they provided a treat for the town instead of a trick by painting over graffiti that had defaced business establishments near the middle school. Appreciative local merchants supplied rags, soap, and paints, and a local sign painter volunteered his help. These activities have become annual events.

Since those early days, BEST has been serving all segments of the community with a conglomeration of projects, many with the participation of teachers, parents, and other residents. They include:

- Building a rest area near the post office on property provided by the bank
- Restoring a local fireman's memorial
- Engaging in town beautification and cleanup programs
- Supervising kids at the polls during elections
- Acting as guides for back-to-school nights
- Serving juice and cookies for participants in school blood drives
- Raking leaves and shopping for homebound local seniors
- Organizing food drives for the needy
- Planning and presenting special holiday shows at a local geriatric center
- Creating valentines for seniors
- Entertaining children in pediatric wards
- Designing and marketing a unique Monopoly-type game to raise funds. Places on the board were sold to local businesses and families.

When the program was first established, the district was on austerity. The community had defeated the school budget. BEST has altered both the community's attitude to the schools and students and the students' attitude to the community. The community now views the schools as more of a focal point and has gained a new respect for the young people. In turn, students, recognizing their debt to the community, have been providing tangible evidence of their appreciation. At the same time, kids' demeanor at school has improved. There are fewer behavior problems. More and more students remain in school at the close of the day to plan activities.

The bank has continued its relationship with the district schools, offering students mock job interviews, assistance in preparing résumés, and opportunities for job shadowing. A few high school graduates have been employed by the bank. Bank officers report that the program has strengthened the bank's relationship with the community.

Although it is still mostly voluntary, Dr. Bonuso notes that the program has had a positive impact on the curriculum. He adds "as important as the academic growth is the affective growth, the curriculum of the heart, the moral fiber we engender in young people."

Other Partnerships

Some of these partnerships have been mentioned in the descriptions of individual schools in the preceding chapters—for example, the highly successful example of the partnership between Kiwanis seniors and Schuylkill elementary students. Some bear further description as examples of the various patterns.

Community ties are woven into the curriculum at the Hillside School in Montclair, New Jersey, where local CEOs helped students at the school set up a "stock market" for their "cookie corporation." In addition, a volunteer program, HOSTS (Helping One Student to Succeed) pairs 50 students with 50 adults— parents or representatives of local businesses—for enrichment in language arts.

In the South Bronx, P.S. 59 participates in a number of partnership programs. A tie-in with the New York City Volunteer Program permits fifth graders to meet regularly with the volunteers, as well as with parents and professionals from Literary Leaders to reinforce skills and to discuss and analyze stories they have read. "I've seen how much the children gain from this program," said resident Cindi Gonzalez, a volunteer who is so enthusiastic about her experience that she is going back to college to become a teacher.

The school also participates in Project BASIC (Business and Students Improving Community), which establishes a forum for local merchants and students to work together to improve their community. As part of this project, students created pictures and wrote compositions illustrating how they could make a difference in their community, at school, and at home. Merchants awarded prizes to the top students at a special assembly at which both students and business leaders spoke.

Many other New York City schools have cooperative arrangements. For example, employees of a law firm work with students at Midtown West Elementary. At Mott Hall Intermediate, employees of corporations and agencies assist in the preparation of students for service.

Students Trained by Organizations

In some instances, not-for-profit organizations invite students into their offices for service learning. While they help with office routines, kids are introduced to work and social skills—how to use office machines such as a fax machine or large copier, filing, telephone etiquette, communicating with clients or employees, dressing for work, and so forth.

Note

1. The National Association of Partners in Education, 209 Madison Street, Alexandria, VA 22314, is a nonprofit voluntary organization that provides training, technical assistance, materials, and other assistance to groups in the public and private sectors interested in establishing partnerships.

CHAPTER 19

Career Exploration

"At the Air Traffic Control Center, we learned that you must pass a test and be trained at the FAA Training Academy, and then get more training on the job if you want to be an Air Traffic Controller."
—Participants in Shoreham–Wading River Middle School Career Exploration Program

Kids may have outgrown the desire to be firefighters or secretaries when they grow up, but for most there is an appalling lack of information about the alternatives that exist. Many kids have little experience with the world of work, little knowledge of the careers out there. Aside from familiarity with family members' careers, students' knowledge may be limited to the professionals with whom they come in contact and to local service and shop people.

Career education is a natural by-product of service learning. Exposing youngsters to settings in which they can scrutinize people in different jobs expands their notions of career possibilities. Teachers deliberately call kids' attention to the careers of adults at the sites in which they are placed, such as careers in health, social services, environment, and teaching.

Youngsters for the first time begin to express more varied career goals, as indicated by these participants in service learning projects.

"I want to be an advocate for the environment."

"I want to work with animals."

"I want to be a park ranger."

"I want to be a doctor for little kids."

"I want to be a teacher."

"I want to be a community worker."

As the kids reflect on their experiences, they are better able to analyze and evaluate different careers. They are urged to indicate in their journals, whether the work suggests career possibilities. In this way their responses become more realistic. Further, they receive a new understanding of what it means to work at a job.

Many schools link career education more formally with service learning. The Redlands Middle School in Colorado invites professionals in architecture, parks service, landscaping, hospitals, media, construction, and other fields to its "Day of Caring," when students engage in a conglomeration of service projects. At that time, many work side by side with these professionals.

Since 1975, the Shoreham–Wading River Middle School has had a program that takes students into the community to observe people at work in different occupations. This pioneering program has evolved into an extension of their comprehensive service learning program. Schedules are arranged so that a block of time is available for students to engage in service projects in the field for a six- to eight-week period. At the conclusion, that same time period is utilized for career exploration. Kids' experiences in service learning placements have prepared them for work settings.

In seventh grade, the class is divided into teams of four. Each team goes into the community once a week for three weeks accompanied by a classroom teacher or community service organizer to investigate work sites. They may go to three different sites or return each week to a single locale, such as Brookhaven Laboratory or the Stony Brook Health Science Center, each time observing a different occupation there. At the conclusion of their visits, each team reports to the entire class about their observations, providing information to the class about twelve possible careers.

Some groups observe the sciences: marine science, energy, medicine and dentistry, agriculture, and veterinary medicine. Others focus on architecture, law and law enforcement, the arts, communication (newspapers, theater, radio, and television), construction, sports, aviation, and small businesses. At the sites, they receive firsthand information on the various jobs in the field with a description of the responsibilities, advantages and disadvantages, a typical day, current pay, educational requirements, and so on.

Before venturing into the field, students complete interest inventories, research various careers, start career booklets, and prepare interview questions. These questions enable the student to assess the pros and cons of a job and its educational requirements. For example, Joanne Urgese, director of the career program, reports: "the student learns what course work will be needed in high school for particular careers. One student who wanted to be a pilot was surprised to learn that pilots should have at least four years of math, including precalculus."

The career program is integrated into the academic program. Students maintain career booklets, write thank-you letters, and compare levels of pay. Speakers are invited into the classrooms throughout the unit.

In eighth grade, during the Home and Career class, students learn to complete applications, scan the classified advertisements, and search for "jobs I never heard of." The emphasis on careers in Shoreham continues into the high school, where students may be given internships and assistance in locating colleges that have majors related to their career interest.

CHAPTER 20

Critical Thinking

"I learned that the world is an awful place for poor people."
—Stephen, fifth-grade student, Johnshill Magnet School, Decatur, Illinois[1]

In the last few decades there has been a spate of material on critical thinking, yet there is little evidence that it has had any effect on students. Reports from industry and evaluations of high school graduates continue to reflect disappointment in the ability of graduates to think critically in job situations. Achievement tests continue to find students lacking higher-order thinking skills. "Conventional education at high school, college and graduate school level," according to Perkins of Harvard University's Graduate School of Education, "has hardly any effect on the development of general reasoning abilities.[2]"

The limited effectiveness of the material may result from the nature of many of the activities designed to promote critical thinking. In some cases, skills are taught in a separate course; but teaching skills in isolation may fail to engender a habit of critical thinking when kids are confronted with real problems.

Theoretically, integrating higher-order thinking skills with all subjects would appear to be the most desirable. However, this too may be problematical. Much depends on the curriculum. If it is concerned with canned subject matter with little relation to kids' real concerns, the chances are that kids will not be challenged to solve the problems presented.

Courses that include service learning experiences that confront students with real issues are particularly well suited to fostering critical thinking. Howe asserts that "providing experiences in real-life situations...increases the probability that (critical thinking) skills will be used."[3]

It is therefore not surprising that evaluations of service projects have almost uniformly pointed to improved critical thinking. It is not difficult to match a service learning project with a taxonomy of higher-order thinking skills and conclude that a well-designed program that fosters guided reflection will include the entire hierarchy. Service projects stress student planning, decision making, comprehension, application, analysis, synthesis, and evaluation through their insistence on reflection.

As students reflect on their experiences, they gain insight. They learn "to see with two eyes." They are forced to confront societal issues. They are encouraged to recognize their responsibility to participate in addressing some of the problems. These are two key components of critical thinking—analysis of real-life problems and consideration of potential solutions.

There are signs that this is in fact happening in many programs. For example, students in the Constitutional Rights Foundation's ACT program, described in

Chapter 5, are asked not only to assess and analyze community policies but also "how they are made and options available to effect change."

Similarly, the CRF City Youth L.A. program, described in Chapter 13, insists that students analyze their community—its institutions, problems, resources, and needs—and then design and implement projects to address the identified needs. The youngsters are directed to examine how decisions made at any one point in history affect later generations.

Although more and more programs are incorporating this kind of reflection, service learning advocates cannot be sanguine. Critical thinking does not develop automatically from service learning, nor can it be taken for granted that it will result from every service project. For example, Ingrid Sausjord of the Constitutional Rights Foundation, writes of another aspect. She notes that there is an expectation that service projects can reduce prejudice and help to improve relations among the many segments of society, and evidence that there have been encouraging changes. Yet she questions whether "we are making the most of the opportunities service learning offers."[4] There are real difficulties:

> *Children begin to become aware of racial and gender differences even before they start school. During elementary school, attitudes about differences begin to gel. By the time children reach age 12, many of them have developed an entire array of stereotypes. After the early adolescent years, it becomes more difficult to change these attitudes.*

Additional approaches are called for, she believes. Among them are "activities that develop critical thinking skills. [They] appear to be one of the more effective tools against prejudice...especially when they lead students to explore issues of prejudice, stereotyping and discrimination."

To generate critical thinking through service projects, much will depend on the quality of students' reflections. In turn, a point can be made that students' reflections are related to the quality of teachers' reflections. More and more, teachers are also being urged to engage in reflection, "to examine their own concepts, theories and beliefs about teaching, learning and subject-matter, and...to monitor their decisions about what and how they teach."[5] Reflection can go beyond questions: "How did the lesson go?" "Should I have taught it differently?"

There are degrees of teacher reflection. Smyth states that reflection "can vary from concern with micro aspects of the teaching-learning process...to macro concerns about political/ethical principles underlying teaching and the relationship of schooling to the wider institutions and hierarchies of society."[6] Teachers who are engaged with macro concerns can be said to be practicing critical reflection. Critical reflection is defined by Von Manen as consideration of the "moral and ethical issues of social compassion and justice along with the means and ends."[7]

Many impediments exist for teachers engaging in this kind of reflection. There is an argument that teachers quickly become socialized into the culture of the classroom and accept for the most part the roles and responsibilities of a bureaucratic system. This system is familiar to them; they were trained in it; to a large extent the ideas they formed came from texts biased in favor of the groups in power at the time. Teachers are not prepared by their own experiences in the school system to challenge accepted customs.

Nevertheless, if we accept as an objective of service learning the development of socially responsible, active, democratic citizens, then it is crucial that teachers guide students to analyze society, to question common practices, and to lead students to explore issues of "prejudice, stereotyping, and discrimination," as suggested by Sausjord.

Teachers can guide students' reflections by the questions they pose to students in the seminars and for their journals. Restricting reflection to kids' personal feelings about their service placements without asking them to consider social issues may be limiting. Just as a teacher who has not learned to ask higher level questions in the classroom will be less apt to induce critical thinking in students, so teachers who have not learned to employ critical reflection will be unable to take full advantage of the tremendous potential of service learning for developing thinking skills and producing effective public citizens.

Notes

1. Quoted in *Star Serve Bulletin* (Santa Monica, CA: Kraft General Foods Foundation, June 1992.
2. D. N. Perkins, "Thinking Frames," *Educational Leadership*, 43, 6.
3. Robert W. Howe, ERIC Report 335232, "Environmental Activities for Teaching Critical Thinking," June 1990.
4. Ingrid Sausjord, "Service Learning for a Diverse Society—Research on Children, Youth and Prejudice: Some Implications for Service Learning," *Network* (Los Angeles: Constitutional Rights Foundation, Fall 1993), p. 1.
5. George J. Posner, *Field Experience: Methods of Reflective Teaching*, 2nd ed. (New York and London: Longman, 1989), p. 25.
6. John Smyth, "Developing and Sustaining Critical Reflection in Teacher Education," *Journal of Teacher Education*, March–April 1989, p. 4.
7. M. Von Manen, "Linking Ways of Knowing with Ways of Being Practical," *Curriculum Inquiry*, 6, 205–228. Quoted in Georgea M. Sparks-Langer et al., "Reflective Pedagogical Thinking," *Journal of Teacher Education*, 41, 4:24.

CHAPTER 21

Personal Reflections

The completion of a project is a time for personal reflection. What has made this project so gratifying for me is that as I worked on the book, I became more and more convinced of the unique potential of service learning to reenergize our schools.

The value of service learning was constantly reinforced by reports from schools. Each new contact brought affirmation of the basic premise of this book—that learning is improved when kids participate in their communities, doing worthwhile tasks that give them an opportunity to apply and test their curricula. In the process, they gain in countless other ways, not only academically, not only in improved critical thinking, and not only in enhanced self-esteem. I found continued evidence of more subtle benefits—compassion and sensitivity to the less fortunate. This was summed up by the statement of one student, "I'll never call anyone a retard again."

This is also a time to reflect on the state of the art, the current status of service learning. There are encouraging portents. Programs continue to expand nation-wide. President Clinton is an ardent champion of service, committed to linking schools and communities and introducing students to the world of work.

Even in a time of dwindling resources, Congress has passed legislation providing funds for service learning. Through the Corporation for National and Community Service, funds have been allocated to each of the 50 states, a number of Native American tribes, and U.S. territories for programs that "integrate service and service learning into daily academic life for students..."

Politicians have been enthusiastic. Senator Harris Wofford of Pennsylvania states:

Service learning must be a critical element in education reform at all levels...[It] improves student achievement by making classroom learning more meaningful. It can reengage students turned off by traditional teaching methods. Service learning promotes teamwork, leadership and problem-solving. In successful programs of service learning, students replace alienation with enagement, boredom with excitement, and learn the exhilaration of making a difference.[1]

Overseas, service learning is also being recognized as an important component of the curriculum. For example, the British Isles bestows a prestigious Schools Curriculum Award on exemplary schools. In its report of these schools, it is evident that community participation is a key criterion of the award. This is illustrated by its description of award-winning schools:

[They] campaigned against litter and other forms of pollution. They planted trees, flowers, plants and shrubs; they preserved and extended the habitat of insect, fish, reptiles, birds and animals by digging ponds, conserving woods and hedgerows and

clearing land-sites and beaches. Children worked not only with parents and adults outside the school, but also with "green" organizations ...[2]

In this country, there are additional factors that appear particularly propitious for school reform at this time. There is a growing demand for change. New approaches are being tested. Service learning is among these and is also a component of many other suggested reforms. The trend toward interdisciplinary programs in middle schools provides additional opportunities for service learning. Middle school organization facilitates the introduction of service, either as a part of a unit or as a topic for the unit.

As it has attracted more proponents, service learning as an educational program has matured. It has been expanded from disparate community service activities to become a key part of the curriculum, a change that bodes well for its durability. Also decisive is the inclusion of reflection as an essential component, augmenting the development of higher-order thinking skills. Already, service learning is included in the curriculum guides of various states.

Nevertheless, there are dangerous currents as well. This remains a critical period for public education. Students come to schools with almost insurmountable problems, which overwhelm even the most dedicated educators. In frustration, parents are turning away from public schools, seeking vouchers for private schools or inviting corporations to manage their schools.

The weakening of public education will only strengthen the divisions in our society. On the other hand, service learning, through its emphasis on inclusion, blurs divisions, inviting participation by all kids. Service is not graded by pen-and-pencil tests. Students find talents in each other that were well hidden in an atmosphere where "What did you get on that test?" is a common mantra. Here, too, service learning can be a positive force. Competition based solely on academic achievement is lessened.

As I ruminate on my experiences, certain recollections remain particularly vivid, reminding me once again of the impact of service experiences. The first is of an interview with a group of eighth-grade Latino girls describing their service learning project. After extensive training, they were presenting skits to students in their school on preventing HIV infection. I clearly recall the expression of pride on the face of one of the girls, as she exclaimed, "We can save lives!"

That girl helped me realize that teachers are part of a most fortunate profession, because we too "can save lives." I recalled the middle school at-risk youngsters in San Antonio who, statistically, should have dropped out of school before high school, but who, as a result of a service-learning project in that district, not only remained in school but "began to view themselves differently as valued and important."

I visualized the dignity with which the African-American students in the Turner Middle School in Philadelphia were going through hospital hallways in their white coats, fulfilling their service assignments. I thought of the Turner students who organize health fairs for their community performing authentic tasks. I remember the quote of a parent, who, after observing his daughter taking blood pressure at a health fair, stated: "I never thought my daughter could do this. I will treat her differently from now on."

The images continue: Exceptional kids in Albuquerque, some with severe disorders, organizing their entire school to contribute to a homeless shelter. Bilingual students in Fort Myers, Florida, who help their Hispanic community complete emergency health forms. A district bilingual specialist observing those students stated: "What a boon to self-esteem when they can find they can also be givers."

There are so many more kids who believe they too *can save lives*, by protecting the environment or campaigning against smoking or substance abuse or helping the homeless.

Ultimately, however, it is the adults who will determine the fate of service learning. To establish a program with goals as ambitious as those of service learning is not easy. A beginning has been made. It is up to us to nourish it. Service learning is not a fully-formed concept. All education programs have to be forged in individual classes, adapted to local needs. But it may be that we owe it to kids to give it a try.

I recognize that not every teacher is ready to engage in service programs. I am aware of the day-to-day demands on teachers. Many are now working on overload. Service learning projects of any magnitude require a significant commitment in both time and energy. It is my hope, however, that this book, with the many varied activities described, including short-term ones that can be incorporated relatively easily, will permit teachers to get started. I trust you will find the effort justified.

Notes

1. Senator Harris Wofford, "Reform and Renewal: The Promise of Service Learning," *The Generator: Journal of Service Learning and Youth Leadership* (St. Paul, MN: Fall, 1993), p. 17.
2. *School Curriculum Award* (London: Longman, 1993), p. 30.

APPENDIX A

Books for Students

Grandparents

Picture Books

Ackerman, Karen. *The Song and Danceman.* New York: Knopf, 1988.

Bahr, Mary. *The Memory Box.* Morton Grove, IL: Albert Whitman, 1992.

Brusca, Maria Cristina. *On the Pampas.* New York: Holt, 1991.

Bryan, Ashley. *Turtle Knows Your Name.* New York: Atheneum, 1989.

Bunting, Eve. *Sunshine Home.* New York: Clarion, 1994.

Delton, Judy, and Tucker, Dorothy. *My Grandma's in a Nursing Home.* Morton Grove, Il: Albert Whitman, 1986.

DePaola, Tomie. *Now One Foot, Now the Other.* New York: Putnam, 1981.

Dodds, Siobhan. *Grandpa Bud.* Cambridge, MA: Candlewick Press, 1993.

Dorros, Arthur. *Abuela.* New York: Dutton, 1991

Flourney, Valerie. *The Patchwork Quilt.* New York: Dial, 1985.

Fox, Mem. *Wilfred Gordon MacDonald Partridge.* New York: Kane/Miller, 1985.

Franklin, Kristine, L. *The Old, Old Man and the Very Little Boy.* New York: Atheneum, 1992.

Greenfield, Eloise. *Grandpa's Face.* New York: Putnam/Philomel, 1988.

Hest, Amy. *Weekend Girl.* New York: Morrow Junior Books, 1993.

Johnson, Angela. *When I Am Old with You.* Orchard/Richard Jackson, 1990.

Johnston, Tony. *Grandpa's Song.* New York: Dial, 1991.

Keller, Holly. *Island Baby.* New York: Greenwillow, 1992.

Limb, Sue. *Come Back, Grandma.* New York: Knopf, 1994.

Polacco, Patricia. *Thunder Cake.* New York: Putnam/Philomel, 1990.

————. *Mrs. Katz and Tush.* New York: Bantam, 1992.

MacLachlan, Patricia. *Through Grandpa's Eyes.* New York: Harper & Row, 1983.

Reddix, Valerie. *Dragon Kite of the Autumn Moon.* New York: Lothrop, Lee & Shepard, 1992.

Say, Allen. *Grandfather's Journey.* Boston: Houghton Mifflin, 1993.

Schertle, Alice. *William and Grandpa.* New York: Lothrop, Lee & Shepard, 1989.

Spinelli, Eileen. *Somebody Loves You, Mr. Hatch.* New York: Bradbury, 1991.

Stevenson, James. *That's Exactly the Way It Wasn't.* New York: Greenwillow, 1991.

Novels

Bacon, Katharine Jay. *Shadow and Light.* New York: Macmillan, 1987. (7+)

Butterworth, William Edmund. *Leroy and the Old Man.* New York: Four Winds, 1980. (7+)

Calmenson, Stephanie. *Hotter Than a Hot Dog*. Boston: Little Brown, 1994. (3–6).

Cleaver, Vera, and Cleaver, Bill. *Queen of Hearts*. New York: HarperCollins 1987. 5–8.

Cole, Norma. *The Final Tide*. New York: Macmillan, 1990. (5+)

Donnelly, Elfie. *So Long, Grandpa*. New York: Crown, 1981. 4–6.

Elge, Lillian. *The Kidnapping of Mister Huey*. New York: Harper & Row, 1983. (7+)

Gardiner, John Reynolds. *Stone Fox*. New York: HarperCollins, 1980. Grades 3–5.

Griffin, Peni R. *A Dig in Time*. New York: Macmillan, 1991, (4–7)

Griffith, Helen V. *Grandaddy's Place*. New York: Greenwillow, 1987. (2–3)

———. *Grandaddy and Janetta*, 1993. (2–3)

Hartling, Peter. *OMA*. New York: Overlook Press, 1990. 3–6. (translated from German)

Herman, Charlotte. *Our Snowman Had Olive Eyes*. New York: Puffin, 1989. 4–6.

Hermes, Patricia. *What If They Knew?* New York: Dell, 1981. 4–6.

Hest, Amy. *Nana's Birthday Party*. New York: Morrow Junior Books, 1993. (2–4)

Hobbie, W. D. *Bloodroot*. New York: Crown, 1991. (5+)

Houston, James. *Akavak*. San Diego: Harcourt Brace Jovanovich, 1990. (5+)

Maser, Norma F. *After the Rain*. New York: William Morrow, 1987. (7+)

Palacios, Argentina. *A Christmas Surprise for Chabelita*. Mahwah, NJ: Bridgewater Press, 1993. (2–5)

Radley, Gail. *The Golden Days*. New York: Macmillan, 1991, (5+)

Roberts, Willo Davis. *What Are We Going to Do about David?* New York: Atheneum, 1993. (5+)

Ruckman, Ivy. *This Is Your Captain Speaking*. New York: Walker, 1987. (5+)

Shannon, George. *Unlived Affections*. New York: HarperCollins, 1989. (7+)

Smith, Robert K. *The War with Grandpa*. New York: Dell, 1984. (5+)

Taha, Karen T. *A Gift for Tia Rosa*. Minneapolis: Dillon, 1986. (2–5)

Zindel, Paul. *A Begonia for Miss Applebaum*. New York: Harper & Row, 1989. (8+)

Environment

Picture Books

Anholt, Laurence. *The Forgotten Forest*. San Francisco: Sierra Club Books for Children, 1992.

Baker, Jeannie. *Where the Forest Meets the Sea*. New York: Greenwillow Books, 1987.

Burningham, John. *Hey, Get Off Our Train*. New York: Crown, 1989.

Cherry, Lynne. *The Great Kapok Tree*. San Diego: Harcourt Brace Jovanovich, 1990.

———. *A River Ran Wild*. San Diego: Harcourt Brace Jovanovich, 1990.

Cole, Babette. *Supermoo!* New York: Putnam, 1993.

Ernst, Lisa Campbell. *Squirrel Park*. New York: Bradbury Press, 1993.

Fife, Dale H. *The Empty Lot*. Boston: Little, Brown, 1991.

Geraghty, Paul. *Stop That Noise*. New York: Crown, 1992

Glimmerveen, Ulco. *A Tale of Antarctica*. New York: Scholastic, 1989.

Himmelman, John. *Ibis, a True Whale Story*. New York: Scholastic, 1990.

Kraus, Robert. *How Spider Stopped the Litterbugs*. New York: Scholastic, 1991.

Lewin, Ted. *Amazon Boy*. New York: Macmillan, 1993.

Luenn, Nancy. *Mother Earth*. New York: Macmillan International, 1992.

Madden, Don. *The Wartville Wizard*. New York: Macmillan International, 1993.

Meeks, Arone Raymond. *Enora and the Black Crane*. New York: Scholastic, 1991.

Rose, Deborah Lee. *The People Who Hugged the Trees*. Niwot, CO: Roberts Rinehart, 1990.

Van Allsburg, Chris. *Just a Dream*. Boston: Houghton Mifflin, 1990.

Werenko, Lisa V. *It Zwibble and the Greatest Cleanup* Ever. New York, Scholastic, 1991.

Williams, Karen Lynn. *Galimoto*. New York: Lothrop, Lee & Shepard, 1990.

Novels

Christian, Mary B. *The Mystery of the Polluted Stream*. St. Louis, MO: Milliken, 1991. (1–3)

Coleman, Janet Wyman. *Fast Eddie*. New York: Macmillan, 1993. (3-5)

Collier, James Lincoln. *When the Stars Begin to Fall*. New York: Delacorte, 1986. (7+)

Cone, Molly. *Come Back, Salmon*. San Francisco: Sierra Club Books for Children, 1992. (2-6)

Danziger, Paula. *Earth to Matthew*. New York: Delacorte, 1991. (5-9)

George, Jean Craighead. *One Day in the Tropical Rain Forest*. New York: Crowell, 1990. (4–7)

———. *Who Really Killed Cock Robin? An Ecological Mystery*. New York: HarperCollins, 1991, (4–7)

———. *The Missing 'Gator of Gumbo Limbo: An Ecological Mystery*. New York: HarperCollins, 1992. (4–7)

———. *The Fire Bug Connection: An Ecological Mystery*. New York: HarperCollins, 1993. (4–7)

Giono, Jean. *The Man Who Planted Trees*. Chelsea, VT: Chelsea Green Publishing, 1985. (6+)

Harpe, Susan. *Waterman's Boy*. New York: Bradbury, 1990. (5-9)

Heide, Florence Parry. *The Wendy Puzzle*. New York: Dell, 1990. (5-9)

Lasky, Kathryn. *Home Free*. New York: Macmillan, 1985. (7+)

Lawrence, Louise. *The Warriors of Taan*. New York: Harper, 1988. (6+)

Levin, Betty. *The Trouble with Gramary*. New York: Greenwillow, 1988. (5–9)

Mendoza, George. *Were You a Wild Duck, Where Would You Go?* New York: Stewart, Tabori & Chang. Distributed by Workman, 1990. (3+)

Pearson, Susan. *The Green Magician Puzzle*. New York: Simon & Schuster Books for Young Readers, 1991. (2–4)

Peet, Bill. *The Wump World*. Boston: Houghton Mifflin, 1970. (3–5)

Pritts, Kim D. *The Mystery of Sadler Marsh*. Scottsdale, PA: Herald Press, 1993. (3–6)

Steiner Barbara. *Oliver Dibbs to the Rescue*. New York: Macmillan, 1985. (3–5)

Swindells, Robert. *A Serpent's Tooth*. New York: Holiday House, 1989. (4–7)

Taylor, Theodore. *The Hostage*. New York: Dell, 1991. (5+)

Tchudi, Stephen. *The Green Machine and the Frog Crusade*. New York: Delacorte, 1987. (6–9)

Nonfiction

Bellamy, David. *Our Changing World: The Forest*. New York: Crown Young Readers, 1988. (1–4)

———. *Our Changing World: The Roadside*. New York: Crown Young Readers, 1988. (1–5)

———. *Our Changing World: The Rock Pool*. New York: Crown Young Readers, 1988. (1–5)

Burleigh, Robert A. *A Man Named Thoreau.* New York: Macmillan, 1985. (4–7)

Dolan, Edward F. *Our Poisoned Sky.* New York: Dutton, 1991. (6+)

Foster, Leila M. *The Story of Rachel Carson and the Environmental Movement.* Chicago: Children's, 1990. (5–7)

Goodall, Jane. *My Life with the Chimpanzees.* New York: Pocket Books, 1988. (5–9)

Hamerstrom, Frances. *Walk When the Moon Is Full.* Freedom, CA: Crossing Press, 1975. (2–6)

Jaspersohn, William. *How the Forest Grew.* New York: Greenwillow, 1980. (3–5)

McNulty, Faith. *Peeping in the Shell: A Whooping Crane Is Hatched.* New York: Harper, 1986. (3–7)

Miller, Christina G., and Berry, Louise A. *Coastal Rescue: Preserving Our Seashores.* New York: Macmillan, 1989. (6+)

Morrison, Marion. *The Amazon Rain Forest and Its People.* New York: Thomson Learning, 1993. (5+)

Pringle, Laurence. *Rain of Troubles: The Science and Politics of Acid Rain.* New York: Macmillan, 1988. (7+)

———. *Living in a Risky World.* New York: William Morrow, 1989. (7+)

———. *Global Warming: Assessing the Greenhouse Threat.* Boston: Little, Brown, 1990. (5+)

Vogel, Carole G., and Goldner, Kathryn A. *The Great Yellowstone Fire.* San Francisco: Sierra Club, 1990. (5+)

Resources

Caduto, Michael, and Bruchac, Joseph. *Keepers of the Earth: Native American Stories and Environmental Activities for Children.* Golden, CO: Fulcrum, 1988. (1–6)

Earthworks Group. *50 Simple Things Kids Can Do to Save the Earth.* Kansas City, MO: Andrews and McMeel Books, 1990.

Foster, Joanna. *Cartons, Cans and Orange Peels: Where Does Your Garbage Go?* Boston: Clarion, 1991. (3–6)

Lowery, Linda, and Marybeth Lorbiecki. *Earthwise at School: A Guide to the Care and Feeding of Your Planet.* Minneapolis, MN: Carolrhoda Books, 1993. (5+)

Pellowski, Anne. *Hidden Stories in Plants: Unusual and Easy-To-Tell Stories from Around the World Together with Creative Things to Do While Telling Them.* New York: Macmillan, 1990. (5+)

Rockwell, Robert E., Sherwood, Elizabeth A., and Williams, Robert A. *Hug a Tree: and Other Things to Do Outdoors with Young Children.* Mt. Rainier, MD: Gryphon House, 1983.

Sisson, Edith A. *Nature with Children of All Ages: Activities and Adventures for Exploring, Learning and Enjoying the World Around Us.* Englewood Cliffs, NJ: Prentice-Hall, 1990.

Homelessness and Poverty

Picture Books

Barbour, Karen. *Mr. Bow Tie.* San Diego: Harcourt Brace Jovanovich, 1991.

Bunting, Eve. *Fly Away Home.* Boston: Clarion, 1991.

DiSalvo-Ryan, DyAnne. *Uncle Willie and the Soup Kitchen.* New York: Morrow Junior Books, 1991.

Spangler, Ruth. *Mandy's House.* Louisville, KY: Society of St. Vincent de Paul, 1990.

Novels

Ackerman, Karen. *The Leaves in October.* New York: Macmillan, 1991. 3–6.

Aiello, Barbara *Hometown Hero.* Frederick, MD: Twenty-first Century Books, 1989. 3–6.

Anderson, Mary. *The Unsinkable Molly Malone.* San Diego: Harcourt Brace Jovanovich, 1991. (7+)

Barre, Shelley A. *Chive.* New York: Simon & Schuster, 1993. (3–6)

Colman, Hila. *Rich and Famous Like My Mom.* New York: Crown, 1988. (5+)

Fox, Paula. *Monkey Island.* New York: Orchard Books, 1991. (4–7)

Grove, Vicki. *The Fastest Friend in the West.* New York: Putnam, 1990. (5+)

Hahn, Mary Downing. *December Stillness.* Boston: Clarion, 1988. (7+)

Hamilton, Virginia. *The Planet of Junior Brown.* New York: Collier Books, 1986. (5–9)

Harris, Mark Jonathan. *Come the Morning.* New York: Bradbury, 1989. (7+)

Herzig, Alison C., and Mili, Jane L. *Sam and the Moon Queen.* Boston: Clarion, 1990. (6+)

Holman, Felice. *Secret City, USA.* New York: Scribner, 1990. (5+)

Hughes, Dean. *Family Pose.* New York: Atheneum, 1989. (3–6)

Johnson, Scott. *One of the Boys.* New York: Macmillan, 1992. (7+)

Jones, Adrienne. *Street Family.* New York: Harper & Row, 1987. (7+)

Nasaw, Jonathan Lewis. *Shakedown Street.* New York: Delacorte, 1993. (6+)

Nelson, Theresa. *The Beggars' Ride.* New York: Orchard Books, 1992. (6+)

Pinkwater, Jill. *Tails of the Bronx.* New York: Macmillan, 1991. (5+)

Sachs, Marilyn. *At the Sound of the Beep.* New York: Dutton, 1990. (3–7)

Thompson, Colin. *The Paper Bag Prince.* New York, Knopf, 1992, (2–6)

Tolan, Stephanie S. *Sophie and the Sidewalk Man.* New York: Four Winds Press. (3–5)

Wojciechowski, Susan. *Patty Dillman of Hot Dog Fame.* New York: Orchard Books, 1989. (5+)

Nonfiction

Berck, Judith. *No Place to Be: Voices of Homeless Children.* Boston: Houghton Mifflin, 1992. (5+)

O'Connor, Karen. *Homeless Children.* San Diego: Lucien Books, 1989. (5–8)

O'Neill, Terry. *The Homeless: Distinguishing between Fact and Opinion.* San Diego: Greenhaven Press, 1990. (3–6)

Seymour-Jones, Carole. *Homelessness.* New York: New Discovery Books, 1993. (6+)

Shachtman, Tom. *The President Builds a House.* New York: Simon & Shuster Books, 1989. (3+)

Exceptional Children

Arnold, Caroline. *A Guide Dog Puppy Grows Up.* San Diego: Harcourt Brace Jovanovich, 1991. (picture book)

Cairo, S. *Our Brother Has Down's Syndrome.* Willowdale, ON: Annick Press, 1985. K–2.

Dodds, Bill. *My Sister Annie.* Honesdale, PA: Boyds Mills Press, 1993. (4–6) (Down's syndrome)

Emmert, Michelle. *I'm the Big Sister, Now.* Chicago: Albert Whitman, 1989. (3–5) (cerebral palsy)

Fassler, Joan. *Howie Helps Himself.* Chicago: Albert Whitman, 1975. (1–3) (cerebral palsy, wheelchair)

———. *One Little Girl.* New York: Human Sciences Press, 1969. (1–3) (mental retardation)

Gilson, Jamie. *Do Bananas Chew Gum?* New York: Lothrop, Lee & Shepard, 1980. (4–6) (learning disability)

Girion, Barbara. *A Handful of Stars.* New York: Scribner, 1981. (7+) (epilepsy)

Gold, Phyllis. *Please Don't Say Hello.* New York: Human Sciences Press, 1975. (2–4) (autism)

Kerr, M. E. *Little, Little.* New York: HarperCollins, 1981. (6+) (dwarfism).

Laird, Elizabeth. *Loving Ben.* New York: Delacorte, 1989. (5+) (disfigurement)

Lakin, Pat. *Dad and Me in the Morning.* Morton Gore, IL: Albert Whitman, 1994. (hearing loss) (picture book)

Levine, Edna S. *Lisa and Her Soundless World.* New York: Human Science Press, 1984. (1–4)

Mathis, Sharon Bell. *Listen for the Fig Tree.* New York: Puffin Books, 1990. (7+) (blindness)

Payne, Sherry Meuwirth. *A Contest.* Minneapolis, MN: Carolrhoda, 1982. (3–5) (cerebral palsy, wheel chair)

Powers, Mary Ellen. *Our Teacher's in a Wheel Chair.* Chicago: Albert Whitman, 1986. (pre-K–2)

Rosen, Lillian. *Just Like Everybody Else.* San Diego: Harcourt Brace Jovanovich, 1981. (6+) (hearing loss)

Rostkowski, Margaret I. *After the Dancing Days.* New York: Harper, 1986. (6–9) (disfigurement)

Roy, Ron. *Move Over, Wheelchairs Coming Through.* New York: Clarion, 1985. (3–7)

Shyer, Marlene. *Welcome Home, Jellybean.* New York: Macmillan, 1988. (4–7)

Slepian, Jan. *The Alfred Summer.* New York: Macmillan, 1980 (6–8) (four friends with varied impairments: cerebral palsy, epilepsy, deformed limbs, mental retardation)

———. *Lester's Turn.* New York: Macmillan, 1981. (6–8) (sequel to above)

Zelonky, Joy. *I Can't Always Hear You.* Madison, NJ: Raintree/Steck-Vaughan, 1980. (2–5)

MULTICULTURAL

African Americans

Novels

Banks, Jacqueline Turner. *Project Wheels.* New York: Houghton Mifflin, 1993. (5–7)

Boyd, Candy Dawson. *Charlie Pippin.* New York: Macmillan, 1987. (4–6)

Cohen, Barbara. *Thank You, Jackie Robinson.* New York: Lothrop. (3–6)

Hansen, Joyce. *The Gift Giver.* New York: Clarion, 1986. (4–6)

Jordan, June *Kimako's Story.* Boston: Houghton Mifflin, 1981 (K–3)

Moore, Emily. *Whose Side Are You On?* New York: Farrar, Straus & Giroux, 1988. (4–6)

Naidoo, Beverly. *Journey to Jo'burg.* New York: HarperCollins, 1988. (4–7)

Tate, Eleanora E. *The Secret of Gumbo Grove.* New York: Franklin Watts, 1987. (4–7)

Taylor, Mildred. *The Song of the Trees.* New York: Bantam, 1989. (4–6)

———. *Mississippi Bridge.* New York: Bantam, 1992. (4–7)

———. *Roll of Thunder, Hear My Cry.* New York: Puffin. (5+)

Williams, Vera B. *Cherries and Cherry Pits.* New York: Greenwillow, 1986. (K–3)

Walter, Mildred Pitts. *Have a Happy.* New York: Lothrop, 1989. (4–6)

Nonfiction

Deane, Patrick. *Martin Luther King, Jr.* New York: Franklin Watts, 1990. (4–6)

Miller, Marilyn. *The Bridge at Selma.* Englewood Cliffs, NJ: Silver Burdett, 1985. (7–9)

Smith, Kathie Billingslee. *Harriet Tubman.* New York: Simon & Schuster, 1988. (3–6)

Asian Americans

Novels

Andrews, Jean. *The Secret in the Dorm Attic.* Washington, DC: Gallaudet, 1990. (4–6) (Pakistani)

Betancourt, Jeanne. *More Than Meets the Eye.* New York: Bantam, 1990. (2–4) (Cambodian, Chinese, Korean)

Choi, Sook Nyul. *Halmoni and the Picnic.* Boston: Houghton Mifflin, 1993. (2–4) (Korean)

Coerr, Eleanor. *Sadako and the Thousand Paper Cranes.* New York: Putnam, 1977. (4–6) (Japanese)

———. *Chang's Paper Pony.* New York: HarperCollins, 1988. (K–3) (Chinese)

Crew, Linda. *Children of the River.* New York: Delacorte, 1989. (7–9) (Cambodian)

Demi. *The Magic Tapestry.* New York: Henry Holt, 1994. (2–4)

French, Fiona. *Little Inchkin.* New York: Dial Books, 1994. Picture Book. (Japanese folktale)

Girard, Linda W. *We Adopted You, Benjamin Koo.* Chicago: Albert Whitman, 1989. (K–3) (Korean)

Godden, Rumer. *Great Grandfather's House.* New York: Greenwillow, 1992. (2–4) (Japanese)

MacMillian Dianne, and Freeman, Dorothy. *My Best Friend Duc Tran: Meeting a Vietnamese American Family.* Englewood Cliffs, NJ: Julian Messner, 1987. (4–6)

Pascal, Francine. *Out of Reach.* New York: Bantam, 1988. (7–9) (Chinese)

Paterson, Katherine. *Park's Quest.* New York: Dutton/Lodestar, 1988. (4–7) (Vietnamese)

Paek, Min. *Aekyung's Dream.* Chicago: Children's Press, 1988. (K–3) (bilingual edition—Korean)

Uchida, Yoshiko. *Journey to Topaz.* New York: Scribner, 1971. (7–9) (Japanese)

———. *A Jar of Dreams.* New York: Atheneum, 1981. (4–6) (Japanese)

———. *The Best Bad Thing.* New York: Macmillan, 1993. (4–7) (sequel to *A Jar of Dreams*)

Yep, Laurence. *Child of the Owl.* New York: HarperCollins, 1977. (7–9) (Chinese)

———. *Sea Glass.* New York: HarperCollins, 1979. (7–9) (Chinese)

———. *Dragon's Gate.* New York: HarperCollins, 1993. (7–9) (Chinese)

Latino Americans

Novels

Adoff, Arnold. *Flamboyan.* San Diego: Harcourt Brace Jovanovich, 1988. (K–3)

Atkinson, Mary. *Maria Teresa.* Carrboro, NC: Lollipop Power, 1979. (K–3)

Beltran Hernandez, Irene. *Across the Great River.* Houston, TX: Arte Publico Press, 1989, (7–9)

Brown, Tricia. *Hello Amigos.* New York: Holt, 1986. (K–3) (nonfiction)

De la Garza, Phyllis. *Chacho.* Syracuse, NY: New Readers Press, 1990. (7–9)

Hurwitz, Johanna. *Class President*. New York: William Morrow, 1990. (4–6)

Martel, Cruz. *Yaqua Days*. New York: Dutton/Dial, 1987. (K–3)

Mills, Claudia. *Luisa's American Dream*. New York: Four Winds, 1981. (7–9)

Mohr, Nicholasa. *Felita*. New York: Dutton/Dial, 1979. (3–6)

————. *Going Home*. New York: Dutton/Dial, 1986. (3–6)

————. *El Bronx: A Novella and Stories*. Houston, TX: Arte Publico, 1986. (7–9)

Sonneborn, Ruth A. *Friday Night Is Papa Night*. New York: Puffin, 1987. (K–3)

Taylor, Theodore. *The Maldonado Miracle*. New York: Avon, 1986. (4–6)

Native Americans

Picture Books

Jeffers, Susan. *Brother Eagle, Sister Sky—A Message from Chief Seattle*. New York: Dial, 1991.

Luenn, Nancy. *Nessa's Fish*. New York: Atheneum, 1990.

Martin, Bill, and John Archambault. *Knots on a Counting Rope*. New York: Henry Holt, 1987.

Scott, Ann Herbert. *On Mother's Lap*. New York: Clarion, 1992.

Yolen, Jane. *Sky Dogs*. San Diego: Harcourt Brace Jovanovich, 1990.

Novels

Cannon, A. E. *The Shadow Brothers*. New York: Delacorte, 1990. (7–9)

Chandonnet, Ann. Chief Stephen's Parky: *One Year in the Life of an Athapascan Girl*. Niwot, CO: R. Rinehart, 1993. (4–6)

Davis, Deborah. *The Secret of the Seal*. New York: Crown, 1989. (4–6)

George, Jean Craighead. *The Talking Earth*. New York: HarperCollins, 1987. (4–6)

Girion, Barbara. *Indian Summer*. New York: Scholastic, 1990. (4–7)

Gregory, Kristiana. *Jenny of the Tetons*. San Diego: Harcourt Brace Jovanovich, 1989. (4–7)

Goble, Paul. *Her Seven Brothers*. New York: Bradbury, 1988. (K–3)

Gregory, Kristiana. *Jenny of the Tetons*. San Diego: Harcourt Brace Jovanovich, 1989. (7–9)

Highwater, Jamake. *Anpao: An American Indian Odyssey*. New York: HarperCollins, 1977. (7–9)

————. *Legend Days*. New York: Harper Collins, 1984. (7–9)

Hobbs, Will. *Bearstone*. New York: Atheneum, 1989. (7–9)

O'Dell, Scott. *Black Star, Bright Dawn*. Boston: Houghton Mifflin, 1988. (7–9)

O'Dell, Scott, and Hall, Elizabeth. *Thunder Rolling in the Mountains.* Boston: Houghton Mifflin, 1992. (4–7)

Pitts, Paul. *Racing the Sun*. New York: Avon, 1988. (4–6)

Richardson, Jean. *The Courage Seed*. Austin, TX: Eakin-Sunbelt, 1993. (3–6)

Wallin, Luke. *Ceremony of the Panther*. New York: Bradbury, 1987. (7–9)

Nonfiction

Aaseng, Nathan. *Navaho Code Talkers*. New York: Walker, 1992. (6+)

Legends

Crowl, Christine. *The Hunter and the Woodpecker.* Chamberlain, SD: Tipi Press, 1990. (all ages)

———. *White Buffalo Women.* Chamberlain, SD: Tipi Press, 1991. (6+)

Flood, Renee S. (Ed.). *A Legend from Crazy Horse Clan.* Chamberlain, SD: Tipi Press, 1991. (all ages)

Anti-Semitism

Arrick, Fran. *Chernowitz.* New York: Dutton, 1983. (5–7) (A ninth-grader becomes the victim of the school bully's anti-Semitism.)

Cormier, Robert. *Tunes for Bears to Dance to.* New York: Delacorte, 1992. (5+) (story of a Holocaust survivor)

Greene, Bette. *Summer of My German Soldier.* New York: Bantam, 1986. (6+) (A Jewish girl strives to save the life of a World War II German prisoner of war.)

Levitin, Sonia. *The Return.* New York: Atheneum, 1987. (7+) (A young Ethiopian Jewish girl escapes famine at home and struggles to reach Israel.)

Lasky, Kathryn. *Prank.* New York: Dell, 1986. (6+) (A young girl helps her brother understand his responsibility for not stopping the desecration of a synagogue.)

Lowry, Lois. *Number the Stars.* New York: Dell, 1989. (7+) (A young girl in Copenhagen helps to save her Jewish friend from Nazis during World War II.)

Matas, Carol. *Lisa's War.* New York: Scribner, 1989. (7–9) (Describes efforts of Danish people to save Jews from Nazis during World War II.)

Roth-Hano, Renee. *Touch Wood: A Girlhood in Occupied France.* New York: Four Winds, 1988. (7–9).

Miscellaneous

Buss, Fran Leeper, and Cubias, Daisy. *Journey of the Sparrows.* New York: Lodestar, 1991. (7+) (Maria, 16, and her brother and sister are smuggled to Chicago from El Salvador in crates.)

Springer, Nancy. *They're All Named Wildfire.* New York: Atheneum, 1989. (4–6) (Interracial friendship leads two young girls to take a stand against bigotry and racism.)

Taylor, Theodore. *The Cay.* New York: Doubleday, 1987. (5+) A young American boy traveling on a freighter is blinded during an attack by a Nazi U-boat and is stranded on a Caribbean island with an aging West Indian who becomes his friend.

APPENDIX B

Resources for Teachers

The organizations listed here are excellent resources for those interested in establishing and sustaining service-learning programs.

Corporation for National and Community Service
1100 Vermont Avenue, N.W., Washington, DC 20525
202-606-5000

Federal body created by the National and Community Service Trust Act of 1993 to "increase service opportunities and civic spirit throughout the country." Of particular interest is the Corporation's Serve-America program, which supports K–12 school-based service, including grants to service-learning programs.

National Service-Learning Cooperative

The National Youth Leadership Council (NYLC) was selected by the Corporation as the national Serve-America K–12 clearinghouse. It organized a cooperative with other groups involved in service learning to provide information, training, and technical assistance to teachers, administrators, and others working to involve young people in service.

The Cooperative maintains a database of programs, resources, and training and consultant referrals. It has established a toll-free hotline for anyone interested in service-learning, Monday through Friday, 8 A.M. to 4 P.M. (central time) 1-800-808-SERV.

The Cooperative also includes a support network of fifteen service organizations, "Partners for Technical Assistance," listed below.

Partners for Technical Assistance

Arkansas Department of Education
4 State Capitol Mall, 405 B
Little Rock, AR 72201
501-682-4399

Center for Experiential Education and
   Service Learning
VOTECH Education Building
1954 Buford Avenue
St. Paul, MN 55108
612-624-2258

Close Up Foundation
44 Canal Center Plaza
Alexandria, VA 22314
703-706-3640

Constitutional Rights Foundation
601 South Kingsley Drive
Los Angeles, CA 90005
213-487-5990

Community Service Learning Center
258 Washington Boulevard
Springfield, MA 01108
413-734-6857

East Bay Conservation Corps
1021 Third Street
Oakland, CA 94607
510-891-3900

Michigan K–12 Service Learning Center
Michigan State University
31 Kellogg Center
East Lansing, MI 48824
517-432-2940

National Dropout Prevention Center
Clemson University
205 Martin Street, Box 345111
Clemson, SC 29634
803-656-2599

National Indian Youth Leadership Project
650 Vandenbosch Parkway
Gallup, NM 87301
505-722-9176

Pennsylvania Institute for Environmental
   and Community Service Learning
Philadelphia College of Textiles and
   Science
Henry Avenue and Schoolhouse Lane
Philadelphia, PA 19144
215-951-0343

National Youth Leadership Council
1910 West County Road B
Roseville, MN 55113
612-631-3672

Project Service Leadership
12703 N.W. Twentieth Avenue
Vancouver, WA 98685
206-576-5070

HAAS Center for Public Service Stanford
   University
P.O. Box 5844
Stanford, CA 94309
415-723-0992

Teacher Education Department
School of Education
Furcolo Hall, University of
   Massachusetts
Amherst, MA 01003
413-545-4185

National Information Center for Service
   Learning
University of Minnesota
College of Education, Room 290
VOTECH Education Building, 1954
   Buford Avenue
St. Paul, MN 55108
612-631-3672

In addition to above the organizations, the following groups are resources for service learning programs.

Independent Sector
1828 L Street, N.W.
Washington, DC 20036
202-223-8100

National Center for Service Learning in
   Early Adolescence
25 West 43rd Street, Suite 612
New York, NY 10036-8099
212-642-2946

Maryland Student Service Alliance
200 West Baltimore Street
Baltimore, MD 21201-2595
410-333-2427

National Association of Partners in
   Education
209 Madison Street, Suite 401
Alexandria, VA 22314
703-836-4880

SerVermont
P.O. Box 516
Chester, Vermont 05143
802-875-2278

State, city, and local offices of volunteers frequently have information about programs. See also the Notes for resources related to specific topics.

APPENDIX C

Suggested Forms

Informing Parents about Program

(The following letter is sent in English and Spanish to parents of eighth-grade youngsters by Myrna Schiffman, service coordinator of the Mott Hall Intermediate School in Manhattan, prior to the start of the school year.)

Date _____

Dear Parents of Eighth-Grade Students:

The school year is just beginning and we are anticipating fantastic new educational experiences for our students. As you know, the instructional program at Mott Hall is dedicated to the belief that our students deserve differentiated programs that teach, challenge, and expand their knowledge. To this end, we have added a service learning program to the eighth-grade curriculum.

Service learning is a unique form of community service that connects classroom learning to real world experience. Community-based organizations reach out to adolescents, creating for them a positive role in their communities. The school structures a program that combines meaningful volunteer work with training and ongoing reflection, whereby the student is constantly learning from his or her experience.

For the young person who does community service, there are multiple benefits. In addition to an increase in self-esteem and a sense of accomplishment, community service provides opportunities for career exploration and for learning the attitudes and behaviors needed in the world of work. It challenges the student to work well with others and to learn to compromise and communicate successfully.

Starting on _____ , all eighth-grade students will leave Mott Hall at _____ , once a week to work at prearranged agencies in their community. The students will have the opportunity to discuss the placement with you before making a final selection.... At the sites, the students will be supervised by the director of the agency with guidelines established by Mott Hall. At Mott Hall, the program will be monitored by on-site visits by teachers, weekly evaluation sessions with students, and journal writings. Community service time is regular school time, and appointments should not be scheduled during this time.

We will keep you informed about the experiences the students are having. If there are any questions, please contact me at the school.

Sincerely yours,
Myrna Schiffman
Coordinator

Approved _____

Dr. M. Acosta-Sing, Principal

Placement Questionnaire

Name of Organization or Agency _____

Address _____ Telephone Number _____

Placement Supervisor _____

Title _____ Telephone Number _____

Students will be available on the following days and hours: _____

Commencing (date)_____ and ending _____

Number of students needed _____

Please describe your work setting and the tasks you would expect our students to perform. The service assignment is part of their regular curriculum. We hope that it will enable our students to learn new skills while performing worthwhile service.

Any additional information we should have about your placement:

Any special student skills or talents desirable (computer literacy, art or music, ability to speak another language, particular subject competency, etc.):

Student Assignment and Parental Consent

Student _____

Address _____

Telephone Number _____

Assignment

Organization or Agency _____ Telephone Number _____

Address _____

Responsibilities at Site

Method of Transportation to Site _____

Schedule of Service: Days _____ Hours _____

Commencing (date) _____ and ending _____

Parent/Guardian Consent

I hereby give permission for the above student to participate in the service learning assignment described above.

_____ Date _____

(SIGNATURE OF PARENT/GUARDIAN)

Student Service Evaluation

The following evaluation will enable us to help our student achieve his or her full potential for growth from participation in the program. Please feel free to share the evaluation with the student.

Thank you for your assistance. We would appreciate your returning the form in the enclosed envelope by _____

Student _____ Placement _____

Please indicate the activities in which the student has been involved:

_____

_____

_____

Please rate the student's performance using the following codes: E—excellent, VG—very good, S—satisfactory, LS—less than satisfactory

Attendance/Punctuality

_____ Reports regularly

_____ Is consistently on time

Attitude

_____ Is appropriately attired and groomed

_____ Is interested in work of school/ agency

_____ Is courteous and cooperative

_____ Relates well to a variety of people

_____ Accepts suggestions

_____ Exercises good judgment

_____ Shows initiative

Performance

_____ Begins work promptly

_____ Completes assigned tasks

_____ Follows directions

_____ Accepts responsibility

_____ Progressively requires less supervision

_____ Can work independently

_____ Has made progress in placement

Additional Comments

Please use reverse side, if more space is needed.

Supervisor's Signature _____

Adapted from Central Park East Secondary School Program.

Student Placement Evaluation

Student Name _____

Placement _____

Period of Service _____

1. Describe your activities:

2. What did you like best about this placement?

3. Was there anything you did not like?

4. What would you have done differently?

5. Do you believe the program could be improved, if so, how?

6. Would you recommend this placement to another student?

7. What did you learn from this experience?

Index of Schools and School Districts

General Index